ISLAND SCHOOLHOUSE

Schools are the glue that hold island communities together. Eva Murray provides passionate descriptions of why the islands' one-room schoolhouses have not only survived, but continued to thrive in the Internet era.
—Philip Conkling, Founder and President, Island Institute, and author of *Islands in Time: A Natural and Cultural History of the Islands of the Gulf of Maine*

I had the good fortune to educate my children in island schools and served for many years on our school board. And, while North Haven is much bigger (350 year-round) than our neighbor Matinicus, I found that Eva's beautiful writing accurately captures the challenges and gifts of island life. What a wonderful book!
—Chellie Pingree, Congresswoman, 1st District of Maine

T0099230

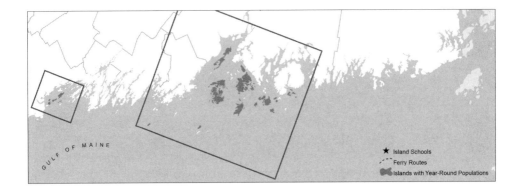

TILBURY HOUSE, PUBLISHERS
GARDINER, MAINE

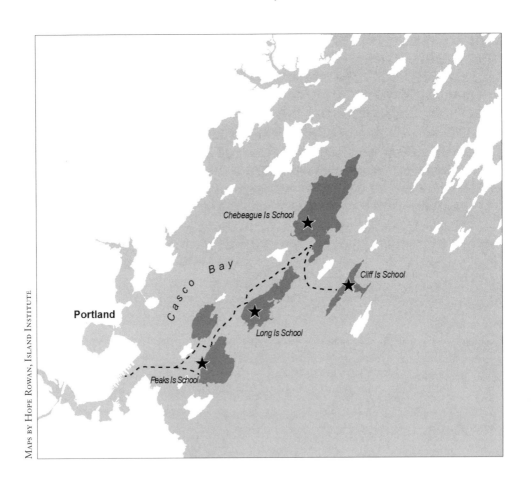

MAPS BY HOPE ROWAN, ISLAND INSTITUTE

ISLAND SCHOOLHOUSE
One Room for All

Eva Murray

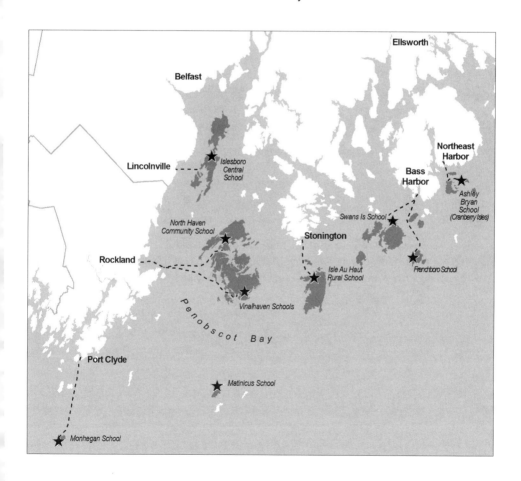

Tilbury House, Publishers
103 Brunswick Avenue
Gardiner, Maine 04345
800-582-1899 • www.tilburyhouse.com

First edition: September 2012 • 10 9 8 7 6 5 4 3 2 1

Cataloging-in-Publication Data
Murray, Eva, 1964-
  Island schoolhouse : one room for all / Eva Murray. -- 1st ed.
    p. cm.
  Includes bibliographical references and index.
  ISBN 978-0-88448-340-3 (pbk. : alk. paper)
  1. Education--Maine--Matinicus Island. 2. Rural schools--Maine--Matinicus Island.
  3. Matinicus Island (Me.) I. Title.
  LA299.M38M87 2012
  371.0109741--dc23
                        2012027765

Front cover: Emma Van Dyne uses a lobster trap for a bench outside the Matinicus Island school while she works on her laptop and pats Rossi the golden retriever. Photo by Eva Murray.

Back cover: The Matinicus students of 2010-2011, after a hike on island trails. Left to right: Ryan Twombly-Hussey, Isabella Bryant, Gardner Griffin, Fiona Twombly-Hussey, Emma Van Dyne, Max Van Dyne, and Ezekiel Bryant. Photo by their teacher, David Duncan.

Copyediting: Genie Dailey, Fine Points Editorial Services, Jefferson, Maine
Printing and Binding: Versa Press, East Peoria, Illinois

This is dedicated to the memory of John Monroe (1913–1988). John taught in several one-room schools in South Thomaston, Maine, in the late 1930s. His sister, who was my grandmother, wrote of John:

> He didn't mind teaching. He liked the kids and the parents but he didn't like the school system. He had to dress well and be neat. I know that he preferred not to.

John was my neighbor in South Thomaston in the 1980s. I would walk up to his house for supper, where the meal consisted primarily of boiled potatoes cooked on the woodstove and a big slab of ice cream cut from the half-gallon block with a carving knife. Over that meal, he'd tell stories of his experiences teaching in one-room schools, which included tangling with some of the "big boys." About teaching school, John told me, "I don't think you're going to like it, but I understand why you're doing it."

With special thanks to Anne Bardaglio and Lana Cannon.

CONTENTS

HOW DID YOU GET HERE?

TERM LIMITS, SECESSION, AND CONSOLIDATION

TWELVE-YEAR-OLD COMMUTERS AND HIGH SCHOOL "AWAY"

PILOTS, RANCHERS, MINERS, AND LOGGERS

LOOKING AHEAD

Oral History
Everybody is doing a story on the one-room schools.

INTRODUCTION

The Twenty-First-Century One-Room Schools of Maine

When most of us hear the word "school," an image comes to mind. For many, the picture in the mind's eye will be of a large, dull, flat-roofed building containing hundreds, maybe even thousands, of students. There are cinderblock hallways, steel fire doors, and lots of signs indicating rules and regulations. Our mental ear likely detects either the chaotic din of a packed schoolyard or a crowded, locker-lined hallway, or perhaps the enforced silence of exams and neat rows of nervous-looking scholars. If we are very lucky and have fond memories of our own education, it may be an image of a colorful classroom filled with construction paper and paint, and with tables surrounded by energetic students making things together or debating some idea.

Bells ring and nothing, absolutely nothing, can override that bell to indicate that an activity must end. Children and staff learn to pay a great deal of attention to the clock on the wall. Despite having all these adults around, bullies still threaten other kids without any adult intervention. Despite all the regulations and lineups and schedules, a noisy hubbub is the default state. With experts aplenty and advanced degrees not at all uncommon among the adults, some students cannot read, and sometimes nobody notices. Advanced students are bored, students new to this country are scrambling to manage with their marginal English, and one-size-fits-all fits relatively few.

What defines a school? How many of these acknowledged realities have anything to do with education? Is the size of the physical facility what makes it a school? Do there need to be bells, or hallways, or classrooms where all the students are the same age (for in no real case are they truly all working at the same level, despite our traditional assumptions about how age represents academic level). Does there need to be a principal or a chain of command evident to the students? If the students all know each other, does that seem somehow abnormal? If siblings are in the same classroom, is that even more peculiar? If everybody, adult and child, male and female, used the same toilet facilities (in turn, of course), would that seem shocking? Why? Why?

Why? "Because that's just not how it is at school."

If we think about it, most of the customs, routines, and conventions associated with "school" (or at least public school) have a lot more to do with crowd control, public safety, logistics, daycare, the bickering down at city hall, and the scheduling of sports than with educational goals. It's not that the schools are at fault; cities and larger towns need large schools, and large schools need administrations and safety rules and bus schedules. Still, it is not those things that make them "real," that make them schools. We make a mistake when we confuse the unavoidable logistics challenges of a building where 500 people work with the real intentions, objectives, and accomplishments of an educational facility. Nobody goes to school just to learn how to slam a book shut and run like a madman to another room when a buzzer goes off. Yet we still think of schools that manage to do without those traditional, institutional marching orders as just a bit odd. Somehow, we may think, they aren't "real school."

I know this because I have heard that expression dozens of times in the past twenty-five years since I came to the island of Matinicus to teach at a one-room school.

My children, born several years after my term as "island teacher," attended the one-room school on Matinicus beginning in kindergarten, and lived year-round on Matinicus until they left to attend boarding high schools at age fourteen. Prior to that, our family had numerous encounters with well-meaning folks who wrung their hands and worried, "How will your children manage when they have to go out into the *real world*? When they have to go to a *real* school?"

"This island," I could only assure them, "is in the real world."

I hope to dispel a few myths, defy a few clichés, and unravel a few stereotypes, chief among those the notion that tiny rural schools must, by definition be impoverished, antiquated, substandard, and inevitably headed for the scrap heap of history. That simply is not the case. The one-room schools of Maine are not strange holdovers from the past. They are not anachronisms, and the islanders who send their children to be educated in those schoolrooms are not peculiar hermits who have denied the progress of time. They—or, if I may be so bold—

"we" (as I have lived on Matinicus Island for a mere quarter century, practically nothing in the eyes of the real natives), just happen to reside where commuting is often not an option, school consolidation is not physically possible, and the notion that a larger school must, by definition, be "better" (and therefore anybody with children ought to move) is easily proven incorrect.

It is important to emphasize that the families who send their students to these schools do not make that choice because they consider it a hobby, or a history lesson, or something cute, or because they want their children to get a nineteenth-century education. Far from it; the tiniest rural schools in Maine are quite possibly the most tech-savvy, the most computer literate, and the most "connected" schools anywhere. They just don't happen to have very many students. The schools I describe here are regular, taxpayer-funded public elementary schools. There are also private one-room schools in this country, tribal schools, Amish schools, and other special circumstances, but the islands of Maine include none of those.

I have tried to be sensitive to circumstances where students, teachers, and parents would prefer not to be in the spotlight. There are no lurking, ugly secrets, but you can be sure that there are a few topics that are not appropriate for detailed discussion in the public square. Small-town politics, special-education confidentiality rules, and disagreements between divorced parents of students mean that not everything is on the table. Occasionally I need to describe a situation or an individual only in a very general sense; the reader will, I trust, understand. I also respect my neighbors and my colleagues too much to treat them like subjects of an anthropological study. After this book is done, they will still be my neighbors and my colleagues.

I am not a journalist who looks at these schools as an outsider might, seeking something cute or charming for a Sunday-supplement story, and for darn sure, this isn't a graduate thesis or some kind of objective sociology-class term paper. I resent—and can disprove—the assumption that a one-room school is nothing but a quaint anachronism, moribund and peculiar. I have been a one-room-school teacher, was the mother of students attending a one-room school not that long ago, and I am still certified to teach kindergarten through eighth grade in Maine. For nine years I kept the books and wrote the checks for the Matinicus Island school district (so I know how things work behind the scenes), and I am currently an elected member of our school board, involved with hiring teachers and sorting out special-education and building-maintenance issues. I listen as teachers both celebrate and cry, as taxpayers worry, and as bureaucrats pontificate—and to children as they play happily with classmates much older or younger than themselves.

I do not presume to call myself an expert teacher. Many of our current island teachers are truly experts in the field of multi-age education and have far more professional experience than I. Neither do I argue that all students would be better off in a one-room school. In fact, I don't argue anything—except that our last remaining one-room schools are quite real, they work well, they still exist and should exist, and they change and adapt and improve with the times.

It must be emphasized that each island, each island school, and each island teacher (for they enjoy more autonomy than do many pub-lic-school educators) is different, and that these differences are worthy of respect. There is no template or one-size-fits-all methodology for teaching multi-age, multi-ability groups of students. There is certainly no single process for dealing with a sometimes dizzying array of logis-tics complications, or for managing isolation, adolescents, ferry sched-ules, preschoolers, special education, bossy school boards, inadequate furnaces, rough seas, computer glitches, shortages of milk, kerosene, and substitute teachers, or what happens when a teacher falls deeply in love with his or her new island home.

I was fortunate to have had the chance to visit Maine's last two mainland one-room schools before they were closed, and I have enjoyed corresponding with several one-room schoolteachers in west-ern states; I included a chapter on the last days of these up-country Maine schools and I share a bit of that correspondence from our Alaska, Montana, Colorado, and North Dakota one-room-school teaching colleagues. A few of Maine's island schools are a bit larger than one room, but not by much; we will briefly visit those schools as well.

I have not taken inventory of every existing one-room school in the country. I cannot answer questions with authority about the issues facing small rural schools in the western states except to the extent that they may share concerns with Maine. Having corresponded with a few teachers in those states, however, I believe that we are more similar than we are different, and that rural educators will find a lot here that is familiar—perhaps except for the details of traveling over stormy seas to get to school!

In these pages, you will experience the real world of the one-room schools of recent years and of today. No barefoot children writing on slates, no designated boys' and girls' cloakrooms, no recitation benches or dunce caps, and we no longer have to worry about frozen inkwells—but yes, the older students do still help the younger ones, children of all ages play together at recess, and the teacher might easily be working on algebra with an eighth-grader preparing for high school right beside a kindergartner learning to write his name. And, despite what we think of as "normal" or "real" school, meaning enormous buildings filled for the most part with strangers, instruction on that small, intimate scale works just fine.

We will talk a little bit about islanders and island life, because a lot of what is unusual about these schools, their students, and their teachers has more to do with their location (and their physical isolation) than simply the fact of their being multi-age classrooms. We will hear a few memories of one-room school from a couple of generations ago, when tiny rural schools were common in Maine (and this is the experience most living former one-room-school students share), and proceed into a short early history of the school on Matinicus Island, and some teachers' accounts from the 1960s and 1980s. Admittedly, there is much more here about Matinicus than about the other islands, but that is where I taught school, raised my children, got to know many of the other teachers, and where I still live and work year-round. We will spend a day in each of the island schools and see how these students work in very modern, technologically advanced, twenty-first-century classrooms.

It is important to me that I write only about what I know. This is a work of research, to a limited extent, or at least "oral history," but it stems from and largely contains my firsthand knowledge, observations, and experience. The academic reader may find some of my storytelling rather casual. The recreational reader may wonder why it is so important that I squeeze in every detail. It is important because those details are assembled nowhere else, and as these schools become increasingly rare, I wish to describe the experience as ordinary daily reality, not as history.

Let me invite you into our workday and our school day, and welcome you into our island communities. You might imagine yourself stepping off the mail boat or the Casco Bay Lines ferry or the small Cessna four-seat airplane, and then being met at the lobster-trap-covered wharf or the dirt airstrip by an islander in a dilapidated (and likely uninspected) pickup truck filled with children's belongings, power tools, and a ridiculous number of slobbering friendly dogs. Welcome to the island.

Students at the K–5 Chebeague Island school tend their school garden.
Eva Murray

LIVING AND LEARNING ON AN ISLAND

Going to School on Little Cranberry Isle
On an island, we rely on each other.

The town of Cranberry Isles is a cluster of five inhabited islands, although the year-round town is basically on two, Little and Great Cranberry. Each of these has a school building and until recently, each had enough resident students to keep its own school going. In recent years Little Cranberry, also called Islesford, is where students from both islands attend school. The children who live on Great Cranberry make a short daily commute on the passenger boat along with work-men, tourists, lumber, and mail.

The Ashley Bryan School is a historic schoolhouse with modern attributes and a new name honoring an island artist/writer. It has the traditional look, with a cloakroom area, creaky hardwood floors, and high ceiling; then we notice the Tandberg teleconferencing unit, which resembles a wide-screen TV, the array of laptop computers, and the Smartboard. The two classrooms are filled with color, and various areas are set up for specific activities. A real boat—a rowing skiff lined with cushions—sits in the library section; an area where a science proj-ect involving growing plants remains set up; and the "morning meet-ing" rug is designated for certain activities through the day. Rainforest models, posters, and dioramas indicate a recent science topic. The Pre-cambrian to Quaternary timeline high on the walls is the same project that can be seen on the walls of another one-room school to the south-west, on Monhegan Island. This indicates a collaborative science unit where the two schools aligned their work so that students could expe-rience a larger "class."

When I first visited, there were three middle-schoolers, two third-graders who are both advanced students and prefer to do much of their work with the older group, and five "youngers." During math, the older three sat at a table together and worked on algebra, tackling concepts like expanding expressions, the distributive property, and factoring. A third-grader tackled area and perimeter problems and factored prime and composite numbers (the other third-grader was off the island with family that day). The Ashley Bryan School is fortunate to have two teachers at this point, which allows them to break up the group into olders and youngers for activities, and allows each to teach her strongest subjects. Lindsay Eysnogle goes back and forth between the three older students and the third-grader offering assistance. The older three bicker theatrically with one another, not really arguing, but maintaining a steady teenage banter. One of them occasionally looks a bit impatient with this. Seventh-grader Meg is the only middle-school girl. Lindsay leans over a student, interrupts the nonsense, and reviews "like terms."

While the older students are doing math, the younger group is with the visiting French teacher; they each hold a copy of *First 100 Words* as they count out loud in French. The younger group includes pairs of siblings, Xander and Beatrice, and Sanna and Whit. Later the two groups will switch, and as the olders have French, the youngers will work on English and language arts with the school's other full-time teacher, Donna Isaacs. The schedule changes daily, depending upon "specials" such as French, but is posted and reviewed during each day's morning meeting.

The children join their reading groups, hovering over their laptops to communicate online with students from Monhegan, Matinicus, and Cliff Islands. Since it happens to be Tuesday, it is time to meet on Skype with the others in the four-island group, each group led by one of the island teachers. Sofie, a third-grader, read *The Incredible Journey* by Sheila Burnford with Olivia from Cliff Island and Ezekiel from Matinicus. Louise, another third-grader, is in a group with Emma from Matinicus, Julian from Cliff, and Quinn from Monhegan; they are reading *Walk Two Moons* by Sharon Creech. The three older students are reading *Trouble* by Gary D. Schmidt, joining with Dalton from Monhegan and Isabella from Matinicus; David Duncan, the Matinicus teacher, leads this group. Jessie Campbell, the teacher from Monhegan, discusses "theme" with her group. She is actually calling in from Portland, rather than the Monhegan school, as both of her students have gone to Alaska for the week to visit family and so she is taking the opportunity to go off-island to do some professional-development work. This year Monhegan has only a pair of brothers in

The two-room Ashley Bryan School, Little Cranberry Isle. Voters agreed in 2012 to rename the Islesford school in honor of author, artist, and storyteller Bryan, who lives on the island. SALLY ROWAN

the elementary school. All this teleconferencing means a lot to them.

A speech pathologist has come to Islesford on the morning boat, and is in the back office with two of the students as they discuss their reading.

Donna mentioned to me that she has heard the older students say that they think the younger kids are better off having the older ones around to help. She has seen that the older kids enjoy having the little ones there as well, despite their occasional comments about all the noise. The students here are conscious of the advantages of having a mixed-age group. At recess, the children run around in the snow with minimal supervision. They play a little freeze-tag; the older kids chat while the younger ones roll in the snow.

After recess, while the older students have French, Donna works with the younger group. They assemble on the rug, where the poem "Velvet Shoes" by Elinor Wylie is written out on a large pad with blue marker. She reads it first, and they talk about the imagery, go over vocabulary, and try reading with expression. They act out the poem, which is about walking in snow. She reminds them not to wrestle, touch, or crash into one another; our little poetry students are still boisterous kindergarten, first-, and second-graders. They read a second poem, and one young student is reminded that she can't read the poem aloud with a good strong voice while she is lying down. "Sit up and breathe so you have a nice voice." This student receives compliments from the others after she reads.

After lunch the younger group has science, and they check on their plant experiment. They are growing seedlings under a variety of different conditions. Then they sit in a circle while Lindsay reads aloud a picture book about deserts and leads a discussion of desert conditions; she talks about "rain shadow" and describes how the Colorado River in Arizona runs dry before it reaches the ocean. The young students have a lot to say about fairness when the discussion turns to water rights.

The older group is working on cell division, and they watch a short online video on the Smartboard. They talk about mitosis and related biology terms. They plan to construct a visual representation of cell division, and consider doing a "Claymation"-type stop-action video.

For social studies, the older students are about to begin a large collaborative unit with several of the other schools about Maine Native Americans (this topic is required by the state). Donna begins by giving the students several blank maps showing the outline of the state of Maine, and asks them to fill in one with what they know of geographic features—rivers, mountains, etc., and another with where they think, or know, that the Europeans settled when they first came to Maine. This activity is intended to determine what the students already know and where the teachers should start in a discussion of how geography affects the movement and location of populations.

The older group spends some time working on its "public service announcement," a service-learning project having to do with trash and recycling on the island (sometimes a problem with tourism in the summer). Lindsay goes over a "contract" with each of the five participating students, reviewing their specific roles and responsibilities within the PSA film project.

The younger students clearly see themselves as a group and seem to really enjoy that dynamic. The older students are each very different, with different needs and levels of interest. The two third-graders in the middle are sort of a group on their own, half the size of the older students but both eager, articulate girls who are academically ahead of their years. Seventh-grader Meg is a prolific reader and writer; her recreational reading tends toward classics such as *Pride and Prejudice.* She writes lengthy reading response letters to Donna about the books she reads on her own. From time to time, she might be a little bit bored. She looks forward to more art and music activities when she goes off-island to high school.

Donna Isaacs, a special-education teacher from Vermont, and her husband Henry, an artist and retired college professor, had come to the island for many summers but began staying through the winter when this teaching opportunity became available three years ago. Teacher Lindsay Eysnogle has married an island man and plans to settle here long-term. Lindsay lives over the schoolroom in an apartment within the schoolhouse; she and her husband are building a house on the island. She mentions that during her first year on Islesford as a young, second-year teacher, she had to handle all sorts of serious behavior issues, "problem students who might have been suspended anywhere else." There is no evidence of any such trouble this year, and with seven years' experience on the island, Lindsay has become a one-room (or two-room) school master teacher of sorts, an example and an inspiration to many of the others.

On the third day of my visit, school is out early because the adults have to take the boat to the mainland for meetings. On the wharf, we try to stand out of the way as a load of 4 x 8 sheets of plywood are unloaded first. Everybody keeps an eye on any younger children who are around; the Islesford wharf is a busy place. The kids are used to the boats, however, and know the routine well.

Islesford teacher Donna Isaacs related this account of her students in 2011:

> I would like to say something about our middle-schoolers—we have two, one boy, one girl. Often we worry about all the social, sports, and cultural opportunities they might be missing by being isolated in our two-room island school. One is musical; one is athletic; both are extremely social and miss being with kids their age. What is the tradeoff? This year we are fortunate to have a completely symmetrical school—even numbers in each grade. There-

fore, we are able to split into two even "teams"—each one headed by an eighth-grader with identical grade-level configurations. Various learning, social, and routine activities are crafted around teams, and sometimes teams are used as an impromptu support device, e.g., if a younger student needs help with a problem, they automatically go to an older student on their team—the eighth-graders are the ultimate place where the buck stops, and only occasionally do conflicts reach our—the teachers'—attention.

I've observed these middle-schoolers build their teams this year and effectively lead the school. There is hardly a minute in the day when they are not facilitating a discussion, mediating a dispute, or guiding a younger student—all with the skill and grace of professional facilitators. Every voice is heard. Every opinion is valued. Nobody talks over anyone else with these older students overseeing the process.

On Wednesdays our students have art and music in the afternoon. Before the Veterans' Day holiday, we asked the art and music teachers to end their lessons twenty minutes early so we could end the day with our usual end-of-the-week ceremonial "wrap-up." Lindsay was in the back room in a conference with a parent, and I was meeting in the hall with our principal (whom we seldom see), when I realized it was 2:55 P.M. and we had both lost track of time. The kids had only five minutes to clean up and wrap up, and we had promised them we could end the day with a dance.

I rushed into Lindsay's classroom, where I saw all the students huddled together near our one desktop computer. In my calmest herding voice, I said, "Okay, everyone, let's go into the other room; everyone get in a circle for a quick wrap-up!" As one body, they turned to me and looked at me like I'd just grown an extra head. One of the eighth-graders said, "We've already wrapped up. You were both busy. We're just getting the song up on the computer now for our dance."

I looked around. Sure enough, the classrooms were clean, neat, and tidy. I could see the chairs still arranged in a circle in my classroom where the wrap-up had just ended—without us. Lindsay was still in the back room in her conference. The principal and I looked at each other. I felt a surge of pride mixed with embarrassment at my lapse in attention to the time. The song they had chosen came on: "When I get older, I will be stronger. . . ." There was nothing more to do. So we danced.

Melissa Amuso, the mother of two Islesford students, describes the difference between a common perception of a one-room school and her children's experiences:

> My father and his family are from Maine. When we found out that we would be moving to Maine (more specifically, to Islesford), I thought my father would be thrilled that I was moving there. To my surprise, his comment wasn't as supportive as I had hoped. He said, "Why would you want to move there—the one-room schoolhouse will not be a good spot for your kids to get their education." He went on to tell me how he grew up going to a one-room schoolhouse, and—trust him—the education wasn't going to be as good as [that offered in] a big public school.
>
> I asked him why.
>
> "Well," he explained, "the teachers aren't supervised as closely, there are multiple grades in one classroom, the kids won't get the attention to their grade level, it will be more generic. In more remote areas people tend to forget about the quality of education."
>
> Now, before anyone gets upset, he meant well enough. Education is very important to me and to my family. My father is a college graduate, my stepfather graduated from Yale Law School, I graduated from Russell Sage College, and we all agree that it is very important to get that education. But my father also lived and grew up in a different time; he was in school in the 1950s when education as a whole was different, let alone in rural Maine.
>
> What I've found in the year and half since I've moved here is just the opposite of what he said I'd find. The first day of school each year, the entire island gathers at 8:00 A.M. in the schoolyard, pictures are taken by all, and well wishes and warm hugs are given out. Just before the kids go into the school for the day, a line is formed, with the residents of the island on either side of the walkway going up to the schoolhouse door, and the residents cheer on the kids as they walk through. They take pride in the quality of the education that these kids get. There are twelve students in the school and two teachers, and then there are the "special teachers"—French, PE, music—and everyone works together to help

the students in their every need. The big difference in the "one-room schoolhouse" is that there aren't so many kids in need of the teachers' attention, so the teachers can and do give that all-important one-on-one time each and every day.

But the teachers and staff go well beyond that. They are your neighbors. You know them personally. On an island, we rely on each other. We live on a rock that is a mile wide by a mile and a half long. We live, work, and play together. The kids at school become like siblings or cousins. They laugh, play, work, and argue like siblings.

I watched my son, without his knowing it, leave the library one day. He was behind the kindergartners, and seeing that one of them needed help on the stairs, he just simply and gently took her hand, smiled at her, and walked down the stairs and down the road to school still holding her hand. Another example: Last year one of our eighth-graders, after being "annoyed" all morning by one of the first-grade girls, was found tying the shoe of the same little girl. When told that he didn't have to do that because one of the teachers could do it, he said, "No, it's okay, I don't mind." How many eighth-graders even notice the little ones anymore?

So, moving to an island and putting my kids in a one-room schoolhouse—was it a good idea? You bet, and I would do it all over again. My kids are learning what it is like to really be a part of a small community. They learn to talk to adults, they learn that there are different personalities, and they are getting an education that is unparalleled. They also get to do really cool things that other schools just can't, due to the size of the school. When they have to dissect something for science class, it is a tradition on Islesford to dissect a lobster—and then eat it for lunch afterward!

A first-grader who lives on Great Cranberry Isle and commutes daily to Little Cranberry to attend the Ashley Bryan School offered the following observations (dictated to a teacher):

Every morning my mommy wakes me up—because if I sleep late, I'll miss the boat to school.

I go down to the dock and get on the mail boat, which is also used as a ferry to get from the island that I live on, Great Cranberry Island, to Islesford where I go to school. I carry a life jacket, because the school says that any child under twelve has to wear a life jacket on the boat [actually, that's a U.S. Coast Guard regulation].

On the way I see an osprey's nest. In the summer the ospreys are usually there. They lay eggs, and sometimes if you are lucky you get to see the mother osprey feeding her babies and teaching them to fly. I ride in between a lot of workmen. The workmen are going to work on a big house on Islesford. They're usually wearing painty clothes and usually have baseball caps on. Each one carries lots of tools and a lunch box. Some of them say "Hi" to me when I get on the boat and look for a seat for me. When I first get on the boat, I look to see if any of my dog friends are on the boat. Some of the workmen bring their dogs. I have a lot of petting to do. I always ride with a teacher. If the boat newspaper is around, we read the funnies. A teacher is already on the boat when I get on, and she gets off with me and walks with me up to the school, unless it's rainy or yucky [when] somebody comes down to the dock with a car and takes us to the school. As soon as it gets to be 3:45 I go down to the mail boat to go home. The workmen are all going home, too. . . ."

The Numbers on One-Room Schools
You can't Google this.

Writer and Island Institute Education Fellow Anne Bardaglio and I have independently discovered the one thing (so far) we believe mankind cannot successfully learn by means of an Internet search engine: How many one-room public elementary schools are still open in the United States?

It's more than you might think, but we have no idea exactly how many that is. Neither does anybody else.

In hopes of satisfying our curiosity and that of our readers, we both started where most twenty-first-century researchers begin, which is to say we "Googled" it.

That didn't help much.

Of course, the first online resource to pop up is the Wikipedia entry on one-room schools, which is reasonably enlightening as long as you are looking for photographs from the 1940s, Amish schools, education in the Shetland Islands, the historical preservation of cherished local buildings, or memories of lugging in buckets of coal and water for the school day in Kentucky in the earliest part of the twentieth century.

So, moving on from Wikipedia, we came upon a 2006 National Public Radio series on the subject. It included a piece on the Monhegan school, and informs us that there were "fewer than 400" one-room schools then. I know firsthand that some schools have closed since 2007; the last two mainland one-room schools in our state, located in the tiny towns of Rockwood and Shirley near Moosehead Lake, both closed in June 2009. I was able to visit both of them that spring, and happened to be at the Shirley school the day after the town voted to close it. Being around those few students that day was like going to a funeral.

Thinking that surely each state would keep records of its own one-room schools, I began examining state websites and writing to the boards of education in states like South Dakota and Montana, Vermont and New Mexico, where I knew that one-room schools had occasionally been described in articles in teachers' magazines and other publications. Sometimes my e-mail inquiries would get bounced around the office to several state employees before somebody replied to me. The replies would sometimes include interoffice notes to other state officials such as, "Is this something you can help with?" and "Well, I know there's at least one."

Alaska's website included an exhaustive list of every school in the state—all 507. They suggested I write to the schools directly to inquire. I figured perhaps I ought to begin with those schools that listed their street address as "general delivery."

I contacted the Rural School and Community Trust to get my question answered. They were able to provide national data on one-teacher schools from 2007 (from the *Digest of Educational Statistics*), which indicated that there were 283 such schools in 30 states at that time. However, I recognized the number given for Maine as incorrect, so I have no idea how accurate the rest of the list might be. I wrote to the RSCT to let somebody know the numbers might not be just right; somebody wrote back, "Thanks for letting us know. We wish you the best in your endeavor."

A 2009 Associated Press article I found about a twenty-student, K–5 one-room school in northern California threatened with closure because of state budget cuts indicated that there were 335 one-room schools in 2006, according to the National Center for Educational Statistics (the same source as the iffy 2007 numbers above). In any event, it sounds like we lost 52 schools between 2006 and 2007.

Admittedly, this isn't always a simple question. Are we literally talking about rooms in the school building? No. In Rockwood, Maine, before that school was unfortunately closed, the beautiful (and relatively new) school building had excellent facilities and multiple rooms for different purposes—just not enough students to justify it all. The question is more about classes—do all of the students study together under one teacher or not? Sometimes "one-room" school student populations are split into two groups when there happen to be two teachers available, as is the case some of the time on Maine's islands. As I like to remind people, it isn't about the architecture.

South Dakota's website listed sixty-nine one- and two-teacher schools. Somebody at the Vermont state office wrote to me and said there was exactly one; I wrote to that school but never heard back. Perhaps it is deluged with letters from people asking about the last one-room school in the state.

(There are five, six, or seven one-room island schools in Maine, depending upon how you figure it.)

It's Not About the Architecture
A one-room schoolhouse?

"One-room schoolhouse." The expression brings up mental images of an American icon, a piece of our common history, but something that for most people, is assuredly a thing of the past. One-room schools are included in the exhibits at living history museums, historical society displays, and period reenactments. They make us think of barefoot boys and long-skirted girls rolling hoops for fun, herding livestock, or churning butter—and a lifestyle we think of as gone forever. Even for those among us who attended one-room schools in the 1940s and 1950s, in small towns all over the country, childhood seems a world away, and "things were different then."

For a few students, however, a one-room school (or a two-room school, for there isn't that much difference) is still a fact of life and a perfectly ordinary, thoroughly modern experience. A few of the ranchers and miners in the western states, who live far from large towns, still send their children to one-room schools, as did a few log-ging and farming families in northern New England until recently. On the isolated offshore islands of Maine, where tiny communities of fifty to a few hundred people withstand rough seas and winter winds to make their livings year-round (while most of the country only thinks of these islands as summer vacation spots), islanders educate their small handful of children in the only practical way available: in multi-age, multi-grade, one- or two-room elementary schools.

You may notice that I don't usually call them "one-room school-*houses*" myself. I am not talking about the architecture.

I'm not especially concerned about the "-house" part—the tall, single-pane windows, the well-worn wooden floors, the classic styling with separate boys' and girls' entrances, the bell tower or cupola high on a steep pitched roof. Hundreds of these structures still exist around the country; many belong to historical societies, some are libraries or municipal offices, and some have become private homes. A small handful of them are still in use as taxpayer-funded public schools.

One book that does not portray one-room "schoolhouses" quite so affectionately is Jonathan Zimmerman's *Small Wonder: The Little Red Schoolhouse in History and Memory* (2009). Zimmerman's book was published after I began this oral history, and in a touch of irony, *Small Wonder* was assigned to a group of Bowdoin College students in 2011—a group that included my daughter, who had attended Matini-cus Elementary as a child. Zimmerman discusses the "little red school-house" as a symbol, a bit of Americana used and manipulated in various ways over the years. He offers some useful data but harbors no sentimentality about the one-room schools of the past:

> In 1913 . . . fully one-half of the nation's schoolchildren attended one of its 212,000 single-teacher schools. [p. 17] By 1925 nineteen states had passed laws to encourage one-room schools to merge into larger ones. . . . Between 1918 and 1928, Americans aban-doned one-room schools at the rate of four thousand per year. . . this trend echoed broad demographic changes [more people mov-ing to cities] [p. 47] By the 1950s, only 1 percent of children in the United States went to a single-teacher school. [p. 52]

Some of Zimmerman's observations on history could well be observations of a typical modern-day town council meeting or school board meeting:

Charged with keeping order in the school and keeping parents happy, new teachers often found that they could not do both. [p. 43] Other common sources of community friction included the site of the school and, not surprisingly, the taxes to pay for it. [p. 44]

Zimmerman also describes how the symbolism of the "little red schoolhouse" can be manipulated and used as either a positive or a negative example, and as an iconic piece of American history, it can be adapted as needed to represent all sorts of things:

> To promote school consolidation [Progressive] advocates released a massive barrage of statistics, testimonies, and photographs about the evils of the little red schoolhouse. Compared to their consolidated cousins, one-room schools were unsanitary. . . . Even more, Progressives argued, they failed to teach. . . . [But later], Progressive education held that schooling should be child-centered, not teacher-centered; active, not passive; and based in experience, not simply in books. In most historical accounts, the one-room school embodied the antithesis of this philosophy. Yet by the mid-1920s, the *New York Times* observed, some progressive educators had begun to rethink their long-standing rejection of the little red schoolhouse. Unlike students in large urban high schools and consolidated rural schools . . . pupils in the one-room school received individual attention and recognition. Each child could advance at his or her own pace. . . . [p. 91] Like the Progressives before them, New Deal critics condemned the single-teacher school as a holdover from a pre-modern era; by sentencing children to lives of deprivation, the critics said, these schools also violated America's founding ideals of equality and opportunity. When the nation entered World War II, however, it transformed the one-room school into the emblem of democracy. [p. 99]

A one-room school can exist in a variety of physical settings. In Ripton, Vermont, in 2001 the tiny nonprofit North Branch School was formed by a teacher and a few parents and supporters to provide a "one-room-school"–type experience specifically for middle-schoolers who would otherwise have had to move on from their neighborhood elementary school to a large school where it was easy to get lost in the crowd. With twenty-six seventh-, eighth-. and ninth-graders enrolled in 2011, the students and staff at North Branch all know each other well, and that is exactly the point.

I have heard that the children affiliated with the Big Apple Circus, performers themselves or the children of performers and other staff, attend a "one-ring school" where a teacher is engaged to travel with the troupe and to instruct the multi-age group between rehearsals. A one-room school, to me, is the people involved—the students, teachers, and community members who need them, respect them, and make them work—and not the buildings. My purpose here is to invite the reader into the world of the teachers and students who work and study in the modern-day one-room school, whether in an old, traditionally styled, recognizable schoolhouse or in a newer structure. The historical preservation of cherished local architecture is a story for another place.

Matinicus
Home of the pirates!

Five weeks into the 2009–2010 school year, Matinicus Island School teacher Heather Wells was almost wishing things would get a little more—humdrum. "Well, not really," she smiles, "but we haven't had a single full week of regular school yet."

Her six-student class had recently attended the Inter-Island Event on Islesford. They had learned about how sheep-herding dogs really work, marched in the Garden Parade, and considered the biology of composting at the Common Ground Country Fair. They had observed and learned about migratory patterns with ornithologists from the University of Maine and U.S. Fish and Wildlife Service as they banded songbirds on Metinic Island, and they had attended the opening of their own art show, "Matinicus: The Place Beyond," at Julia's Gallery for Young Artists in Rockland. "The Place Beyond," by the way, is the title of a song about the island composed by the school children and their music teacher, Nat Hussey.

Sometimes people assume that island students, because of their physical isolation, miss out on the artistic and cultural exposure and experiential learning opportunities important for a well-rounded elementary education. "Not these days," maintain the teachers, parents, school committee members, volunteers, island fellows, mentoring neighbors, and local artists who have gone out of their way to make certain that the kids from Matinicus get a lot more than "the three Rs."

For example, the show of photographs at Julia's Gallery, part of Rockland's Farnsworth Art Museum, was the culmination of a two-year Building Bridges arts project involving island schools, local artists, the Farnsworth, and Maine Media Workshops. Matinicus artist and mentor Maury Colton worked closely with the children throughout the year. The photography project continued through the academic year, and students began the second year of the project with a specifically scientific focus. Combining art with study of environmental science makes perfect sense when students are blessed with such ready access to marine, intertidal, woodland, and cultivated land biomes. Learning to be a good steward of the environment, in the words of Island Institute Fellow Lana Cannon, who brought her scientific background to the classroom, parallels the development of an aesthetic sensibility.

Matinicus is the island farthest from the mainland in Maine that still has a year-round population. According to Philip Conkling, president of the Island Institute in Rockland, Maine, there used to be full-time residents living on three hundred of Maine's islands; now, there are year-round communities on fifteen. After hearing that I live on Matinicus, people often ask me, "How many people live on the island?" and I am at a loss for an accurate answer, as it changes so much through the year. From a peak of a couple of hundred during the summer, the head count drops to a low point of perhaps thirty-five in February, when many residents are away (we take our vacations in the winter). "A hundred," I might answer, "plus or minus seventy-five." The odd thing is that isn't really a joke.

Twenty-three miles south-southeast of Rockland, Matinicus Island has never been an idyllic summer getaway, a tourist haven, or an easy place to visit (not to mention live). We are not an artists' colony, a national park, a suburb, or an intentional community of like-minded idealists. Unlike many of the other, more well-known and busier Maine islands, we have no daily boat service, no "commercial downtown," no public facilities, minimal accommodations for tourism, and now, no store. More like Newfoundland than Nantucket, Matinicus is sometimes said to resemble the rest of Maine fifty years ago. I have also heard this island described as "the most Alaskan place in the lower forty-eight," although never having been to Alaska myself, I cannot vouch for that! At any rate, the few people who spend

A lobster boat and the *Sunbeam* at the wharf, Matinicus Island. The economy of Matinicus is still dependent upon the lobster fishery, and most schoolchildren have at least one commercial fisherman (or woman) in the family. EVA MURRAY

their summers here, retire here, or choose to move here and attempt to make a living do so with the knowledge that nothing will be convenient, much will be difficult, and some things are simply impossible.

Islanders live at the mercy of the weather. We are not in control of when and if and by what means we come and go; we are not even entirely in control of whether we will get to the doctor when ill, how we will manage an emergency, or whether or not the Valentine's Day flowers or the birthday present or the Thanksgiving turkey will be here on the appointed day. Dealing with the complexities of expensive travel, uncertain transportation, constant freight handling, thwarted plans, seasickness, and complex logistics of all sorts is the tie that binds year-round islanders together. While the vacationer and the seasonal resident may wax rhapsodic about peace and quiet and natural beauty, or the potential for eating lobster every day, we who live here all the time worry about getting the sick child *off* the island and the furnace parts *on*. If it's foggy or raining or snowing or the wind is blowing too hard or the airstrip is too icy or too muddy, the mail plane will not get here. Much of the time there is no scheduled boat, and even when there is, sea conditions can easily interfere with those trips as well. Nothing is simple on Matinicus, here in the "simple life."

Maine as a whole is not a wealthy state. Aside from parts of the southern coast, a few suburbs of Portland, and a couple of other isolated spots, most of Maine shows its poverty alongside its beauty. For many Mainers, part-time seasonal employment and economic uncertainty is more the norm than the exception. Many of the traditional industries such as logging, papermaking, shipbuilding, and fishing have either disappeared or have evolved to require a far smaller workforce. Tourism services—mowing grass, waiting tables, working as a chambermaid or on a summer boat crew or as a registered guide or in a gift shop—make nobody a wonderful living.

The lobstering community of Matinicus Island has been, recently, something of an economic anomaly. Some of Maine's islands host wealthy summer homeowners, folks who refer to their thirty-room mansions as "cottages." Matinicus is oddly, perhaps uniquely, middle-class. We have neither a summer community of great wealth nor a year-round community in significantly depressed straits. We have neither a population on public assistance nor one that can make large monetary contributions to community projects. A few elderly residents on fixed incomes do struggle, and a couple of homeowners are of substantial means (although they may not show it). For the most part, though, we range from the just-getting-by, multitasking, working parent to the "highliner" fisherman who does very well some years—but neither is truly outside the economic middle.

Therefore, readers should understand that our one-room school is not an artifact of economic status. We are neither "stuck with it" because of economic need, nor do we support a school for just a few children "because we can we afford the luxury." This is a very important point. Maintaining the little community school simply makes sense educationally. It is an anchor for a sense of community in general, and we find we are able to provide a perfectly adequate, up-to-date program without extraordinary cost. Our program is hardly gold-plated, but we are not lacking in the basics and can sometimes offer a few extras. Some of the other islands described here are the beneficiaries of some of that summer wealth, but all of these schools are basically supported by the same mechanisms as any public school.

We enjoy more local control than many other public schools, and obviously we do without large physical facilities such as football fields, but let there be no mistake: the one-room schools of Maine are "regular schools" in every way that matters.

Matinicus Island has a reputation in Maine, a reputation grossly exaggerated by the media, lovingly cultivated by the lobstermen, and either humorous or troublesome when some citizen is trying to arrange for an appliance repairman or plumbing inspector or even sometimes the in-laws to pay a visit to the island. People searching for information online about Matinicus or asking questions in nearby communities are as likely as not to be given accounts of violent crime, general lawlessness, hostility toward outsiders and an all-around "uncivilized" attitude on the part of the island's residents. We are, by most local accounts, the "pirate island." A real estate appraiser recently commented that a banker for whom he worked asked, "Are you *really* going to Matinicus? That's like something out of a Stephen King novel!" In early 2012 I happened to be in Rockland and needed a taxi. The cab driver was a retired Rockland police officer, and when he found out that I lived on Matinicus, he laughed and shared with me that when he was with the police department, they used to refer to Matinicus Island as "Six-gun City."

Lana Cannon, an Island Institute Fellow who worked for two years on Matinicus from 2008–2010, relates the story of attending the opening of an art exhibit in Rockland that involved island students and, when another woman saw her "Hello my name is" nametag indicating that she was from this island, remarked loudly, "Matinicus? Why, that's a HORRIBLE place!"

True stories like those three make the rounds in the community and everybody has a good laugh at our purported "dangerous" reputation, but sometimes the stereotype grows wearisome. The rough, defiant, unregulated, and cutthroat reputation Matinicus Island has within the midcoast Maine region serves a very specific purpose. It is not an accident of history, nor is it completely undeserved, although it hardly represents the majority of us who live here. The fact is, this place has but one industry, one economy, and one means of making a year-round living, and that is commercial fishing for lobster. Maine's lobster fishery is one of the very few fisheries nationwide that is still stable; many others have been through an enormous crash over the past few decades. Maine lobstermen are owner-operators, each fishing his or her own boat, commonly with one or two employees (called sternmen), and are not part of a fleet or larger corporate entity. The lobstering grounds around Matinicus are healthy, and this fishery is potentially quite profitable (although some recent years have been a struggle). Our harbor is full of lobster boats; there is room for no more. If many more people fished this area, all would suffer. Since the law in the State of Maine says that anybody with a valid lobster license can fish anywhere they like (within a certain large district), informal local territories exist to prevent "everybody" from descending on any spot that seems to be a lucrative lobstering sector. "If you don't live here, you can't fish here" is the basis of the system. These territories (with one exception, that being Monhegan Island) are not supported by any regulation; they are, in fact, illegal, although unofficially acknowledged as part of the industry by the Department of Marine Resources.

The best way to prevent dozens if not scores of fishermen from nearby mainland communities insisting on fishing Matinicus bottom (and taking their profits back to the mainland) is to encourage them to fear the Matinicus boys. In the late 1980s teacher Tom McKibben picked up on the local humor as well as the tradition of schools boostering their sports team's names when he created a masthead: "Matinicus Isle Elementary: Home of the Pirates."

Criehaven, Matinicus's Neighbor
A cautionary tale.
Island Institute President Philip Conkling tells the following story about our neighboring island of Criehaven in his book *Islands in Time:*

> Shortly after starting the Island Institute, I met the venerable octogenarians of Criehaven, Dorothy Simpson and Elisabeth Ogilvie. Simpson had grown up on Criehaven and Ogilvie had summered there in her youth during the 1930s and '40s. They told me Criehaven's instructive story.
>
> After the start of World War II, the islanders could not find a schoolteacher—back then, almost always a single female—who was interested in living on such a remote island. Without a schoolteacher, the women and children were forced to go ashore for the school year. Without the women and children on the island, the

store could not afford to stay open. Without the women and children and store, the mail boat couldn't afford to keep running during the winter. Without the women and children and store and mail boat (and next, the post office, too), the lobstermen eventually moved ashore.

These island towns are old communities, not uncertain outposts populated by idealistic homesteaders or antisocial, escapist cranks; nor are they the exclusive domain of wealthy summer residents in their enormous vacation homes. Instead, Maine's islands have supported stable fishing communities for hundreds of years, and many generations of children have been born, raised, and educated far from the mainland. Some of them have done exceedingly well.

A town (and by this I mean a community that self-identifies as a town, no matter the legal name of its form of incorporation) is not likely to survive without a few basic institutions. Matinicus Isle, its legal name, is technically a "plantation," which (having nothing whatsoever to do with Scarlett O'Hara) is an archaic name for a form of government sort of halfway between being a complete "town," with all governmental obligations and powers, and what in Maine is called an "unorganized territory." As a plantation we collect and spend our own property taxes, and we have an elected town council, called the Board of Assessors, made up of people who are most certainly not professional administrators. We hold elections, we plow at least some of the roads, and we sell hunting, fishing, and dog licenses on behalf of the relevant state agencies. That's about it. We don't have a planning board or a code enforcement officer or a full-time town office staff. We cannot create local ordinances without the state legislature's involvement. As of this writing, we don't have a town website, and we can't even successfully tell people where they ought to park. We have minimal public works (no street lighting or sidewalks or downtown area); an informal volunteer fire department that essentially includes every able-bodied resident; seasonally troublesome dirt roads; no physician, no high school, and no law enforcement personnel on the island whatsoever. We have a basic-level EMS service but no paramedics. In the winter, transportation usually means a flight in a small airplane from a dirt strip on the island to the county airport over twenty miles of water. No transportation, by plane or boat, is ever inexpensive.

The move toward school consolidation nationwide, described as an economic necessity in most cases, has led many to believe that bigger is obviously better, that any child would be better off in a large institution because the physical plant might offer so many things that a tiny rural school cannot (and besides, who can afford all these little schools all over the place?). In some cases, those arguments make sense—but not always. It is a mistake to assume that just because a school is very small, or because the building perhaps lacks a cafeteria and a gymnasium and an auditorium, or because students of various ages work side by side under the tutelage of one or two instructors, that the education provided is in any way substandard.

The people of Matinicus do without a lot. There's certainly no stopping for a coffee on the way to work in the morning. Still, in order to function as a freestanding municipality and a functional year-round community, we agree that a few things are not negotiable. We must have a post office (this community fought and lobbied hard to keep our post office open in 2011 when it was threatened with closure for being too small). We must maintain our little power company (there is no cable to the mainland). We eagerly support the small mainland flying service that delivers our freight and groceries, and carries our sick and injured as well as healthier passengers. We are grateful for the charter passenger boat captains who make that trip in fog and rain, even if only during six or eight months of the year. The state-run vehicle ferry, for truck freight, serves our harbor but thirty-two times a year. The small-airplane pilots and the small-boat operators who are willing to cross twenty miles of Penobscot Bay make living and working here possible.

The fact that we maintain a school makes raising children here a reality, too.

The importance of the island school is not questioned. It is not optional. It is not a luxury. There is no way for a student (or anybody) to commute to the mainland from Matinicus on a daily basis. On Matinicus Island, this is not a matter of parental choice or sports schedules or convenience or even expense; it is simply not possible to guarantee transportation to and from the island in any weather. If we let the school close, we believe, it would not be long before the entire wintertime community dried up. If that were to happen, the power company would not have the ratepayers it needs to stay operational.

Without central electricity, we would lose the telephone and the Internet. Nobody—at least nobody trying to run a business on the island—wants to go back in time that badly.

Matinicus Elementary is the only school in its district—Maine Regional School Unit #65—and its budget is covered almost entirely by funding from local property taxes. It employs one full-time certified K–8 teacher, one full-time educational technician, a part-time bookkeeper, and a very part-time superintendent. A special-education consulting teacher visits from time to time, and she bills for the time and expenses. Two local music teachers provide lessons. A guidance counselor from another nearby district visits occasionally, and a technology specialist on another island gets new equipment and programs in place and assists as needed. That is the entirety of the staff, and it is a lot larger than it used to be.

Those last five specialists, and the ed tech, and even the on-island bookkeeper are relatively new positions for Matinicus. When I taught here in 1987, I worked entirely alone. The superintendent did the books. He rarely visited the school more than once or twice each year and then mainly to preside over the annual budget meeting. The district employed no technicians or aides or assistants or specialists of any kind; there was no substitute teacher, no special-education advisor, no high-quality music instruction, and nobody from the community came in regularly to offer their art or their assistance.

Things are very different now. Rather than being the last remaining holdouts—or a few old stragglers who cling to a relic of an institution—the one-room-school teachers of Maine have become professional specialists. Multi-graded classrooms, differentiated education, and expeditionary learning are what modern educators call these techniques, but they are not new. Thankfully, they are becoming recognized as valuable and, indeed, mainstream. This small handful of very special teachers can teach the rest of us a lot.

Island Logistics
You can't get there from here.

The old joke in Maine goes as follows: A tourist from New Jersey or somewhere is driving around off the beaten track in rural Maine and gets lost. He stops and asks a farmer/clam digger/old woodsman/fisherman (depending upon where the joke is told) for directions to some sizeable town. "Well," replies the local, "take this road for a few miles and then—well, no—actually, go back to the last fork in the road and take that right and go along that way for—well—no, uh, maybe you should—uh. Actually, you can't get there from here." You have to imagine the heavy down-east accent in the delivery: You can't get they-ah from hee-yah.

On Matinicus Island, the joke is: "'You can't get there from here' isn't lame Maine humor, it's the weather report."

Island logistics and the complicated transportation routines that must be learned by each new island visitor (and teacher!) are probably the biggest real difference between an islander's lifestyle and everybody else's. Whether you live on seafood or eat a strict vegan diet, whether your children run barefoot in the fields all day or play violent video games all night, whether you've grown up in the stern of the boat or you get terribly seasick, and whether you make your living catching lobsters or making art or pecking away on a computer—those things do not define an islander. You can do any of those almost anywhere. Islanders are not all alike. However, when you try to explain to your dentist that you have absolutely no way of knowing whether you can honor an appointment two weeks from next Thursday; when your friends send you oranges or take-out Chinese food for your birthday because you can't get either of those where you live; when you have to move Thanksgiving back four days because the seas are too rough to travel; or when you read five newspapers in one day because the mail has been delayed that long due to an extended rainy spell, you know you are living an islander's life.

The common assumptions are that all inhabited islands have ferry service, and that all islanders own a boat. Neither is always true, and "having ferry service" doesn't mean the same thing everywhere. Peaks, Long, Chebeague, Cliff, Great Diamond, and Little Diamond Islands in Casco Bay are served by Casco Bay Lines, a private company that runs multiple ferries a day, although with a complex schedule that takes a bit of experience to puzzle out. Getting from one island to another can be easier said than done. Chebeague is additionally served by a second boat company, which leaves the other side of the island for service to Cousin's Island, which has a bridge to the mainland town of Cumberland (most middle- and high-school students make this trip twice a day). Peaks Island, considered by some a suburb of Portland, gets a ferry nearly every hour for most of the day and through the evening. The trip is short and the sea conditions are rarely severe, but should you be on Peaks and get sick in the middle of the night, you are reminded that you are still on an island.

Monhegan Island has a regular private boat service that, during the winter, makes three round trips a week starting from the peninsula village of Port Clyde (about half an hour from Rockland) on Mondays, Wednesdays, and Fridays. That schedule is subject to change if necessary due to bad weather. Island residents must tailor their mainland appointments and commitments to this schedule. Summer brings lots of boats from several mainland ports, carrying hundreds of visitors a day: artists and tourists who find the iconic island charming and unspoiled (while they wait in long lines to buy a lunch because the crowds are so large, everybody trying to catch a glimpse of Jamie Wyeth or some other famous painter). This busy schedule and crowded commercial whirl ends with the onset of cooler days, however, and the winter population dwindles down to fewer than fifty people.

When I visited on a fifteen-below-zero January day, I was grateful that the vessel *Elizabeth Ann* had a reasonably heated passenger cabin, and I plopped down in a seat and waited to depart from Port Clyde into the sea smoke. A few others came aboard, standing and chatting with each other about frozen pipes, bad colds, and other wintertime concerns. During the summer when boatload after boatload of strangers make the trip to world-famous Monhegan daily, nobody is especially noticed; even celebrities appear from time to time. In January, however, a stranger is conspicuous, and I knew I was out of place.

As the *Elizabeth Ann* started away from Port Clyde and out past Marshall Point Lighthouse, the seas began to pick up. We rolled side to side in a motion that, thankfully, I had become used to after two and a half decades on Matinicus. The standing, chatting Monhegan people began to resemble city commuters on a subway as they flexed their knees to adapt to the motion. Suddenly, I heard a very loud crunching, crashing sound overhead that I did not recognize. My first fear (my "worst case scenario" thought) was freezing spray: I feared for a moment that waves and spray splashing onto the boat in this temperature were instantly freezing, which could result in a dangerous build-up of ice on the upper parts of the vessel. Of course, nothing dangerous was actually happening, and a moment later I figured out what the sound was: the large plastic storage bins which people use these days for freight, stowed but not attached in any way, were sliding back and forth across the slippery, snow-coated deck over the passenger cabin, the sound resonating through the steel. I was just glad it wasn't my freight bashing back and forth like that; noisy, but not worrisome.

The boat trip is not assured, however, when the weather is bad. Island students, parents, and teachers on the mainland for anything from medical appointments to swim-team practice to meetings with other islanders for a variety of reasons sometimes find themselves having no choice but to stay another night or two on the mainland. This means sleeping on friends' couches, paying the cost of motel rooms (some local inns have special discounts for island residents), and dealing with another interruption to the planned work or school day. Islanders are never in complete control of their schedules.

Frenchboro has a complex schedule where those who need to get back and forth often have to work with both the state vehicle ferry (the Maine State Ferry Service f/v *Henry Lee,* from Bass Harbor, also serving Swan's Island) and a private passenger vessel ("the Gott boat"). As of this writing, the state ferry runs once daily from Bass Harbor and back on Wednesday, Thursday, and Sunday. The Frenchboro board of selectmen (the town council) has asked the Maine State Ferry Service to approve a second trip on Wednesdays so that islanders could go to the mainland, deal with an appointment, and get home the same day, and repairmen, etc., could get to the island, do a job, and get back off within the workday. In the words of a Frenchboro resident who participated in a meeting of the Maine State Ferry Service Advisory Board by conference call from Frenchboro Island, "The teachers . . . said this is a benefit for the school because it will allow staff to come out [such as speech therapists, etc.], and when kids have to go off [for the dentist, etc.] they'll only miss one day and not two."

The reality, though, is that this extra ferry would somehow have to be squeezed in between the regular trips to Swan's Island, and to do this would put such a time constraint on the Swan's Island mail and freight delivery on Wednesdays that they are (as I write) still trying to sort out what's fair. Swan's is a large island with a year-round population of roughly 300 people who expect uninterrupted mail, etc. The island also supports several lobster-buying businesses that need to ship live lobsters out (and bait in) on large trucks on a daily basis; changing the ferry schedule is not just a matter of tourists having a few minutes less to watch the birds. On the other hand, at this point, Frenchboro residents must miss a lot of work or school if they need to go to the mainland for anything, and the island itself hosts almost no services of any kind. No solution seems evident that is convenient for all. Given one small hitch—a delayed delivery truck, a mechanical problem, especially rough seas—and the whole tight schedule could be a shambles. Summer visitors think business on their beloved islands just flows along of its own accord, without stress or anxiety for anybody, but nothing could be further from the truth.

Matinicus is in the fortunate position of having an airstrip. The 1,500-foot gravel strip is by no means an "airport"; there is no electricity, no radio communications with anybody on site, and for many years it didn't even have a windsock. There are two reasons for this: one, the boats on moorings in Matinicus Harbor also act as wind vanes, so a pilot can check what the wind is doing by observing them; also, the airstrip is private property, dangerous to those not used to it and completely without services, so random uninvited private pilots should not use it. Some thought it best not to make it look too welcoming. Wind conditions are peculiar, the strip is very short, and mud, ice, and especially crosswinds can be real dangers. The municipality of Matinicus does not own the airstrip, and landing here requires permission of the owners.

For the past half-century there has been an air taxi and freight service linking Matinicus and the Rockland area. Generally, the same pilots and often the same aircraft have been under the auspices of the half-dozen business entities that have been "the flying service" over the past few decades. Many of the flyers are former Alaska bush pilots; some were game wardens, commercial floatplane pilots from the woods of northern Maine, former commercial airline captains, or retired military pilots who now enjoy a more relaxed group of co-workers. None is a beginner.

These days, islanders rely on Penobscot Island Air. "The flying service" has the contract to bring the mail, UPS, and FedEx; they also carry other freight delivered to their tiny office at the Knox County Airport in Owls Head outside Rockland (anything from furnace parts to legal paperwork to birthday cakes). They carry boxes of groceries

Mail plane landing on the 1,500-foot gravel airstrip at Matinicus. Penobscot Island Air carries passengers and delivers freight and supplies to several Maine islands. PETER BANKSON

ordered by fax from a Rockland supermarket, prescriptions and other health-care needs, and they are essential transportation for everybody from the visiting nurse, the funeral director, or the state police to very large unaccompanied dogs—and, of course, they carry passengers. The passengers are all of us, traveling for every purpose—dealing with business and family obligations and recreation just like our mainland counterparts. Children of divorced parents go back and forth to spend time with each. High-school and college students hope to spend their breaks at home, but worry about getting stuck on the wrong side of the water because of weather. There are folks visiting a sick grandma or getting the snow tires put on the car or shopping for Christmas or going in for a root canal.

On Matinicus, everybody is a bit obsessive about the weather. I used to think it funny that when you asked a longtime fisherman if he'd heard a forecast, he might well reply with something like "They say it's gonna come around to the south'ard." From the wind direction, we are expected to extrapolate the next few days' precipitation, visibility, temperature, etc. After a few years' experience, we can.

Getting the Job Done

Our teachers had better understand the business end of a wrench.

Instructing in a multi-age classroom, and having to fill in as the boiler man from time to time, might stretch most teachers' idea of their job description, but those things are entirely doable by the right people. What makes the position especially difficult is not what goes on within the schoolroom, but what happens in an island newcomer's head when he or she realizes that the weather is bad, the neighbors are peculiar, the store is closed, the storm is coming, and they are well and truly "stuck on the rock."

Our tiny island communities make up for the inevitable shortages, aggravations, and thwarted travel plans with other things that may seem wonderful to the suburbanite. Children can, if they so desire, spend long stretches of time just playing outside—unstructured, unsupervised, unplugged, and unhurried. Quiet, even lonely winters are offset by highly social summers. Kids play on beaches, swim in the harbor, learn to go lobstering with their relatives, build structures of driftwood and scrap lumber, mess around in kayaks, or make money mowing grass or bagging bait in the stern of the boat. Adults generally seem to be in good spirits and involved in all sorts of community gatherings.

But after summer ends, and the brilliantly colored days of September and October fade into the dark gray of November, the hard work of island life begins. Teachers in the past have found that the cheery, supportive, enthusiastic group of parents and school committee members with whom they interviewed in the spring might be a good deal less cohesive and cooperative come winter. The weather, not to mention the ups and downs of the lobster fishery and the general economy, take their toll on every islander's mood, and the idyllic "one big happy family" impression of an island community can easily deteriorate into "one big junior high school," with the mean girls, the bullies, the stoners, and the show-offs all heavily represented. Such is life in a very small town.

The teacher will find him- or herself responsible for things that were never anticipated in an interview, never explained in a handbook, and most certainly never taught in college. "Our teachers had better understand the business end of a wrench," quipped one school administrator in a meeting in 2007 when the possibility of island schools being consolidated into larger mainland districts came up (and the talk was of a mainland-based maintenance person being responsible for an island school's furnace). With or without such consolidation, the more an island teacher can manage the physical plant, the less stress they will probably feel when things go wrong. Things will go wrong. Generally, they will be very small things. One island teacher mentioned the time the reset button for the school furnace was pushed and it fell completely into the switch box. Power failures happen, the Internet goes down, propane runs out, diesel fuel furnaces shut down when temperatures dip so low the fuel gels in the filter, and the microwave telephone link, usually reliable, is occasionally subject to strange, weather-related problems. The teachers are not expected to fix these things, but they are expected not to panic. They are expected to keep calm and take it all in stride. The children have seen this all before.

Island communities often have complex sets of traditions and customs that involve the school or the children, but sometimes no one remembers to explain them to a new teacher. It is just assumed that "everybody knows how we do things." Mechanisms for obtaining groceries and heating oil, whether or not motor vehicle laws are generally followed, what to do with trash, and how to call for help with any number of problems are also certain to be different than they were in the teacher's mainland hometown, and often nobody will think to start at the beginning and explain. The teacher is advised to be courageous and outgoing, or else risk sitting in the cold.

In some places, the burden is heavy because the school offers the bulk of the wintertime social life in the community. Isle au Haut teacher Paula Greatorex observes that "The school often is the only social leveler on the island. Just about everybody will gather at the school for a special event, no matter what their agenda or who is upset with whom or what 'island social group' they belong to or who's speaking or not speaking to who. They will all come to a school potluck or a school play. All differences are put aside for the kids." Former Frenchboro teacher Rebecca Smart Lenfestey recalls that when she taught, "There were no knitting groups, no book discussions, there was no community stuff to go to unless the school did it."

Holidays can get tricky for the newcomer. On Matinicus there is a bit of a wry wisecrack about how "if you do something the same two years in a row, people will say 'that's how we've always done it here.'" In small towns, a change to even the most miniscule detail is sometimes looked upon as tantamount to mutiny. Christmas plays, patriotic holidays, Halloween, and end-of-school celebrations are filled with local expectations. The teacher may or may not have the authority to decide how these occasions will be celebrated.

On Matinicus, a crop of fresh new little American flags has always appeared in the cemetery, one flag at the grave of each veteran, on the days preceding Memorial Day. The school kids traditionally set them out in order to learn a bit about their ancestry, honor the vets, and do a small community service, but where the flags came from, nobody knew. For years, they just appeared on the island each May, until one year when they did not. The teacher, having no idea how any of this worked, of course didn't know that anything was missing until she began getting stern lectures in the road from community members.

"Why haven't those kids done the flags?"

"What flags?"

Evidently, somebody from a veterans' organization, perhaps the VFW in Rockland, perhaps somebody else, arranged for a few dozen small flags to be sent to Matinicus each year, and perhaps that person retired or moved or passed away. Nobody knew. At any rate, nobody from the island had ever ordered any flags, and nobody really knew from where one *would* order flags. The teacher was berated, at any rate, because tradition is tradition. (Since then, a member of the cemetery committee has made sure the flags are obtained.)

Sometimes, the attempt to make improvements to the school is viewed more than just a little skeptically by members of the community. There arises, in any small town from time to time, an exaggerated sense of "I didn't have (whatever) when I went to school here, so why do they think they need it now?" Whether the talk is about special-education services, computers and technology, improvements to the building, additional staff, field trips, or anything else, there will be townspeople who only look at the bottom line (and not the real available funds, the future costs of not doing the work, the education of the children, or, occasionally, the law). One former teacher remembers that "A couple of years ago our school budget had gone up; we had kids who had special needs and everybody in town knew it, and they wanted names. They wanted to know who was making them spend that extra money."

Sometimes the teacher, new to the island, feels him- or herself working against a current of pointless custom or apathy or local power struggles. It must be said that these exist in any workplace, and they certainly exist in large schools as well, so they need not be considered "the bad side" of a one-room-school job. Still, being new in town obviously makes dealing with these things harder. A teacher who worked on Matinicus a few years ago wrote about her frustration with trying to get rid of old books, trying to find some peer support without confiding too much in neighbors outside the school staff group, and the lack of help with students who arrive with difficult attitudes (and, quite possibly, relatives on the school board):

> I did not find many of the texts or books that I needed when I arrived. I couldn't find more than a few reference books that were published after 1981. A priority was to get the library pulled together. We sent boxes of books that were ripped, duplicates, boring, never going to be opened due to their age, etc., off on the *Sunbeam*. I'll say that caused some consternation among some folks! Why were we getting rid of books? How did we make a decision which books to let go? How and why were we letting books go if they had the names of former students in them and were therefore considered of historical caliber? We were asked to take books to the Town Office to be reviewed by Historical Society members. With their okay, we were then allowed to remove them from the island. . . .
>
> The children [that year] had had fairly disjointed educations [previously]. For a variety of reasons, their academic needs were great. This was really nobody's fault. Discipline issues and needs often exceed the abilities of one teacher. It happened to me in my first semester of teaching on Matinicus. The issue of discipline in a one-room schoolhouse is huge, and every island teacher [that year] was frantic for help. One teacher on another island would work herself into a somewhat depressed frenzy over it. Because of the size of the community and the interrelatedness of parents, relatives, school board members, etc., it was a difficult problem. There is really nobody to go to for help. I could not go home, unwind, or talk to anyone on the island. In a mainland school the same issues

come up, but there is more backup for the teacher.

Another teacher, sharing some of the more difficult parts of her job, mentions the reality of being bullied by a student: "If I wasn't doing something according to this ridiculous handbook that they had, a school board member's son would come to school and make sure that I knew that I could be fired—because his mom could do it."

I have myself observed, perhaps fifteen years ago, a grade-school girl looking straight up into the face of her teacher, a quiet young man who stood at least twice her height, and sassing him thus about some minor change in plans or point of procedure: "You can't do that! You have to ask my mother first!"

A BIT OF THE HISTORY

We'll look briefly at what a one-room school experience was like in the past when such schools were common on the Maine coast, and share a few unusual experiences of Matinicus Island teachers who worked in the middle of the twentieth century, a time we rarely think about in this context—not the storied "old days," to be sure, but still an era before computers, when island children were more isolated than they are now. First, let's take a peek into the Matinicus Island classroom of today.

A Day in School on Matinicus
Skiing to school.

It is Monday morning. Emma (grade five), Max (grade two), and Ryan (kindergarten) are here to start the day. By time I arrive, they have already hoisted the flag outside and said the Pledge of Allegiance. Isabella, Ezekiel, and Gardner have not yet returned from a weekend trip to the mainland. This is late January, and there is no boat this time of year; all travel is by small airplane, and there can be no landings on the island when snow obstructs visibility. Fiona is also out; she may also be on the mainland or she may not be feeling well.

Emma is on her laptop working on her graded book-group project. She will be starting to read the young-adult novel *Walk Two Moons* with students from several other islands, and this week, they are to read the first eleven chapters. Each student is expected to be prepared to discuss and share thoughts at the end of the week, and to respond online to the discussion questions posted by the group's leader, Monhegan teacher Jessie Campbell. Emma, like all the students in the book groups, also has an individual assignment each week. Emma moves around the quiet classroom, walking between her computer and the printer in slippers. She gets some advice from Mr. Duncan when she has a bit of trouble with the printer.

Teacher Dave Duncan is teaching a math lesson to Max and Ryan. Gardner, our first-grader, will be part of this little group when he returns. The little boys are learning to measure, and they move around the room measuring things in inches and in centimeters.

Robin Tarkleson, the ed tech, who had also gone to the mainland for the weekend (something she does much less frequently than do her students!), has just arrived back on the island on the morning mail plane. The airstrip is about three-quarters of a mile from the school. She stops to check in at school before hurrying home to unload her groceries, and drops off a couple of gallons of milk for Dave Duncan—islanders are always bringing milk back for each other; without a store, that seems to be the hardest grocery item to keep on hand. She will be back in a few minutes.

Dave and the little boys use the Promethean Active Board (a brand name) to work on a telling-time lesson as Emma begins reading the new book-group selection. Dave works hard to keep the boys "on task"; he speaks clearly and deliberately and gives them lots of attention.

As the younger students work on clocks in an electronic form on the whiteboard, the real schoolhouse clock chimes 8:30 A.M. This

Teacher David Duncan and his family, Grace, Rachel, and Micah. The Duncans moved from Wisconsin to Matinicus with their two babies in 2010 and soon became fast friends with many islanders. EVA MURRAY

beautiful clock was built for the school by Ralph Gould of Cape Elizabeth, who made and donated clocks to a number of Maine schools a few decades ago. Not long ago the striking mechanism failed, but an islander fixed it.

The new furnace kicks in to warm the room. It is very loud, but there are no complaints, because today is very cold and all are grateful to have a furnace that works well. This unit was just recently installed, and replaces a furnace that gave the school staff constant trouble. Of course, getting a furnace delivered and installed on a remote island is a story in itself! You don't just call up the contractor and expect it to happen with the snap of a finger.

The Matinicus school was built in the late 1960s, and therefore does not have the "old schoolhouse" design elements common in many one-room schools. Instead of hardwood floors there is new, commercial-grade vinyl floor tile; instead of a high ceiling, perhaps even decorative pressed tin, there is a newly rebuilt insulated ceiling bright with fresh paint, and new, energy-efficient lighting fixtures. Today is a sunny day, and with the light reflecting off the snow, everything

Matinicus students; from left to right: Ryan, Isabella, Gardner, Fiona, Emma, Max, and Ezekiel. Courtesy of Dave Duncan

looks good. The room also looks good because neighbor (and custodian) Cynthia has just cleaned the school. She has left a lollipop on each child's desk as a surprise.

Mr. Duncan talks to the boys about the metric system, and prompts them to measure certain items—their pencil, their book, a pair of scissors—in centimeters. He then checks on Emma and speaks with her for a few moments about her reading. She is a fast reader and will finish the week's assigned chapters in a day or two. The boys move on to counting money and doing some activities with the value of coins. They do some addition problems with money, working with Mr. Duncan, and then he sends them off to measure anything they want in the room. They are to write down their finding and draw a picture of what they measured. Emma moves on to a spelling assignment in a language arts book after some discussion of the lesson with the teacher.

The only other sound in the room is the pump for the saltwater aquarium. A special license had to be processed for the schoolchildren to have a baby lobster in their saltwater tank, since Maine has an "undersize" limit on which lobsters are legal to possess. The little lobster turns out to be quite a predator and has already done in many of his tank-mates!

Ed tech Robin arrives back at school on cross-country skis. She lives a fair distance from the school, down a long, narrow road that is not plowed, but she is an avid outdoor athlete and expert skier. The conditions are wonderful for playing in the snow—and that is rare for Matinicus, where winters are often muddy, icy, and gray.

Max and Robin go into the small back room to work together on some of his lessons. They stop first to look into the aquarium, and find that one of the sea stars has died. Dave works one-on-one with Ryan on a reading lesson, checking on Emma from time to time. Normally, this classroom would be busier, but during the winter it is also not uncommon for half the class to be out. It only takes one family struck on the other side of the water to nearly cut the student population in half.

Emma's math involves the nine times table, which she insists is tricky. Mr. Duncan shows her several tricks and patterns that help.

At 9:20 A.M., Gardner arrives. He takes off his boots and coat and goes to the table with Ryan. Mr. Duncan welcomes him: "You're almost just in time for snack. Are Zeke and Isabella on their way?" He invites Gardner to come listen to Ryan read. Emma is on her laptop with a headset on. "Can I be done?" she asks. A few minutes later, Fiona arrives, all bundled up. She starts undoing all her winter gear, probably just in time to put it all back on for recess. She goes right to where the laptops are stored and gets hers from the recharging area. Mr. Duncan tells the kids it is time for snack, and he reminds the little boys to wash their hands. Fiona asks Gardner about his brother and sister. "They're coming; they are just putting on warmer clothes. I came straight!"

At recess, with all seven children present at last, they play with sleds on the slight hill behind the school. Rachel Duncan, Dave's wife and a teacher herself, brings their two preschoolers by for recess with the "big kids."

After recess, the class goes through some of the activities that might ordinarily have taken place earlier, but were delayed in hopes more kids would turn up. The group gets together on the stage to "share," each given the opportunity to show, announce, or talk about something. Emma has looked up the meaning or derivation of everybody's name. Fiona talks about her trip to the mainland and staying in a hotel. "We swam seven out of the twenty-two hours we were there!" Ryan describes how he stepped on a thumbtack. Dave shows the students a short video he found online of somebody "slam-dunking" himself through a basketball hoop. For the benefit of the older students, there was brief discussion of items from the news, including the current unrest in Egypt and how civilians surrounded the National Museum in Cairo to protect the Egyptian antiquities from rioters. The children have studied a little art history with Mrs. Duncan so they know a bit about ancient Egyptian art. After "share time" the students go to different parts of the room to work.

Robin takes Gardner, Max, and Ryan to a small rug in the library area where she reads them a picture book called *George Washington's Teeth*. The older four gather at a table with Mr. Duncan to work on math. He does a quick multiplication fact review with all, and then they work on their own assignments. Emma works on division and multiplying three-digit numbers on the Promethean Board. Zeke and Fiona work on ALEKS math, an online program. Dave talks with Zeke about greatest common factors. Isabella and Emma work in

Saxon math books, where each chapter reviews many previously taught skills.

Dave, while discussing the commutative property in math, mentions the word "commute." Fiona has no idea what the word means, as in, "I have to commute to work." On the island, that would be an alien concept.

Sometimes, a younger student will have more interest in a subject than his or her older classmates and may be ahead of them. Fiona likes math and does well. The younger students hear what the older kids are working on and learn from the exposure. For example: The back wall is covered with skeletons; each of the students has assembled a life-size paper human skeleton and the group is working on learning about internal organs, which they cut out and color and attach in place on their models. In a multi-age science activity like this, older students are expected to do more in-depth research and use more advanced vocabulary than younger students, but all can participate to some degree

With all three of the younger boys together, it takes an effort to keep order. Silence is not demanded, but reasonable "school manners" take a good deal of reminding. Robin spends a lot of time working one-on-one with Max. Ryan likes to be serious much of the time. The three boys "run as a pack" but have very different personalities; all are funny, all are endearing, and all are eager students.

Dave begins a writing lesson with the younger children. Gardner is writing about his father's birthday, which they celebrated on the mainland over the weekend. "We got to go to a restaurant. He taught me how to draw a cube."

As we prepare to go home for lunch, Dave asks me whether I might bring a couple of items back from my kitchen for the science experiment that afternoon; of course, it's not possible to just run to the grocery store.

After lunch, a check of the weather instruments and posting to the weather blog online, and a read-aloud session, Dave quizzes the group on the science topic they have just finished: the human body and, in particular, the skeletal system. Gardner, the youngest, announces that, "Your skull is in your head." Fiona mentions bone marrow. Emma talks about the tibia and fibula, and the radius and ulna. They talk about different types of joints. Zeke asks, "What kind of joint is your jaw?" Dave asks Fiona, "What connects your muscles to your bones?" She replies, "Tendons." He asks Max, "What connects bones to bones?" "Ligaments!"

Then, the students cluster around the big table where science equipment is already set up. Each child brings a food item. The students do not know what the lab activity will be; they are just beginning a unit on nutrition, and this experiment will test foods for fat content.

After the science lesson and lab activity, they clean up the area and proceed to the saltwater tank to feed the rock gunnel, an eel-like fish who likes to "hog all the food," and the sea anemone, both of which eat bits of scallop. The children find this entertaining.

Before long, it is time to begin pulling on the many layers of winter clothing to get ready to leave for the day. Dave encourages them to dress first and talk later, to make the process go faster, but the little boys like to blurt out random pointless facts or things they've heard somewhere ("Hey! Did you know you can die with your eyes open?"), which start complex debates or get everybody laughing. Eventually, they are all out in the snow. Robin calls to one or another of the youngest children with a reminder about mittens or hats. The children head home, Dave Duncan starts for his rented house and Rachel and their young children, and Robin is soon headed down the middle of the road on her skis.

Memories of Years Ago
That teacher ate moose meat all winter and never knew it.

Maine is filled with people who went to one-room schools as children, or whose parents did. Many communities, including some of the islands, had three, four, or five schoolhouses because they couldn't be so far apart that small children couldn't walk from home to school in the winter. One-room schools were common all over Maine in our grandparents' generation, and what seem like the "old days" to some of us are childhood memories for others.

Almeda Urquhart (as I write, nearly a hundred years old) of Scarborough, Maine, speaks for most when she tells us, "We walked. It was almost a mile, and we walked winter and summer. We got home in the dark. I remember walking in the trolley-car tracks, until the [trolley] car came." She indicates that not everybody grew up with exactly the same lifestyle, and explains:

I remember I wouldn't go to the outhouse or drink water from the dipper water pail because we didn't do that at home and I wasn't used to that. It was "primary school" for grades one to four, and "grammar school" for five to eight. I had a good teacher for that and when I got to high school I didn't feel lost at all.

Nick Snow of Spruce Head, Maine, remembers, "In the winter of 1932 . . . there were three of us in the first grade. . . . Maynard Post lit the fires in the stove every morning and wrote jokes on the blackboard. Inkwells froze."

Hal Owen, who attended a one-room school in New Hampshire, told of the harried teacher having to "fight off an amorous six-footer and change the underwear for the littlest kids, and constantly making cocoa and bouillon." Students either too old or too young to really be in elementary school made a day focused on academics nearly impossible, but they managed.

Lucy (Rackliff) Judecki of Spruce Head offered extensive recollections of her South Thomaston school. Her experience is in many ways typical "classic" Maine one-room school experience and reflects the memories of many others with whom I have spoken"

When I started school in 1934, the kindergarten was called sub-primary. There were nine grades in one room. In the town of South Thomaston, there were five schools. This one was called the Backstreet School—I never knew why. My house was a half-mile away from school, but [the walk] was safe.

The schools were spaced more or less evenly according to population, because there were no buses or other transportation. The students had to walk to school, since few families had cars.

I remember my first day of school well—as a scared almost-six-year-old. I had a new pair of black shoes, which was quite exciting as my younger sister Amy and I only wore shoes in the summer when we were going somewhere nice. The rest of the summer, until cool weather, we went barefoot. The soles of our feet were so tough, we could walk on the roughest places and never feel pain.

In those days there was no orientation, so I had no idea what to expect. By the time I had walked the half-mile to school, my new shoes had made blisters that were so painful that I sat on the steps of the school with my shoes off. The teacher came out and rang a little handbell that signaled the children to come in, but I just sat there, not knowing this, and the teacher came out to get me after a short while. I'm sure she took care of my sore feet.

My first teacher was Ethel Holbrook, later to become Ethel Godfrey. She boarded with my family for a number of years. In those days, a female teacher was not allowed to teach if she was married, so Ethel and Von's marriage remained secret for some time so that she could finish the school year. I think the rules relaxed in a few years, because when Ethel was home with her sons, the new teacher was Ellen Nelson, who was married with a daughter. Ethel came back as a teacher when I was in eighth grade.

She made school an interesting place to be. In the spring we would have wildflower contests to see who could find the greatest variety of wildflowers, which we would identify from a book we had. One time, I won and my prize was two goldfish! I was so proud.

Sometimes in the spring we would have our lessons outdoors on a nice sunny day.

A little about the school itself: There was a small entryway with a water cooler. Every morning, one of the big boys was assigned to go to a well across the road to get a bucket of water and fill the water cooler. The woodstove was near the front of the room. I don't know if the big boy who carried the water started it or if the teacher did, but I think it was the teacher. There was a door in the back of the room that led to the woodshed and a short divided corridor that led to the boys' and girls' bathrooms. They were always called backhouses. They were wooden one-holers. Even if you were blind you could still find them, if you know what I mean.

We each had our individual desks, and inside of the top was a compartment that held crayons, notebooks, pencils, etc. Down front near the teacher's desk were seats where the lessons were given. In one room everything could be heard, so children in the lower grades could often absorb much of what the older children were being taught. In my opinion, there is much to be said for this method.

In the whole school (nine grades) there were at no time more than twenty students. If the teacher found a student who was anxious to read and learn, she would encourage this and give him or her extra help and guidance. When I started high school in Rockland, I found I was ahead of my class in some subjects.

There were older boys, maybe fifteen or sixteen, pretty sexually mature. Us littler girls got a "sex education" pretty fast about how to get rid of those boys! [I recall] a wrestling match between big boys and the teacher, which was scary for younger kids to watch.

Lucy said she has no memory of homework.

Those were easier times, really. It was pretty typical for parents to have a hands-off attitude about schoolwork. Some of them were pretty overwhelmed just trying to feed their kids. There wasn't always a lot of education. It seems to me that nobody ever got held back, even the students who didn't even try to learn.

We played kick the can, we played hockey, some kind of hiding game, hopscotch—not really organized sports. We threw a ball over the schoolhouse roof to the team on the other side, and if the ball was caught, they'd run around and try to catch the other team. The big boys could be mean; sometimes they threw ice balls.

I'll refer to the teacher [I'm describing here] as Mrs. Godfrey, because I don't know at what point she married. She was a woman ahead of her time. She started for the winter months what might have been the only hot-lunch program for rural one-room schools in the state. This was only one day a week, but eagerly anticipated. In a small community, each family's means of earning a living was known, and she took this into consideration when planning the hot meal. My family was money-poor, but we had a productive farm that supplied our needs—poultry for eggs and meat, pigs for winter meat, cows for milk and butter, and a big garden for fresh and preserved vegetables. If Mrs. Godfrey planned to make a corn chowder, for example, she might ask children whose families had cows to bring in a jug of milk or a quarter-pound of butter. Or from children whose families had it harder, she might ask for two potatoes or an onion. From the school's meager treasury she would buy a few cans of corn, and along with the donated items would make a delicious corn chowder, which for some children may have been their only real meal of the day.

To add to the tiny fund in the treasury she devised a money-maker called a "Penny Carnival," which was held in the fall. It was held in the school with the desks put in the woodshed, I think, and was well attended. She cut strips of construction paper, the students printed "Penny Carnival—1 cent" on them, and we took them to residents in our area to sell. More often than not, people would say, "I'll buy fifty tickets, or a hundred tickets. Here is your money, but take the tickets and sell them to someone else because I don't need more than one." We were so excited to see so many people in our school. It was decorated and there were various games—I don't remember, but nothing cost more than a penny. Of course, if you didn't want change for a dime, that was great. I suspect some people were very generous for such a good cause. I remember Mama made molasses popcorn balls to be sold for a penny.

This carnival funded the purchase of foodstuffs that could not be easily donated by parents. This program was over and above what was expected from a teacher. It showed what a caring person Ethel was, though it was many years before I fully appreciated this.

But, boarding with my family as she did, she got to know my younger sister Amy and me very well, and now I realize I was a special favorite of hers. She was careful not to show it; in fact, I was not allowed to get by with anything in school, lest she should be accused of favoritism and I'd be called the dreaded "teacher's pet."

She was harder on me than on any other kid. The slightest deviation from her strict rules would send me to stand in the corner in utter humiliation to endure the other kids' snickers. [Lucy told me she remembered no corporal punishment.] In her school, rules were made to be obeyed, and you stayed in your seat until you had permission to leave it. She had ultimate authority and all parents backed her 100 percent.

In the winter we brought our sleds to school because there was a small hill by the schoolhouse that seemed quite large to us. There were not many people on the Waterman Beach Road who had cars, so it was fairly safe to slide in the road. The road commissioner was very considerate when they sanded the schoolhouse hill (this was done with a small dump truck and men with shovels in the back). He had a child in almost every grade. He made sure the men with shovels would only spread sand on one side of the road, so we had half the road for our Olympic sled runs.

Boarding the schoolteacher gave my parents a little extra money to help out, but at times it created major problems. As I said earlier, farm people sometimes found it hard to get by and feed a family. Part of our winter protein depended on venison harvested in November, the open season on deer. My older brother Maurice, who was probably in his late teens, was hunting deer in the woods not far from our house when a moose walked in front of his rifle and committed suicide. Well, my parents knew it was against the law and didn't approve of this, but the animal was dead and the vast amount of meat could not be left to go to waste. But what about the teacher? She could not find out about it. What a dilemma!

Mama had a two-burner kerosene stove in the shed that she used to heat water to do laundry. Papa moved the stove down cellar. Papa and Maurice would bring, probably, a quarter of the moose, or whatever two men could carry, to the bushes by the road. After dark, they would take it to the cellar. Fortunately, the teacher was usually pretty tired after a hard day at school and retired early. After she was asleep, my mother, after a long eight- or ten-hour day of laundry, cooking, etc., would go to the cellar. She would put the meat that my father had cut up into jars. She would put lids on the jars and process the meat in a boiling-water canner for probably two hours. The next night and for many nights afterward the process was repeated. The teacher ate moose meat all winter and never knew it. One day she said [to my mother], "Edna, I don't know how you make a beef stew taste so good." Mama later told me, "You never realize how big a moose is until you process the meat seven quarts at a time!"

Early Schools on Matinicus
Constructed of lumber salvaged from a shipwreck.

The oldest document found so far concerning the schoolhouse on Matinicus Island is an 1833 reference to an already existing structure.

In his book *Matinicus Isle: Its Story and Its People* (original from Lewiston Journal Print Shop, 1926; reprinted by Higginson), Charles A. E. Long suggests that a school had been built "not far from the year 1800."

Matinicus town historian Suzanne Rankin offers an account of earlier days of school on this island based on what old records she has been able to find. Matinicus has a brand-new historical society, and the effort to locate, organize, and preserve such records is still a work in progress.

Regarding the teacher situation on Matinicus years ago, the oldest mention of a teacher [I can find so far] is from 1848. That was in some old town records I found in the back room of the town office. Between 1848 and the Civil War, it looks like there were four sessions a year: spring, summer, winter, and fall. There were as many as forty kids, one teacher, and the ages ranged from four to twenty. Not all the same students came all four quarters; if you look at the record, you see that they were seasonal. Sometimes the older boys were almost never in school because they were out fishing or farming. The older kids sat in the back and the younger kids sat in the front. The four-year-olds would sit closest to the teacher. In the back of the room were the twenty-year-olds, who were there because their father beat them or whatever. Who went to school depended upon money, because they had to buy all the materials—the books, the paper. . . . They were taught very few subjects . . . geography, arithmetic, reading, a little history. . . ."

The teacher obviously had to be single, and she had to board with a family. She would board with a family that had kids, because all families had kids, so she's boarding with parents of her students, *and* she's boarding with the person who bid the least for her upkeep! It's scary when you think about it; what family was going to charge the least for the upkeep of the teacher? What could her accommodations and food have been like? On top of dealing with these bozo boys who were twenty and didn't want to be in school, and the four-years old who probably shouldn't have been there either, and just the number of kids, how would she have had time to teach anything except the basics—readin', writin', and 'rithmetic? We have some old books here that are algebra, so somebody was doing algebra. They read Longfellow.

This was real stuff, reading from the public spectrum. This was real work, this wasn't "See Spot run."

She had to make lists of who was there when—do a lot of record-keeping. We don't have a lot of the records, but I don't know what would have happened to them, because they were certainly kept.

The oldest town meeting warrant I've found is from 1848, when everybody gave money to support the school, but that was mostly for the building, and if you didn't want to give money you could give time—you could sign up to shovel the steps or something. I know that the original school was across the street from the Parmenter [now Griffin] house, by that horse chestnut tree. There is nothing there now.

In 1858 the current "old school" was standing, and my great-grandmother attended there (other sources note the school having been built in 1859–1860). From all the pictures we have of it, it looked exactly the same as now except it had a bell tower on it.

The teachers back then were always young, because the minute they got married they could no longer teach. They were always "Miss So-and-so." It's hard to believe how they had to deal with these older boys. How do you manage the classroom with that many kids? Some of the kids went all year; the kids who you might consider to be better off economically ended up going to school the most.

Suzanne and I talked about the paucity of records from the earlier part of the twentieth century; maybe every time a new teacher came, she threw out all the old stuff, not thinking anybody would want it. They've done that a lot recently, so maybe they did it back then as well.

We discussed how Criehaven more or less dried up as a year-round community in the 1940s. Suzanne says that nearly happened on Matinicus as well; Sari Ryder Bunker, in her research paper "The History of Education on Matinicus Island" (unpublished, 2002), indicates that the school was closed for the 1942–1943 year, when "it was wartime and many families moved to the mainland." Rankin adds, "The war did the same thing to Matinicus [as to Criehaven], but we had a larger population so more people came back. When the men were gone, there was no fishing, there was no growth; the growth stopped. When they came back from the war, people have told me, they would have mainland wives or sweethearts who didn't want to come to Matinicus, so a lot of people moved off, and the whole thing sort of plummeted to where we are now."

Sari Bunker's research provides some other insights into the school community in the nineteenth century:

In early days the length of the term depended upon how much money the inhabitants of the island were able or willing to provide. This was called meeting the school expenses "by subscription." Later, expenses were taken care of by assessment. Each family paid according to 1) the number of students in the family; and 2) the number of days in attendance. Matinicus was incorporated as a plantation on October 22, 1840, and soon after that the school system changed. Each year at the town meeting, a certain sum was appropriated for the support of the school. This amount was raised through taxation, with additional funds coming from the state.

A school register for 1848 lists fifty-two scholars, a great many of whom were teenagers and eight of whom were listed as being aged twenty or twenty-one. The teacher that year was compensated eighteen dollars per month.

A handwritten Annual Report of the school committee dated 1852 indicates that "summer school" was conducted for three months, with total attendance at forty-six students and average attendance at thirty-four. "Winter school," also in session for a term of three months, had a maximum registry of fifty-five with average attendance of thirty-nine students. The report states that there are ninety-nine school-aged residents, or "Scholars in the plantation," and the committee expresses concern over this "want of regularity." It continues, "Although we find a little improvement when our present report is compared with last year's, yet we see further need of improvement." The report notes satisfactory textbooks in some topics but "see the want of uniformity in the Arithmetics in use." Finally, "Your committee finds, as they did at the time of their last report, that our School-House is not large enough, and very inconvenient. . . ."

[Charles A. E.] Long describes the schoolhouse then extant as being far too small for the growing population of the mid-1800s, and "after several years of agitation the plantation voted the necessary funds for a new building which was constructed in 1859–60" [Rankin says she has seen writing indicating that the building was in service in 1858, but it may not have been completed at that time.]

Much of the schoolhouse was constructed of lumber salvaged from ships that had run aground close to the island. Long writes, "February 1859, the brig *Mechanic,* loaded with lumber, was lost on the west shore [of Matinicus]. Part of her cargo was used in the construction of the school-house."

The later decades of the nineteenth century represented Matinicus Island's highest population point, and the school was supposedly full to the rafters with students, several of whom, according to Sari Bunker, were twenty-one years of age. She tells the story, based in historical record and adapted by author Elisabeth Ogilvie in her historical novel *Whistle for a Wind,* of "some of the island's rowdy young men [who] after priming themselves with potent West Indian rum, took it upon themselves to manhandle the schoolmaster and auction him off to the highest bidder."

Long provides us with some interesting extracts from some old school records in his book:

1849: Met and accepted the master, Henry Young, to teach the school for the term of three months, at $20 per month.

1858: Voted to raise 132 dollars for the support of schools, as the law directs, it being sixty cents on every inhabitant according to the last census." [This is interesting because it describes a population of 220 for the—presumably—1850 census, four times what the 2000 census counted!]

1860: On motion of H. T. Philbrook that the teacher's board be set up at auction and struck off to the lowest bidder—H. Young bid off the "mistress" for $1.00 and the "master" for $1.75 [per week].

This "bidding off" of the teacher's board was a change from the "itinerant boarder" custom, where families in turn would host the schoolmaster or -mistress and, we read (and hope!) treated them as a welcome guest. After Matinicus incorporated as a plantation, writes Long, the teacher was settled at one home for the term (although at the home that agreed to charge the least for the food!). Long also gives us cause to sympathize with the difficulty of the teacher's position.

Some children attended for the purpose of absorbing what knowledge the tutor had to offer, and was capable of imparting; others went to school simply because they were obliged to; and still others went for the sole purpose of "baiting" the teacher. This latter element was particularly numerous in the winter, and the larger boys—indeed, some of them were young men—were the culprits. They have caused many a poor creature, toiling for a totally inadequate wage, to long ardently for death—if not for their own, at least for that of their persecutors.

A source of data we've stumbled upon from outside Matinicus is the *Thirtieth Annual Report of the State Superintendent of Common Schools, State of Maine 1883* (Augusta, Sprague and Son, 1994). Statistics for Matinicus Isle Plantation listed for 1883 indicate sixty-six children between four and twenty-one in the town; thirty-seven enrolled in summer school, thirty-nine enrolled in winter school, forty-six different pupils registered with 49 percent annual attendance. Average "summer school" went for sixteen weeks, "winter school" for twelve weeks. One teacher was employed in the summer session, two in the winter session. The male teacher was paid an average of fifty-five dollars per month, not including board, and the female teacher six dollars per week, not including board.

Glenn W. Starkey, in *Maine: Its History, Resources, and Government* (Silver Burdett, 1920), tells us that "A very important law was passed in 1889 which specified that all towns must provide free textbooks for the pupils in the schools."

In the early 1900s, it was decided at last that the Matinicus school would only educate students from first through eighth grade. As Suzanne Rankin points out, records for the early decades of the twentieth century are scarce, but we should realize that a perceived drop in enrollment may only reflect that change from first–twelfth- to first–eighth-grade status, until the 1940s, when the population of all of the islands plummeted.

In her book *Highlights of Life on Matinicus Island* (1960), Celia Philbrook Emmons writes that:

Matinicus maintains a one-room school with a teacher to teach all grades as far as high school. Its standards are on a par with similar mainland schools and it compares favorably with them. Recently, the inside was redecorated and modern moveable furniture was purchased and is now in use. Many students continue on to the high school of their choice on the mainland. MCI, Gould Academy, Camden High School, Rockland High School, and Vinalhaven High School are present choices. A few, after their graduation from secondary school, continue on in college, nursing school, Maine Maritime Academy, and of course military service.

In 1967 Matinicus Isle Plantation formed a school district (Maine School Administrative District #65), according to Bunker, "in order to qualify for construction aid from the state," as a new schoolhouse was already on the minds of the community and "on the drawing board."

School in the Fifties and Sixties

One of the earliest telephone calls to Matinicus.

Jeanette Young Beaudoin is a Matinicus native who lives and works on the mainland now, but went through eight grades of school here in the late 1950s and 1960s. She was sharing some memories with me of one-room-school days, going off to boarding school at Kent's Hill, and landing on Matinicus in the snow in Arthur Harjula's Piper Cub, which was the first iteration of the air service we count on so much now. Jeanette passed on an interesting story. Most everybody old enough can recall their "where I was when JFK was shot" story. Jeanette was in the seventh grade in November of 1963: "I remember when the first telephone was installed in the schoolhouse. Students would be assigned chores, and two students would go get water from [neighboring home] Orrin and Ervena's in buckets for the water cooler. One time Evelyn and I were sent to the neighbor's to get water." (In those days school was held in what we call "the old schoolhouse," the traditional one-room school building, which had no plumbing.)

Jeanette described how, when they got back inside with the water, everybody was visibly rattled and the teacher, Mrs. Betty Carleton, was very upset. It took a minute to ascertain what had happened. One of the earliest telephone calls to Matinicus Island had just been received—the news about President Kennedy, "that he had been shot and he wasn't expected to live." Matinicus had only just started the power company, largely for the purpose of supporting the residential telephone system, and ordinary telephone calls were still something of a rarity. The call shook everybody deeply.

(The actual first telephone call to Matinicus was made in 1929, but that was on a United States Coast Guard line to Matinicus Rock Light Station with an emergency-call-only branch on Matinicus Island. Individuals did not have subscriber lines. That first call was basically a test: Frank Ames saying he was heading back to the island in his new boat, the *Jane*.)

A few days after my 2011 conversation with Jeanette when she mentioned Mrs. Carleton, I got a telephone call from Dave Duncan, our current teacher. He told me that a woman who had taught here many years ago was coming to the island to visit at some point soon, and asked if I'd like to meet her. Of course I would, I told him. "Do you know her name?" I asked. "It was something like—Colton—maybe? I don't think that's her name anymore."

Sure enough, it was Mrs. Carleton, now Mrs. Heald. She described her days as island teacher, and answered questions from the children:

The [gas] mantle lamps—if you put your finger on the mantles they would disintegrate. I see you have a more modern furnace now. We had this great big black thing. [I explained that we'd only recently hauled it away, although it hadn't been used for around twenty years.] In order to start that, you really had to know what you were doing. Charlie Pratt used to come up and start it for me. On the floor, at night—because I was hired to be janitor as well as teacher—you had to sprinkle this green stuff around and sweep it up—that's how we kept the wooden floor clean. Out in the "bathrooms" we had what were known as "two-seaters"—I presume they're still out there—you had to sprinkle lime down in there.

We had the regular subjects—math and English and reading and spelling and social studies and science—and for science, lots of times we'd take a walk down to one of the beaches and pick up shells and things. Then, on holidays, like Valentine's Day, we'd have a party in the latter part of the day, and we'd make sure to invite all the preschool children. We did have a school board out here, but we didn't have a superintendent who came out a lot, so I could do what I wanted to a point. I brought my collie dog; he'd come to school with me, lie down behind my desk, and when it came recess time he'd go out and play with the children. Nobody objected then, but don't pass that on—I'm sure that's not considered proper for a teacher.

We assured her that lots of dogs had hung around in school over the years (although we're not recommending it!).

The first year I taught out here I had two boys that were eighth-graders, Jimmy Johnson and Jimmy Pratt. Jimmy Johnson was very smart, and I had the answer book, so between the two of us—Jimmy Johnson and the answer book—we got Jimmy Pratt through eighth-grade math. Then, for graduation—we held it in the church up here, because that had a stage—every child in the school participated; everybody would either sing a song or say a poem or something. We had parties of various kinds. Sometimes on Saturday I'd tell the children that if they wanted to come, we'd have a treasure hunt. I'd give them something they had to go find, like a blue jay feather or whatever; they'd pair up, and while they were out hunting for the treasure I'd bake some cookies. We tried to do things that all the children would enjoy, not just the ones enrolled in school.

I lived in several different places around the island; at one point I was living in what they called "the red house." It was coming on to cold weather, and at one point the wind was sort of going through the place. One of the fishermen's sons told his parents that he didn't think I ought to have to stay there because it was too cold, so his parents invited me to come stay at their place a while.

After I described Jeanette's story about the phone call following the Kennedy assassination, Betty Carleton added:

At that time they had sort of passed a ban on praying in school and the rest of it. This was one of those times when I did as I pleased. I took the children out and we made a ring around the flagpole; I don't remember what we said (but we had some kind of reverent moment). Technically, legally, I guess I wasn't supposed to do anything, but people were pretty relaxed out here. I can honestly say I loved teaching on Matinicus.

We didn't have electricity, we had kerosene lamps. If you were lucky enough to have a generator you had electricity for your house. We did a lot of walking. The children went home at lunchtime. It was a big deal if I'd announce doing something different, like "tomorrow you can all bring your lunches to school." A lot of the older children would help the younger children; if I was teaching the fourth-graders, maybe a seventh-grader would

Matinicus Elementary, sometimes still called "the new schoolhouse." Built in the late 1960s, this hexagonal building sits beside the historic "old schoolhouse," which is now an office for municipal officials (and still has its attached outhouse). Eva Murray

help the third-grader with his spelling, things like that.

Quite honestly, when I first told my mother that I was coming out here to teach, she didn't think much of that. I wasn't a lobsterman; what was I coming out here for? But I'd always wanted to live on an island. When I saw the ad, that they wanted a teacher out here, I couldn't follow up fast enough. When I married Walter Thompson, he didn't want to stay out here and lobster anymore, so we moved to New Jersey, to where my sister had moved. He took a job as a boatbuilder and I took a teaching job.

Betty told us about the job she took after she left the island (her own son was almost school age and she thought it was best if she didn't become his teacher). As a new teacher in a fairly rough school in New Jersey, she encountered some tough boys who tested her to see if she'd scare easily. One of them announced to her in front of his buddies, "I'm going to hit you." Betty said she thought of her Matinicus boys, some of whom stood way over her head. "You do," she replied, "and I'll mop the floor with you!" Betty then explained that she knew she might get in trouble for that, but,

I didn't really care if I taught in New Jersey anyway. Before the year was out he and his brother were arrested and put into a juvenile place, sort of a jail for kids, because they had been stealing social security checks out of mailboxes. Believe me, Matinicus never came up to that!

I just loved all of it here. For one thing, everybody was very helpful. Parents were helpful, the children were helpful. I'd always wanted to be a teacher, since I was in the third grade. Being here, and this is such a beautiful island, and having a classroom of kids that were good kids—I never really had a "bad child" all the times I taught here—and I had Ameses and I had Bunkers and I had Philbrooks and I had Youngs. The adults also, back then, if the child did do something questionable, or they needed help, the parents were right there to help or to tell a child, "You don't behave that way in school!"

One current student asked Betty, "How frequently did you go back and forth to the mainland?"

Not very often. My father-in-law Charles had a lobster boat, so we could go back and forth on that. If I really needed to get to the mainland, we'd fly. Back then it was the Piper Cub, just the pilot and one passenger. That was the first time I'd ever flown. I loved it. The store in those days [was good]. If you needed something and they didn't have it, you'd just tell them and they'd call up the mainland and have it sent out by boat or by plane.

Did the weather affect my mood? Well, only if I wanted to get to the mainland! The pilot wouldn't come out here if it was too windy and bad, and if it was too choppy I wouldn't go [by boat] because I got seasick. I didn't have to change my trip plans very often, maybe once or twice a year. Usually I was pretty lucky. We had a nurse, Nina Young, so if it wasn't anything too serious, you didn't have to worry about sickness. The *Sunbeam* came out, too.

When the wind would sweep through here [the old school], it was very cold. If it was so cold we had to put our mittens on and the furnace wasn't doing anything to help us, we'd just call school off. I don't know that I had the authority to, but we did.

Teacher Dave Duncan, ed tech Robin Tarkleson, and I assured her, "Not all that much has changed!"

Picket Lines and Flush Toilets
The great one-room-school teacher's strike of 1968.

From a Boothbay Harbor, Maine, newspaper op-ed column by Sidney Baldwin, dated September, 1967:

> When the Portland paper announced that no teacher could be found for the school on Matinicus Island and that ten families would either have to board their children with relatives or move to the mainland, I thought of what an attractive winter some teacher is going to lose.
>
> Mrs. Gilbert Ames, who is the School Board Chairman, says that many applicants change their mind when they find out they have to teach eight grades or see how isolated the island is.
>
> That teacher who is courageous enough to "take on all eight grades" is going to learn as much as she (or he) gives, especially if she should come from inland country. The homes her pupils come from will have been lighted by dawn when their fisherman fathers set out to tend their traps or to man their fishing boats. By nine o'clock, when the children are in their seats, their fathers will have finished a day's work. . . .

Baldwin reminisces about his winters on Monhegan as he encourages somebody, somewhere, to apply for the Matinicus position. Whether helped by his merry depiction of off-season island social life or for other reasons, a teacher finally turned up and accepted the position. Whoever he was, that teacher had to back out before the year began because of a personal or family issue. That fall, at the last minute, the board hired teacher Tadgh Hanna, who had been living in California at the time and saw a story in *Down East Magazine* about the island's difficulty finding teachers.

According to the many newspaper articles that were to shine an unwelcome spotlight on Matinicus later that winter, Hanna went to the Department of Education in Augusta, inquired directly about the job, and was simply offered the position (that is assuredly not how it works these days!). He had not worked as a teacher before and did not hold certification. The thirty-two-year-old Hanna had attended the U.S. Merchant Marine Academy and had graduated from Denver University with a degree in business administration; he had worked in construction, as a writer, and in several administrative positions.

In February, after teaching for six months with the assistance of his wife Jeannette (who worked with the younger students), Hanna notified the superintendent and state agent, Bruce Kinney of Rockland, that he was not resigning, but intended to go on strike to bring attention to some serious shortcomings and unmet needs at the school. According to Hanna's comments to the press, the school board had recently passed a budget that did not include funds for the necessary repairs that Hanna had requested. "No repairs have been made on the school since before the Second World War," the teacher insisted. (The superintendent later cited expense records that indicated things weren't quite that desperate.) On that Monday morning, Hanna opened school at the usual time, gave a week's worth of work to his thirteen students, and sent them home at 10:00 A.M.

Board members replied that some of Hanna's requests were reasonable, but others were financially or otherwise "too much . . . for us to meet."

Hanna mentioned the "indoor" (connected) outhouses as "only one of the many wrongs at the school." He referred to the school as being in "deplorable condition." He listed twelve items that required attention, none of them specifically being the hoped-for flush toilets he said were of primary importance. The list included a state-appointed board of review for the district; fire safety, health, and building inspections; "budgeting for purpose of essential school equipment" and construction of a playground; medical attention for "children with emotional problems"; appointment of "a third party not a member of the district" to hold and account for teachers' records; appointment of a custodian; and compensation for things such as "mishaps caused by the attitude or policies of the school" and "expenses paid by [the teacher] for school items."

"I am not even able to have the kids participate in the President's Physical Fitness Program, because they won't give me the equipment to do it," Hanna is quoted as saying.

The three-member Matinicus school board responded by notifying Hanna by letter that his services were no longer required, and by posting his position as open immediately. They referred to his actions as "arbitrary and high-handed" and said that he closed the school without authority to do so. Hanna, according the news stories, contended that the school's operation was illegal because of the conditions therein.

A few days later, Henry Blagden, an ex-Marine Corps first lieutenant who had been living for the previous three years in Bremen, Maine, was on a Coast Guard boat, along with superintendent Kinney and the town's attorney, headed for Matinicus to meet with the school board about the job. The regular mail boat, the *Mary A*, was not scheduled to run that day and Kinney felt the process should not be delayed. Blagden, like Hanna before him, had read about Matinicus's "teacher troubles" and had initiated contact. A graduate of Yale who had also attended the University of Maine, Blagden didn't have a teaching certificate either, but according to Kinney he was qualified and would receive a temporary certification from the Board of Education.

Hanna maintained he was still the teacher and planned to picket the school when Blagden and the thirteen island children arrived the following Monday morning, hoping that Blagden would have some reservations about "crossing a picket line," even if that line was, in his own words, "imaginary."

"I'm doing what my conscience tells me is right," Hanna was quoted as saying. "I still feel that I am the teacher here." He also mentioned that "They [the local school officials] asked me before they hired me what kind of person I was. I told them I was a renegade and that if I found anything wrong I was going to tell them about it."

At some point, Hanna and Blagden did meet for several hours to exchange student records. The *Portland Press Herald* reported at one time that Hanna said he refused to turn over the keys and the school register to Kinney, but Kinney said he did not refuse. The Hannas, who had been asked to vacate their island rental home ("the parsonage," home to most island teachers for many decades) in thirty days, began preparations to leave. Getting their automobile off the island would take a while. This was before the island received regular vehicle ferry service; the *Mary A* could take an occasional single vehicle with prior arrangement, but it wouldn't be a simple move.

Hanna distributed mimeographed letters to his island neighbors detailing his position. "I can understand where you might be very disappointed in me for taking my recent stand. But if you don't realize it yet that I am fighting for you, your children, and the school here . . . you will eventually in the years to come."

Unfortunately, in the eyes of many on Matinicus, this news wasn't just a local issue. The Associated Press and United Press International picked up the story of the strike at the one-room school, assuming many would find it entertaining, and soon islanders had clippings arriving in the mail from all over the country (and farther; I was told that *Stars and Stripes* also ran the story). The publicity was not pleasant to endure. School board chairman Clayton Young told the *Portland Press Herald* that "the people are sick over this. We didn't warrant this situation." Hanna supposedly made the observation, "I guess they're calling in the Marines!"

The president of the American Federation of Teachers weighed in, labeling Henry Blagden a "scab," according to a March 7, 1968, article in an area newspaper (probably the *Press Herald*). AFT President Charles Cogen sent a telegram to Blagden in which he said that crossing Hanna's picket line was "a deplorable case of scabbing which we protest."

The telegram continued, "While the nation's press treated the American people to Hanna's singular example of nobility, your action provided, in contrast, an illustration of knavery. Hanna made the good fight, and you pilfered his victory."

Cogen added, "You will learn that one of the worst moral offenses on Matinicus Island is to foul a fisherman's line. A picket line is just as sacred and for the same reason."

Several previous Matinicus teachers, upon reading the whole episode in their local newspapers wherever they were then, wrote letters voicing their opinions. Milton Philbrook, a retired Maine high-school principal with Matinicus roots (and a Matinicus retirement home), wrote to defend Matinicus as an honorable, safe, and respectable community with a history of sending its students on to higher education. "My first eight years of formal education were at that island school. Many others who started there have also gone on to high schools and academies and then to college. No one to my knowledge ever flunked out and many have done very well." Philbrook added, "Matinicus is the only community I know of that has the honor system regarding the sale of gasoline and fuel oil. Where else can you find this being done?"

Mrs. Alice McDonald, who taught on the island from 1953–1955, referred to the strike as "a grave injustice for those people on Matinicus." In a telephone interview with the *Press Herald*, McDonald said, "A rural school can get out some well-educated children." She noted the "high morals, good homes, even the wonderful food these people have out on Matinicus. There are no more intelligent, alert, or well-read children than I had out there."

Mrs. Walter Thompson, who taught here in the early 1960s as Mrs. Betty Carleton, saw the stories about her former island home in the news while she was teaching fifth grade in New Jersey. She immediately contacted the *Rockland Courier-Gazette* to express her displeasure: "Why, that story made it sound like the school was a tar paper shack! I feel that a teacher who has such a lack of understanding of the community in which he is teaching and who would take such an outrageous way to make demands lacks personal integrity. Anything I wanted in the way of teaching supplies I got simply by asking Mr. Kinney." Perhaps having noticed Hanna's comment somewhere about the President's Physical Fitness Program and the unbudgeted athletic equipment, she continues, "The children are the healthiest I have ever taught. Any youngster who can row a boat and grow up on an island is not wanting for physical fitness."

A few who wrote letters to the Portland and Rockland papers were in support of Hanna's actions, arguing that it sounded to them as though the Matinicus school board was negligent in not modernizing the facilities before then. The crockery water cooler, according to one reader, was undoubtedly unsanitary. Not everybody thought outhouses were acceptable at all. However, Patricia Harmon, who lived on Matinicus part-time in the 1960s and year-round in the 1970s, made the observation that "People were offended by all this press about the outhouses being so bad, because, you've got to remember, most of those kids went home to an outhouse."

Fundraising for Equipment
We never wanted to see another soup label!

When I first arrived to teach at the Matinicus school in 1987, the community was still buzzing about "soup labels." The expression popped up frequently in conversation, sometimes with a roll of the eyes or a slightly overwhelmed-looking smile. I was not immediately sure what the back story was, but it was clear that there was one. Before long I began to find piles of cardboard boxes everywhere, stored in closets and back rooms and anywhere they might fit around the school and the neighboring "old schoolhouse." Occasionally, packages of labels would arrive for some reason in the mail. Community members made it clear: it was my responsibility, as the teacher, to continue to trim, count, and manage little piles of a hundred Campbell's soup labels, because these were "valuable."

The story went thus: The company that owned Campbell's soups, as well as V-8, Franco-American, and a few other canned-food brands, had a program where, if labels were collected, donated to schools, trimmed carefully with scissors. and stapled into batches of 100, the company would exchange them for equipment for the school. They issued a sizeable catalog of items that could be obtained if one had enough soup labels. These items ranged from small sporting goods and classroom items such as soccer balls and globes to the big-ticket items including, for 83,000 labels, a computer.

The teacher a couple of years before me had begun collecting labels and had procured a few smaller items this way. Before long, however, the "soup label" thing grew to become a piece of Matinicus history. Islanders who were children in school at that time (the early 1980s) still smile and shake their heads as they remember how the collection of soup labels for the acquisition of the Matinicus school's first computer snowballed into a job of monstrous proportions thanks to the accident of nationwide media attention. Thinking back, one local lobsterman, then a middle-schooler, told me, "It got so as we never, ever wanted to see another soup label!"

Students and several teachers spent every spare moment unpacking, sorting, counting, and trimming labels, because most arrived from donor organizations as a random boxful (and could not be turned in this way). By 1987, when I taught, the computer had already been bought and our interaction with the program should have been over, but the labels kept arriving and the island, by then, had come to accept that we were obligated to take this seriously until every last soup label was properly handled, the donor thanked, and the "scrip" used wisely. I suggested we pass our surplus along to another school but not everybody was amenable to that.

Suzanne Winkelman, the Matinicus teacher from 1984–1986 who initiated the collection of the labels, endured the sometimes-difficult media attention, and actually received the first computer, sent me some notes from her journal of those days. The following are excerpts from her account of how this tiny community was inundated with more goodwill than we could handle.

Who could have predicted the chain of events that was catapulted by a simple three-line ad in the paper? *DESPERATE: students from one-room school need labels from Campbell's, Swanson's, V-8, Recipe, Prego, Franco-American, Juiceworks by Feb. 10. Promise to acknowledge all donations. Send care of Matinicus Elementary, Matinicus Island, ME 04851.* At the time I was thinking of sports equipment for the kids. . . . Within a few weeks of the ad being in the paper, we started receiving Campbell's and related labels in the mail. The class journal also indicates we started acknowledging the donations. In the beginning it was short, personal letters from us, and I divvied up the tasks according to grade level. I took the ones that needed more than "thank you"—an old lady on a fixed income sent us two labels and also told a bit about her plight. Some people told about where they lived and sent photos, like the lady who was a professional hog caller out west. Because of the amount of labels that were pouring in, we soon changed our goal to aiming for a computer system.

Once I recognized it was a fountain that wasn't going to shut off any too soon, I got ideas on how to incorporate some new things into the curriculum:

On the laminated map of Maine, we started putting colored dots by each town from which we received labels.

Soon, after the AP wire service spread the story about our quest, we began receiving mail from other states, so another bulletin board displayed a U.S. map and more colored dots.

Then someone constructed a huge thermometer-like graph with 83,000 for the goal (the "cost" of a computer system in soup labels). After cutting labels to size and stapling bundles of a hundred, we stacked them in bigger bundles of a thousand and marked this on the thermometer.

The content of some of the accompanying letters often provided more teachable moments, especially those that sent photos or told of the sender's experiences in a one-room school. . . .

In between descriptions of the soup label work, Winkelman wrote in her journal about the stresses of working on the island:

January 20. Not a state holiday in Maine [at that time]. FOG— no plane, no mail, no UPS. Only on Matinicus. Four kids in, one out hauling. A pony races past down the road. Jody yells out, "Sugar!" She runs [out of the school and] after the pony and Troy runs after her. Meantime, two brothers, Mike and Jay, are reminded to keep busy. . . .

TV people from Boston's Channel 5 here at school taping us for a special they're making on Matinicus. Campbell's labels pouring in.

At the time the [Boston] *Chronicle* show came out to the island, they spent about two hours at least with us, from the early morning pledge outside and as we did lessons and each of the kids was interviewed. They played football with Jay, Mike, Troy, and Jerm. The people were very nice. So it was a sore disappointment to finally see the show, maybe three or four minutes within the school. I wrote to the producer later to express our disappointment and asked if they could give us a tape with the outtakes. The letter I received back from the producer wasn't so nice and basically said, "That's show biz." Evidently they did get the video outtakes, but they were just long shots of birds and scenery.

A man from the Rockland office of the *Bangor Daily News* said he wanted to write an article about us needing soup labels. The Associated Press called and wanted to spread it around the country.

A radio interview spurred on more label donations from the New England area. Not only labels poured in; on one of the radio talk shows someone asked me how I was going to afford to pay for the postage to send all those thank-yous out. So far I'd been paying for that myself.

Among the at least forty-seven groups or schools that "adopted us" [sent boxes of labels and letters stating that we would be the focus of their future collection of labels], there were elementary, middle, and high schools, a volunteer club, college student activity clubs, a telephone company, a Sunday school, three scout troops, Rainbow Girls, an Emblem Club, two granges, Silver Seniors, a women's association, a Coast Guard station, a DAR, a church fellowship, a VFW post, a Junior Women's Club, and a Lion's Club.

A syndicated newspaper columnist wrote sending "leftovers" from a thirty-seven–state mailing (apparently people sent him labels and he forwarded them on to us). Most surprising among the groups that adopted us was a letter from the United States Senate from George Mitchell saying his Maine and Washington staff was saving labels for us. Labels came from as far as a military base in Japan.

Got a call from a lady who wanted to "give us" our computer. The bottom line was she spent five thousand dollars through the Hammett Company [a school supplier] to get us a computer, monitor, etc., a Canon copier, and tons of software. She wanted to be anonymous.

No end in sight. Another newspaper article about us—and then many more labels sent to us from across the country. What a monster I had created! It was becoming overwhelming.

At this point Suzanne Winkelman notes in her journal, "Ad in paper advertising this job." The label saga continued:

John Scully, the president of Apple, wrote a letter that he's giving one. We will now have three computers. On that day, we reached our goal of 83,000 labels, which at that point was kind of a redundancy since we had recently been promised two as donations, but this one would be special because we worked terribly hard for it. Boxes and packages in the mail keep coming with labels. A Sunday writing bee with mothers and kids [doing thank-you notes].

April 8: Nothing moving off or on the island since Friday's mail. Our first computer is due today. Rain, sleet, low ceiling prevent flying. No *Sunbeam*.

April 12: Soon it will be April break, but not before we received all three computers in style. Hammett Company's representatives plus someone from one of the local papers were due to arrive midweek. We went down to the landing field to meet the planes; photos from the newspaper articles document this.

The kids were very involved in helping to unpack the computers and furniture and copier and software. The reporter got me off to a corner and interviewed me "off the record." Never believe that! It was amazing that I got out of bed that day (I was so sick with the flu), much less presented myself as a sane individual. So when [the local newspaper reporter] asked me "off the record" how I felt about all of this, I ran off at the mouth and described the nightmare it had become. Also, Hammett had sent some of the finest and most knowledgeable people in the company, who had chosen to come out to the island to personally deliver all our hard-earned equipment, and in the newspaper story they were just called "technicians."

After the set-up, we were all instructed in a crash course in how to use the computers and some of the software. Technology entered the Matinicus Island school! The kindness of those folks from Hammett that day as they joined in our own exhilaration (even me—through my own fog, still not feeling well) was just so supportive. I think parents were there, too, those who could get away.

Sometime near the end of school, the phone rang, and Mike (fourth grade) ran to answer it. He was there for a little while and then he came to me and said he took care of it. I learned that it was our anonymous donor calling and she wanted to know what else we could use at the school. Dear Mike never thought to come and get me, but proceeded to advise her. He told her that the teacher could use a new desk and so could the kids. Never at any time did we ever discuss needing these things, so I was just amazed when he told me.

The annual town meeting was held shortly before I left the island. I think Mr. Sternberg (the superintendent) attended. It was after we had received—FREE—three whole computer systems, a copier, fifteen hundred dollars' worth of software, schoolroom furniture, money in the bank, and, yes, unwanted notoriety. It was suggested by the Hammett Company that the school/town invest in a maintenance policy for the computers at the cost of about ninety-nine dollars a year. I could not believe the very vocal responses to this: they argued that their kids grew up attending school years before and didn't need computers and extra equipment, and why, now, do they have to pay extra insurance or maintenance fees on equipment they never asked for in the first place? I did a double-take. I'm not sure if they ended up grudgingly agreeing to pay or not.

The newspaper article she mentions indicated that the volume of mail resulting from the label shipments raised the island post office's classification one level.

One other note from Suzanne Winkelman's memoirs bears

repeating, as most everybody alive in this country in 1986 remembers where they were on this day:

> We arranged to have a TV in class to watch the launch of the spacecraft *Challenger* as we sat in our Circle of Quiet on the stage. It was June 2, 1986, and like many people, old and young, our special interest was that one of the astronauts was a teacher from New England. I'm sure, these many years later, when asked what they were doing when they heard about the tragic explosion of the *Challenger,* it isn't hard to remember that each of us was actually focusing on it as we joined in the countdown until takeoff. Maybe they cried. Maybe I did. The rest of the day is a blur.

Figuring It Out for a Year, Twenty-Five Years Ago
He had spelling words like "Czechoslovakia."

When I started work at the Matinicus school, I was pretty much shown the building and left on my own. No one told me what was expected of me as the teacher. There was no curriculum, there was no detailed discussion with the superintendent or the school board or the previous teacher, and there were no academic records from the teacher before me; there were copies of report cards in the files, if I remember right, but no specifics about what topics were covered or how the teacher arrived at those assessments. There was a fairly random assembly of textbooks and materials, but no entire sets from a single publisher and no sense that I was obligated to use anything in particular. Many of the books had names written inside the front covers, names of former students I knew to be adults by then, so they'd been around a while. The kids had a good time finding people's names, but some of those books were pretty old. I'm not someone who thinks that kids need the latest in crisp new flashy math books in order to learn long division, so I wasn't too worried about the textbooks, but it wasn't as good as it is now.

There was a notebook left by one of the previous teachers in the back of a desk drawer. In it an attempt was made to communicate with future teachers. However, at first glance it was clearly too opinionated about my students for me to feel comfortable reading it so early in the year. I think this well-meaning former teacher was going to tell me who the "bad boys" were. I didn't want somebody else's opinions about the kids to affect me, so I stuffed the notebook out of sight and promptly forgot about it. I'd heard that not all of the teachers before me were gloriously happy all the time, and I didn't dare to get tangled up in whatever their problems may have been.

The school board that hired me was made up of three mothers, one of whose kids had graduated from eighth grade and was off in high school, and two with kids in school and preschoolers coming. That was very common; the assumption in those days seemed to be that the school board was logically the place for the mothers. In some future years that got to be a problem—in fact, at the end of my year it was a problem—but I wouldn't have had any reason to know that going in. The board was good to me as a new teacher.

Toward the end of the year, I started to realize that, as parents, they probably wanted things but they didn't explain what they wanted to me. They probably wanted more reports from me; I didn't realize that this was the case. They'd tell me again and again that they were "flexible," as I did things like getting stuck on the mainland and then having to make up school on a Saturday, but actually they'd have preferred that it didn't happen. Communication wasn't structured in any way, and I did not realize that it was part of my job to make sure there would be regular, orderly communication between me, the parents, and the school board. I assumed that in as small a town as this, it wasn't necessary to have scheduled meetings and such. That was incorrect. I also assumed the students kept their moms apprised of school activities, homework, Christmas plans, and the like. That, too, was incorrect.

I did get the impression that they figured that teachers just knew what to do, that there was some arcane technique that we learned in teacher's college that enabled us to work completely alone. We would just know what to teach, even in a sort of academic vacuum. Thankfully, I liked working alone. I like autonomy. I don't mind having to sort of "wing it" sometimes, and I never liked being given orders. Maybe that's why I came to Matinicus in the first place. My teaching experience prior to the island had been substituting, so I was used to working with all ages of students, working somewhere different every few days, working with all sorts of different materials and levels. I really did learn to "make it up as I went along." I was never a substitute who believed I was just there to babysit; I took my role as a teacher seriously, and I never had the privilege of getting into a rut.

Still, I'll admit to not having a huge amount of experience with things like describing the plans for the whole year to parents or supervisors, talking about goals and objectives, using the latest education lingo, grading against an external standard (rather than for effort and progress), or dealing with school paperwork beyond the daily attendance log.

I immediately realized that I had to do some initial assessments of where each student was academically. I had nearly one student in each grade, except no fifth-grader and two sixth-graders who were doing very different work. Many of the kids couldn't find Maine on a map, and in fact didn't know how to use a map at all, so I decided we'd do a lot of geography that year. I have always liked teaching academics through usable skills, so we did lots of things like writing business letters, working with the newspaper, budgeting for and ordering supplies and materials, cooking, making blueprints and scale drawings, and things like that. (Remember, this was before we had the Internet.) One time I was out in the road in front of the school when a couple of islanders stopped to see what was going on, because one of the older boys was up on the schoolhouse roof. The students were measuring the building. I don't think we were really supposed to be doing that, but nobody had ever given me a rule book. I guess the islanders had a good time with that one and the word went around pretty fast. "That new schoolteacher was out there and those boys were up on the roof. Do you suppose she's in trouble?" I don't think they all realized that I'd given those kids permission to be up there.

Even though I had roughly eight kids (and I say roughly because a couple of them came or went during the year), I had basically two groups, because the students in the middle grades were very advanced readers. Megan, my third-grader, and Sam, the fourth-grader, could easily work with the middle-schoolers. I used to describe Sam by saying he was assigned spelling words like "Czechoslovakia." Megan was reading *The Prince and the Pauper*. Their math was advanced as well, and both were really good students. They both had some significant stressors at home, they did not have easy lives, but both were very, very smart kids.

So I had a fairly large "older" group and then the two, sometimes three students in the little kids' group. That's how I taught all those different grades. I did a lot with the students divided into the two groups. Of course, you wouldn't expect everybody in the big group, from third to eighth grade, to respond exactly the same way to an assignment no matter how well they could read, because of course they were very different ages and had very different previous schooling, but I'd assign things that each could understand and each could do—write, do research, reply out loud, whatever—at his or her respective level. One thing I could not do that way was gauge how each student compared to a traditional set standard for his or her grade (except for math, where they used graded textbooks), but I will admit to not being too sure how valuable that was anyway. I graded for effort perhaps more than I should have. I believed that I had a decent sense of each student's capabilities. These days, I doubt a teacher could just decide all alone what the parameters for grading would be. There is a lot more attention to published standards. In those days there was considerably less standardized testing, too.

We did a lot of writing, a lot of English/language arts, and a lot of social studies, but since I didn't use textbooks very much for these things, I'm afraid some parents may have thought we didn't work on these subjects much at all. The textbooks on hand for those subjects were pretty awful, and those subjects were what I was most prepared to teach anyway, so I saw no need for the books. We used them a little, but I didn't have a lot of respect for them. I also believed in teaching whatever seemed necessary at the moment. I'd discover something useful or important that the students hadn't mastered, or something would come up in conversation that indicated a gap in their knowledge, and I'd try to tackle it. We did a lot of grammar, editing, proofreading, and rewriting of drafts, but not with textbooks; I just made up the lessons. I used a grammar textbook with my eighth-grader, but I don't think he was very happy about it. I did want him to see himself as having more advanced work than the rest of them, to start him thinking about high school. I was prepared to teach elementary school English and arithmetic cold, and social studies for any age. I didn't realize that adults would equate studying a subject with being issued a textbook on it.

I wanted the students to gain a lot of real-world communications skills, like feeling comfortable calling up a store and asking a bunch of questions of the adult on the line, using the telephone and the telephone book and a catalog. I wanted them to be able to write a formal letter of complaint and a businesslike letter of inquiry and a nice note to compliment somebody. I wanted them to be able to use reference materials, read the paper, figure out the classified ads—things like that. I wanted them to be able to calculate road miles and gallons of fuel and board feet of lumber and calories and money and time. I wanted them to be in touch with students from other parts of the country and to learn about places far from Maine. I wanted them to hear different kinds of music, to think about politics and life in other countries, to get curious about the rest of the world. We'd even try those strange unknown tropical fruits you can get in the bigger super-markets and talk about what country they were grown.

Have you ever looked at an elementary school social studies text-book from the seventies? They don't deal with anybody's real world. The theme for younger students was usually "My Community," but it was one-size-fits-none. It seemed like, if you lived in the middle of the South Bronx, the unit on "Get to Know Your Neighborhood" would emphasize cute little suburban streets with perky little picket fences, and if you lived on a lobstering island in Maine, it would have the lit-tle guys reading about going to work on the subway.

Instead, we did one project where we found two very, very small towns in each of the forty-nine other states, using an atlas that had population numbers in the index, and we sent a letter to each postmas-ter, asking to be put in touch with a schoolteacher or local historian or somebody who might write back. For months after that we got all kinds of mail—letters, postcards, snapshots, brochures for places, packages with local specialties, really great stuff. Every day we knew there would be something interesting in the mail. I remember we wrote to Crow Agency, Montana, and Annette, Alaska, and they wrote back; those town names stick in my memory. I think those two are both on reservations, but we didn't know that until after we heard back from them. Anyway, the walls of the schoolroom were covered with pictures of the rest of the United States.

Paul Murray, an island man who was more or less the fix-it guy, would come to the school once in a while with a bird that had hit a window and was conked out in a box. The kids would get a close look at it, and if the bird seemed to be okay we'd turn it loose of course, and if it was dead we'd bury it. The other thing he'd bring once in a while was a cake—actually half a cake—a plain chocolate cake in a rectangular baking pan. He did this three or four times through the year until we finally found out what the deal was. He'd have what he called a "chocolate fit," where he'd get a craving for chocolate. He'd wake up in the middle of the night, go to the kitchen, bake a cake from scratch with the recipe his mother had taught him when he was eleven, wait for it to bake, eat half of it, and go back to bed. The next morning he'd decide he really shouldn't eat the whole thing and he'd deliver it to the school kids at snack time. So eventually, whenever the kids would see his electrician's van stopping outside the school (for instance, if he was bringing a UPS delivery from the airstrip), the kids would all clamor around him and demand to know whether he'd made a cake recently.

The other thing Paul had that the kids liked was the power company's bucket truck. He did the line work for the island electric company, among other things, and one time he brought the truck to the school and each student in turn got a ride in the bucket up 40 feet in the air to see the view all around the island. The school is more or less in the middle of the island, but with woods all around and no water view at all. With the boom extended straight up, you could see everything, so he showed everybody the panorama: the Camden Hills, Vinalhaven, Isle au Haut, then Seal Island and Wooden Ball nearby, Matinicus Rock beyond Criehaven, Monhegan, and back around to the mainland. I went up last, and he showed me the whole thing twice around; as it became clear that he was keeping me up there a little longer than anybody else, the older kids began to giggle. Paul and I got married a year and a half later.

By the way, no, we didn't plan the "view from up in the bucket truck" thing as an organized school activity with permission slips first and legal releases and disclaimers and a bunch of moms taking photographs; it was just a sort of short-notice fun thing we did. This was twenty-five years ago.

The flying service would then, as it still does now, sometimes stop at the school with its freight van and deliver a parcel of one kind or another. It was very hard to keep the kids in their seats when any kind of delivery arrived. I insisted on answering the telephone myself, or designating an older student who had rehearsed his line to answer it, because I never did like the way people let small children answer phones without having practiced, without being able to speak loudly and clearly or take messages correctly. Sometimes, though, it would be tempting because some of the calls were from salespeople who had no idea they were calling a one-room school; they would ask for the head of Athletic Purchasing or the office of the choir director or the Industrial Arts Department. I'd say something about one-room school and they would say "Really? Wow!" but of course, they couldn't sell us anything. I had no idea what there was in the budget anyway and I couldn't spare a lot of time on the telephone during school. They could not believe that there was no school secretary. The person on the phone usually had a lot of questions once he or she found out we were a one-room school, but as a sales call, it was generally a failure.

Speaking of telephone orders like that, I remember one time when I tried to order a bunch of school supplies from J. L. Hammett, a major catalog company for classroom materials. They didn't believe I was giving them a real ZIP code. Some small town ZIP codes aren't in some software directories, and this was around the beginning of things like that being computerized. They argued, "You've got to give me a valid ZIP code, lady!"

In the spring, after we'd done a lot of talking about economics, I had the kids do a fairly large art-supply order. I just told them what the budget was, gave them the catalog, and let them discuss and debate the pros and cons of every possibility. Should we get more stuff or better quality stuff? Should we order every color of paint, or should the little kids be expected to mix the colors themselves? Are we stocking up for next year or just getting what this year's class needs? The discussions were quite animated, and they all realized that you couldn't just get what you wanted. Something else would have to give—money was limited. That's the real world. It was a good exercise. That was the kind of teaching I loved, and it certainly was not a problem that the students were of different ages or grades!

For much of the year I would leave the kids at the school at lunchtime, walk the five minutes to my house, make a sandwich or something, and walk back, leaving them alone for twenty minutes or so. It was a deliberate trust exercise and the students and I had discussed it a lot. Nobody ever sabotaged the room or hurt a little kid or fell out of the apple tree and broke his neck. Of course, I was eventually told I couldn't do that, leave the kids unsupervised, even if it was lunchtime and they would be just as unsupervised should they elect to walk home for lunch themselves.

After I stopped leaving at lunchtime, the kids were indignant, saying it seemed like I didn't trust them anymore. That hurt a little. I told them outright that I had my orders from the adults. Soon after, Paul started bringing me lunches at school, big ones. He'd bring a pot of soup, a sandwich on homemade bread, some kind of dessert, and a can of Coke or whatever. More than I could possibly eat. The kids said, "Hey, we don't get hot lunch!" but they grinned and ribbed me about it being cute.

We hosted a school banquet once where the students did all the cooking over at the parsonage (my rented house). We set up tables at the school and all the parents and a few others came. Making nice invitations cards for that dinner was one of the only things we ever used the computers for that year. That was before we had the Internet, of course, and the computers were mostly used for word processing, printing signs, and stationery, things like that. We had a black-and-white dot-matrix printer. Even after all that effort to get the computers, I didn't use them much. I didn't want my students spending a lot of school time playing computer games on discs, even the ones sold to us as "educational." I thought they were mostly just inane time-fillers. I had that old-fashioned idea that if they had spare time, they were better off reading or drawing a picture.

Each morning, while I was doing start-the-day activities with the younger kids, the older ones were expected to settle down and work independently on a short writing prompt that I'd have written up on the board. Yes, I used the real blackboard all the time (although it was green). I also used the old-time purple-ink mimeograph machine; we didn't have a photocopier yet. Anyway, I'd write "Think about . . ." and then write something on the board, and the third- through eighth-graders would write a paragraph or so in response. Of course students of different ages wouldn't be expected to come up with the same thing, but actually, my third- and fourth-graders were a couple of the best writers in the group, so they were fine working along with the middle-schoolers.

Then I'd set the younger children up with something to do where they were supposed to work on their own; this worked better some days than others, but I figured it generally worked best early in the day before they got tired. While they were doing this, the older students and I went over by the big window facing the road and sat on the bookshelf and the table there, really casually, and talked about what had been on the news the night before. They were all expected to watch the news, at least as much as they could, although sometimes parents weren't a lot of help with this. But usually most of them had seen it. We'd discuss current events and some background, and we'd find places on the world map that had been mentioned. Nothing was too controversial as long as we managed to remain polite. We did talk about communism and we did talk about marijuana. That year I remember we heard a lot on the news about Manuel Noriega, Robert Bork, and the girl in Texas who fell down the well and was rescued. It was always a social studies lesson of some kind, but never one that appeared carefully scripted from a lesson plan.

I did a lot of old-fashioned geography stuff with my students. Sometimes it was an activity as basic as taking a blank map of a continent and filling in the countries—with discussion allowed. I also did a lot of language arts. We did what educators call "the writing process," which basically just means working over several drafts, which is often hard for kids. They always seem to think that once they've written something, it is over and done with forever. We did a lot of editing; I'd put a selection up on the board that had lots of errors or awkward style issues and we would "find all the mistakes in this paragraph." We'd write a quick draft and then work on proofreading and on stylistic techniques and strategies for improving writing—maybe going back and adding detail, including what somebody might hear or smell or feel in a scene rather than only what they see, avoiding beginning every paragraph the same way, and so on. I gave them traditional spelling lists with spelling tests, but I didn't get the words from some published source, I just estimated, based on reading their writing every day, what they needed. We did traditional penmanship exercises, too. Not a lot of people teach that now. I wished that my own handwriting was better than it is; that was the incentive to do it with my students.

I decided we should do a literature-based reading program. I wasn't going to put up with those horrible basal readers except for occasional work with beginning readers, so I ordered multiple copies of novels. We got a collection of Sherlock Holmes stories; we got *Never Cry Wolf, Johnny Tremain, The Prince and the Pauper, The Call of the Wild,* and *Captains Courageous* (which was a familiar world for most of them). I think I was usually reading two or three books at a time with different pairs and trios of students. We'd go through the books fairly slowly but thoroughly, and I'd have them write essays, like I'd done in high school. I wasn't about to give them multiple-choice quizzes about what country Farley Mowat was writing about or what Johnny Tremain's middle name was. We weren't skipping English grammar, because I did that with them at other times; I just saw no point in reading textbooks and doing the little reading-comprehension questions.

I wanted to teach those older students to fight city hall. I wanted them to think about ethics and decipher the language in the Pledge of Allegiance and question politicians and read the papers and be responsible for themselves. I had some very bright students and I think I was determined to have a little gifted-and-talented social studies and literature program going here informally. I have no idea whether any of it sunk in, and I never will know. We'd talk about things that were pretty mature—not crude, never sexual, but politics, war, prejudice, and things like that. We also played the "stock market game," where kids invest imaginary money and follow certain stocks they've chosen by checking the newspapers, and then see who makes the most profit at the end.

As for the little kids, I probably had fewer goals for them, less awareness of where they needed to be. I was probably a better middle-school teacher in those days. I believed that what the little ones mostly needed was a lot of being read to, a lot of reading instruction, a solid grounding in basic arithmetic, lots of art, and ways to practice fine motor skills. Of course we started the day, as is traditional, with some calendar work, the weather, anything special going on, a bit of warming up—this while the older kids had their morning writing prompt. I remember spending a long night once every month cutting out little calendar pieces for the coming month—thirty-one construction paper pumpkins in October, construction-paper crocuses for every day in April, or whatever. If a child seemed immature for his grade and needed more time before he could do a lot of independent work, I thought that was okay. Maybe it was, maybe it wasn't.

The little kids were really neat people. One girl was always at the island parties. I assume she was hardly even noticed because she was just a little kid, but she was very perceptive and remembered everything the adults said—and then she'd gossip about people when she came to school, not being mean, but just because she liked to talk. One boy only wanted to deal with things related to boats and lobster fishing, so a lot of his lessons were things like one-on-one writing practice having to do with boats. We sent for a bunch of boat-shop brochures and stuff for him, pored over the marine supply catalogues, and he drew lots of pictures of his future lobster boat. Yes, he is a full-time lobster fisherman now.

I remember this little boy not knowing that the sea creature the lobstermen refer to jokingly as a "whore's egg" had another name; he would talk, totally straight-faced, about crabs and lobsters and starfish and whore's eggs—not knowing what a "whore" was. A whore's egg is a spiny sea urchin, of course.

There were no substitute teachers and no aides or ed techs that year. I did get stuck on the mainland a few times, probably too many times, and we'd make it up on Saturday. It is not as if the children had any other activities on Saturdays. Nowadays, kids go off to participate in various activities more, but they didn't leave the island so much then. Once I called off school for a "snow day" because the heat was out: the fuel had frozen. I learned that diesel fuel will gel up and turn to a waxy substance in an outside fuel filter and should be thinned with kerosene in cold weather. Normally, the little island schools are the only schools in the state that will be open in a big snowstorm, because we don't use school buses.

Having no substitute was hard a couple of times. When I got strep throat. I didn't want to leave Matinicus because I'd already been through the get-stuck-and-cancel-school thing a few times and was attempting not to let it happen again. But a friend on the island insisted that I go to the doctor.

We performed a very elaborate Christmas play that year. I had read a humorous book to the kids and we decided to do an adaptation of it. The only reason I don't mention the title is that we probably should have asked permission, but there wasn't time because I had no idea how to do that (remember, this was before you could just "Google it"). Anyway, I wrote the script, which itself was no small job because this wasn't just a quickie little one-scene pageant, it was the whole story, a real play. We needed everybody. One or two of the kids didn't have the patience for a lot of serious rehearsing or memorizing a lot of lines. We managed, though. I remember my seventh-grade boy, Noah, dramatically pulling off his woman's wig and stomping on it in very theatrical exasperation when one of the little kids made the same mistake for the umpteenth time. It was hilarious. When the schoolroom was full of islanders and we performed the play, I thought it went great. A couple of the older people didn't know what was going on because it was long and wasn't a typical Christmas pageant, but I was delighted; we'd put on an entire play, with sets, costume changes, and loads of memorizing, all a ton of work. It was really funny, too.

We did not have much for organized physical education. When the weather wasn't decent for going outside, the kids liked to play a form of floor hockey with some huge cardboard bricks we had. We didn't have a lot of playground equipment then; there's a lot more now. We did go ice skating a few times that winter, and I remember there were two days when the road was such a glacier that several of the kids actually skated to school. Seriously. I took the kids for walks sometimes, and we messed around with a ball a little, but I didn't know the rules myself for games like soccer, so even if I'd had a more homogeneous group of kids, I wouldn't have been able to teach sports.

We had strict orders from the woman who cleaned the classroom: stocking feet or separate indoor shoes. At the time, the school board only allowed cold water at the sink, supposedly because running the water heater would cost too much. (Later they relented and allowed hot water.) I had also been specifically directed that the children were to call me by my last name. Later, a lot of the Matinicus teachers had nicknames, like "Mister T" for Tom McKibben, or "Teach" for Pat Walchli. I also later found out that some of the other island kids called their teacher by their first name, or had some compromise like "Miss Becky." It wasn't up to me.

A few kids dropped in for a while in the spring; Brock came for a little while, Penny was around a little bit, too. Ikey started the year with us, a first-grader, a sweet little kid; he disappeared about six weeks into the year and nobody told us what happened to him. Finally, the kids started hearing talk around the island that he'd been taken back to the mainland. On the island he lived with his grown half-sister and her family. I don't know who was technically his guardian; I couldn't find out, and none of the other adults at the time seemed to worry about it. Amy and Sam were just there for one year.

Their mom married an islander in September, and she took the kids and left the next summer. Those two were really, really smart kids, too. I hope they went somewhere that had a good school.

Each year we were supposed to take the kids on a two- or three-day–long field trip. Some of the kids didn't get off the island much, although that was starting to change. (Island kids go back and forth routinely now.) For field trips island teachers had been using a passenger van owned and lent to us by the Maine Seacoast Mission. Paul was supposed to go along as the bus driver because the Mission had given him permission or put him on the car insurance or whatever. We went tent camping at Acadia National Park, then to Augusta and the Maine State Museum and State House, and to Scarborough where I knew the previous fire chief so we could ogle the fire trucks. The superintendent had told me to take them to McDonald's and to go roller skating or something, because those are rare treats for the island kids.

I didn't think that these kids would either find trouble or be in danger. My kindergarten student went, too, without her parents, and she was just fine. I remember her, five years old, roller skating on the carriage road at Acadia National Park. Since then we've supposedly had all kinds of issues with little kids going on these long trips, crying at bedtime or whatever, but I guess I was lucky. Of course, they *were* kids—I had to bust up a poker game among the older boys once, but nobody was a flight risk or a genuine discipline problem or likely to get hurt. They didn't get upset or need their parents, and parents in those days didn't seem to think they needed to hover over their kids as much as some do now. Nobody had medications or dietary restrictions, either.

Toward the end of the school year there was a bit of a tug-of-war between some of the parents, and I was being used as the rope. I actually had somebody call me up on the phone and yell, "You better tell that bitch to tell her kid to stay away from my kid!" The kids were arguing, the adults were arguing. Welcome to March on an island. This was all during the infamous late-winter mud season when people here tend to get depressed or easily angered anyway. I had to look at myself in the mirror every day and say, "You are doing a good job with the children," but my job was getting difficult with the adults. I had no coworkers or peer group, the superintendent was almost a nonpresence, and I also knew that I had been hired to tough this out.

What would I have done differently if I had it to do over? I'd have pushed for a ton of parent-teacher conferences and discussions, really forced the issue. I assumed the parents knew what their kids were doing in school, that they looked over the homework, and that they talked about school with the kids. That was a mistake. Kids rarely talk in detail about school under the best of circumstances. I made the mistake of assuming that since I had a relationship with the kids, a working arrangement with the kids, and felt my responsibility was to the kids, that they themselves would be adequate intermediaries between school and their parents. It would have been better if I had involved the parents a lot more, especially once they all got to fighting in the early spring. I've learned that the teacher, each year, has to create and manage and maintain the school's image and place in the community. That takes work.

SO, HOW *DO* YOU TEACH
ALL THOSE GRADES AT ONCE?

Going to School on Frenchboro
This job rocks!

At the Frenchboro School, the children line up and greet every visitor, each introducing him- or herself and shaking hands. Teachers Michelle and Doug Finn have decided that good manners and similar skills useful when dealing with strangers are a worthwhile part of the curriculum. The first time I visit, in 2009, Cadin and Johnny are in kindergarten. Austin, Teressa, Brody, Myron, Bradley, and a little girl named Saylor are in grades one through three; twins Dylan and Cody are in the sixth grade and Lance is in the eighth. He is thinking about high school next year and looking forward to guitar lessons and Spanish. He and his mother, who had once been the Frenchboro teacher, will be moving off the island; they own property on the mainland, and that is where he will attend high school. A twelfth student recently left the island because her grandmother, with whom she lived, had become ill. Frenchboro has had a bit of a "baby boom"; numerous preschoolers and babies on the island make it look like the school population should be steady for quite a while.

Frenchboro, like Matinicus, is a lobster-fishing community; there aren't many other ways to make a living (okay, maybe none), and there isn't much for external entertainment. Although there are summer homes, tourism is not a big part of the island's identity or economy. Transportation on and off the island can be a challenge, as the ferry schedule is a bit strange and rarely convenient (there is no airstrip and no daily scheduled water taxi or mail boat). This is very definitely a working community; unlike some of Maine's other islands, even during the summer there isn't a celebrity in sight.

The Frenchboro School was built in 1907 to replace an older structure. As with the other islands that still make use of their old, historic schoolhouses, it is a striking juxtaposition of old and new. The room trimmed with old woodwork and a pressed-tin ceiling holds a Poly-

The Frenchboro School. Eva Murray

com videoconferencing unit and lots of laptop computers. The teachers here are called Mr. and Mrs. Finn, specifically, to go along with their intention to teach "adult" social behavior in school.

"This job rocks!" grins Doug Finn, and then he stops me. "Probably you shouldn't quote 'this job rocks!'" (He would later give permission.) Mr. Finn moves fast. His eyes twinkle and his enthusiasm is contagious. He comes across as genuinely friendly and approachable but never without complete control of the room. There is a system for everything. The Finns seem to be constantly in motion and the students have no down time. That is intentional; unlike a schoolroom with two or three students, a room with a dozen kids of different ages requires a lot of choreographing. "There is no discipline problem. Never. The kids get no time where they don't know what they should be doing." He confides that his high-school classes in Alaska, where he used to teach, were much rougher and less disciplined. "We're strict," he tells me, and Michelle smiles, but I can see that they both have a sense of humor. The Finns met on Savoonga, a remote Alaskan island very close to Russia, where they both taught. Before that, Doug had been in the Peace Corps in Gambia. In terms of convenience, the availability of groceries, social life, civilization, and comfort, they think Frenchboro is a walk in the park.

The Frenchboro School is part of a school district called Alternative Organizational Structure (AOS) 91, along with Swan's Island, the Cranberries, and the schools of Mount Desert Island (a large, bridged island usually considered "mainland"). The Town of Frenchboro itself is actually a cluster of islands, and in years past, several were inhabited. Now, only Long Island has schoolchildren, and although it isn't extremely accurate, we usually refer to the island itself as Frenchboro now, to differentiate it from the Long Island in Casco Bay.

Doug teaches a lot of science. He laughed when he mentioned that the State of Maine standards for first grade include "learning that the weather changes." For an island child, living with the ocean, where every coming and going is dependent upon (or interrupted by) the weather, nothing could be more obvious. A former middle- and high-school math and science teacher, Doug brings a wealth of science resources and doesn't need to rely on a textbook. He tells me that some of the younger students had been significantly behind in their math skills, but he's working to get them caught up. There is a lot of drill, but with his upbeat delivery, it seems pretty painless. Many of the younger children do math facts drills from a free website that they seem to enjoy. They are eager to show Mr. Finn the work they've done. "Can we try times tables?"

Mrs. Finn rings a traditional old school bell to let the kids know recess is over. Lobstermen often stop by with buckets containing various sea creatures that have come up in the lobster traps—sometimes unusual animals they think might interest the kids. The schoolroom hosts a saltwater tank, "the hotel tank," where these specimens stay for a while to be observed, but nothing is left there permanently to die.

The science lesson for today is about Newton's Laws of Motion. All of the students are involved, from the littlest children to Lance, who is getting ready to leave for high school. They review terminology with lots of examples, and even the little fellows know what *gravity* and *force* and such words mean. The younger ones are really listening to the lessons intended for the older children, although they are also included in the activity and spoken to at their own level; the Finns are expert at multi-age teaching techniques. Doug shows a video on the Polycom's big television screen, a stop-action film of a bullet smashing various things, something gleaned from YouTube. The students find it very entertaining. There is a staged train-crash video produced by the British Electricity Board and some footage of dramatic hockey collisions. Mr. Finn, in talking about Newton's Laws, asks the kids, "Can you break these laws?" "NO!" they laugh. He talks with Cody, a sixth-grader, about a bullet hitting a deer. No need to be terribly delicate with these students; he knows them all personally, knows their backgrounds, and he can gauge what's appropriate—and what would pique their interest. A bullet is a perfectly logical physics example to a child who is growing up among hunters.

Older students have to supplement the fun with research or further reading, for the youngest it's largely a good time, but everybody gets something out of the lesson and nobody is bored. The kids do some action-and-reaction experiments in the classroom, pushing off against each other in rolling chairs and on wheeled dollies; the craziness is just enough to make the little ones laugh and take an interest, but the Finns keep things safe and scientific. Finding that fine line takes some practice, and it is obvious that Doug and Michelle have had plenty of that.

Frenchboro teacher Doug Finn, and "Terrapin" the African basenji, climb the ramp at the dock. Rob Gorski

After school we take a long walk through the beautiful woods of Frenchboro Long Island. Doug grins and says, "The faculty has 100 percent buy-in! We can come out here on the island trails and have faculty meetings or talk about what we want to do next week. We plan a lot while we're out walking around.

"We feel like we belong here but we also feel like we have to keep some professional distance. We've been very conscious of staying out of people's business," he continues. "If we're playing cards at somebody's house, we don't engage in conversation about somebody's kid. There's a school environment for having that conversation. The conversation may go on, but we're not part of it."

"We're both really strict, we run a tight ship," Michelle adds. Both talk, sharing thoughts together:

Ours is not a spur-of-the-moment sort of classroom; we have a set structure, which I think the kids need. It's really important for them to know what's happening next. There's no question about what happens in the morning. Our afternoons have a general guideline—like Tuesday is gym, Friday is art and gym, Thursday is generally library or a large unit where the kids work together on a project. We don't split them up in the afternoon at all.

Frenchboro teacher Michelle Finn. Eva Murray

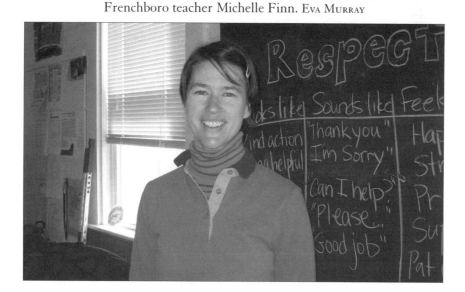

Michelle proudly mentions Doug's great lesson on Newton's Laws and simple machines:

You go ask Bradley, who is six years old, and he can tell you Newton's three laws of motion. You ask different levels of questions to the kids. And, they all have different assessments. Obviously, the eighth-grader is going to be responsible for a lot more information than, say, the kindergarten kids who aren't really writing yet.

We also have high expectations for their behavior. Look out for the youngers, sportsmanship, how to win and lose and be graceful about it.

We've scheduled, we like to have a plan, but we're also very flexible. It might be, "Dang it, I wish that kid wasn't going off on Wednesday." Gym class is important. The adults wanted this for their children because the kids will be going to high school with others who have been playing basketball competitively since they were in pee-wees. We teach the rules of the games.

With this emphasis on sports, the Frenchboro students are unusual among islanders, most of whom don't really learn about team games until high school.

By the time hockey was over this year, everybody knew how to play hockey. We haven't canceled gym, outside class, once so far.

Doug describes how he combines morning weather study with planning the day for outside gym so it doesn't get canceled; he'll move things around to make it work around the weather. As we speak, it is late in the afternoon. Michelle explains:

The island kids are all outside right now; they're in their various "forts" [little structures built in the woods], and probably somebody's down on the beach finding stuff. They all know all the animals, all the reptiles and amphibians. When somebody sent us this big poster of things to identify, they were saying things like, "Yeah, that's the kind of turtle I caught last summer!" Bradley [the kindergartner] goes on walks and he'll ask, "Hey what's this? Let's check this out!" We go hiking with the kids; they love it.

Some of those kids really have a work ethic. They're all working on their lobster traps around now [in the spring]. Myron, he's nine, ten years old, he's out shoveling snow all winter. I wish everybody had a little bit of Myron in them.

We've had some students go from being two years behind

grade level to making up two-and-a-half years in one year. We had a third-grader who was behind, a second-grader, a first- and a kindergartner all doing math together. They got the third-grader caught up to where he could go on, and the younger kids learned the second-grade-level math. The little kids listen to the older kids' lessons, just the way the old-timers describe it.

The previous teachers had dividers up in the classroom, and we took them down. We just have areas. But they were teaching their own children. That's tough.

I spoke with the Finns two years later, and their enthusiasm had not waned. Michelle told me:

We're still so enamored with these children. Our job is our life. We've had a musher from Alaska come out to Frenchboro and do a presentation with the kids with two sled dogs. We've had a Polycom meeting with Vanderbilt University where two scientists are working with us on teaching adaptation and natural selection. We've had authors with the Island Readers and Writers program come out, real authors and illustrators, like Chris Van Dusen and Ashley Bryan, amazing people doing world-class stuff! We have the *Sunbeam*, and we have [its pastor] Rob Benson. We go to swimming lessons at the YMCA in Bar Harbor. We went to visit Swan's Island, and then the entire town came over and played hockey with us. We did cross-country running with Swan's, Isle au Haut, and Islesford. The logistics are hard, yes, but you can do it. These kids walk home in two minutes; I remember as a kid having to be on a bus for an hour.

I've seen a lot of places, and this is one of the prettiest. I love this harbor. I am pretty grateful! I'm not going to be here forever, but I feel really lucky. I don't feel like this is "just a job." Island kids are—hmm—I would say they lack "guile." We have eighth-grade boys running around playing with the little kids. There's none of this, "Oh, I'm too cool for that" in our classroom. They run the whole morning meeting themselves. They're just so up for anything, so helpful and kind—there's a lot of independence that happens, but also some innocence.

Two of our boys have their own boats, their own depth-finders, haulers, everything. Myron was in fourth grade, last year, when he bought his boat. Cody is in eighth, and he is probably going to make more money this year than I make. Everybody, pretty much, in the school has a lobster license, everybody eight years old and above—girls, too. They're 100 percent lobster-dependent, all of our kids. All of their dads fish. There are young kids here who have their own fishing businesses that make ten grand a year, but they might still believe in Santa.

That year, Frenchboro had more children in its school than did any other one-room school in the state, but that has not always been the case. *Hauling By Hand,* by Dean Lawrence Lunt, who grew up on the island, provides a detailed description of the ups and downs of the island population over the last century:

1940: Island population is 119 people.

1963–1964: The school population dwindles to two students, with only two expected the next year. As a mechanism for increasing the population, the island petitions the state for foster children. The man who headed the local welfare office initially assumed it was an unworkable idea, but his visit to Frenchboro convinced him otherwise.

August 1964: The first two foster children arrive on the island. Two more arrive in the fall, and a family of eight siblings arrives in the winter of 1965. Not all of the children stayed, but some did, and some remained on the island into adulthood.

February 1979: The school dwindles to one student. Classes are moved to a private house for the winter to save heating the schoolhouse.

1979: Town of Frenchboro is incorporated (it had previously been called Long Island Plantation).

1980: Island population dips to 43

1980s: The state of Maine approves the grant to begin the Homestead Project, and the Frenchboro Future Development Corporation is organized. Nationwide media attention to the project brings inquiries from far afield; as Lunt puts it, "Unlike mainland towns, an island has no natural flow of people who might live in town and work at nearby jobs. A person must specifically seek to move to an island." He continues, "The FFDC received more than 3,000 inquiries in the first few months. Some letter-writers understood reality; some did not. Some wannabe islanders even planned to commute to mainland jobs."

Frenchboro Harbor. Lobster fishing is still the primary source of income on some of Maine's islands, but summer brings lots of visitors who admire the natural beauty of the Maine coast. Eva Murray

1987: Seven houses are built for the Homestead Project, six for new residents and one for the teacher, with five other lots set aside for outright sale. In 1999, when Lunt's book was published, he says twenty-eight current residents were directly or indirectly linked to the program. In the decade that followed, some of those people left Frenchboro.

1998–1999: For part of the year, the school again had only one pupil.

The Lego Robotics Competition is an important part of the lives of Frenchboro children (and interest has spread to several of the other islands). Explains Doug Finn:

Essentially, the Lego Robotics Competition program was an after-school program to get kids involved with engineering. The program took off like wildfire. There's a theme each year, a task we have to build a robot to do, and we don't find out what those tasks are until the beginning of September. The robot has to drive out, do the tasks by way of the programming, and win points. Then there's a presentation aspect of the program, where the kids have to come up with an innovative solution to the problem. This year the topic was human bioengineering. The team has to come up with a problem and a solution. The problem we came up with was frostbite, so the kids came up with this "lava suit"—basically long underwear with temperature sensors that heat up where they need to. It doesn't really exist, of course, but it was using all these technologies that do exist. You have to present in front of three or four judges and they tally up all the points.

The kids don't have to do it; it's an after-school program, but they all *want* to do it, definitely. This year we had a very informal Lego "track meet," which was more like, "Build a robot that is the fastest, build a robot that can climb the steepest slope, pull the most weight," that kind of stuff. The programming is simple to just make it go forward, but you actually have to build it strong enough. They learn about gears—high and low gears, faster and slower and more powerful.

We got sponsorship from the lobstermen for T-shirts and some extra equipment we needed for the robot. For example, you have to buy sensors. You can either program the robot kind of mathematically, like, "Right wheel goes two rotation, left wheel goes three rotations," or you can say, "Drive until the sensor bumps something, and then turn left 90 degrees." There are different ways to send the robot out. I'm trying to get them to use the sensors more, because the other way is very difficult; any error gets multiplied at every turn, and next thing you know, you're off the table.

We've got a boy in second grade, and because he actually plays with Legos, he knows how to build a car. The older kids don't necessarily know how to build a car. This little guy can show the big kids some things.

Our first meet was in Castine at Maine Maritime Academy. That year they had a northern and a southern [Maine] competition. Now it's one big one in Augusta. It's a big day. Practically the whole community of Frenchboro goes off, and we stay in hotels. I love Legos!

A photograph in the *Bangor Daily News* showed the Frenchboro students at one of the meets, all wearing their team T-shirts with the list of sponsors on the back. Every sponsor was a lobster boat, and several of those belonged to students on the Lego Robotics team.

Sonja Philbrook, an area CPR instructor (and native of another Maine island), describes her experience offering a CPR and First Aid class to the Frenchboro school in 2011:

> After leaving Swan's Island on the 6:45 A.M. ferry, I arrived in Bass Harbor, only to have to wait thirty minutes before lugging all of my equipment onto the Gott boat [a privately run passenger boat]. There were islanders waiting on the Frenchboro side to help me carry my equipment up the ramp and into a parent's waiting car. When we arrived at the school the kids were so excited! The students introduced themselves in order of grade—eighth-graders down to a kindergartner. We started with First Aid and most of them were ready to jump up for the practice sessions. They were sent home for lunch at 11:00 but were told to come back early, at 11:30, so we would have enough time to cover everything. When they came back from lunch they found the tables/desks cleared out of the main area and manikins scattered around the floor. Some of them were very excited, others not so much. A few were worried about "putting our lips on these plastic people," but they became less shy over time. They even cheered on the teachers and adults from the community who were taking the class, too!
>
> While learning to use the AED [defibrillator], the kindergartner told his partner to "back off" when it was time to "clear the patient"—too cute! All of the students did a great job. The littlest ones had a hard time getting enough depth doing compressions on the chest of a manikin, but they gave it their best shot and did everything I asked of them and learned a lot. Throughout the day, they were very respectful and attentive. We had a little extra time before school ended at 2:45, so the teachers quizzed the students with questions and scenarios about what they'd learned, and they were able to answer every question! The children were like sponges and absorbed everything they were taught.

Sonja describes some the logistics involved with presenting this special lesson to the Frenchboro students:

> While the students were being quizzed, I started checking around for a ride off Frenchboro that could take me back home to Swan's Island; I didn't want to wait for the 6:00 P.M. passenger ferry that would take me back to Bass Harbor and strand me there for the night. One possibility was a Frenchboro fisherman who sells his

lobsters on Swan's, but he was on his way there already by the time I was finished. The other lead was a Swan's Island man who was going to come get me, but he'd ended up in the hospital for part of the day, and then couldn't come because he still had a load of traps on his boat and it was a bit rough out. I was just about out of hope of sleeping in my own bed that night, when the people who were helping me take my things to the dock noticed another boat leaving that was taking people back to Bass Harbor. Thankfully, we caught him as he was pulling away from the dock, so I was able to ride a lobster boat back to Bass Harbor and get there in time to catch the 4:30 ferry home to Swan's. What a day!

Differentiation, Standards-Based Education, and Some Observations

How can anybody teach all those different ages at once?

Excellent teachers in any setting find themselves recognizing the differences between their students, even if subconsciously. If you think about the day's work as "teaching the children" rather than as "teaching the subject," teaching multiple ages is less of a stretch of the imagination.

The island teachers use a variety of programs, mechanisms, and strategies, and of course, each year brings a different configuration of students. Very young children rely on a certain amount of routine. Middle-schoolers ought to be given increased individual responsibility. Some special-needs students cannot manage without a very reliable schedule, where other students bristle under such rigidity. Some teachers do a lot of direct instruction, while others like to set up long-term, student-led projects or online activities. What works depends upon the students involved—their ages, academic background, maturity, and personalities—and the nature of the student group can change significantly from year to year in a school this small. There is no "typical" template for running a multi-age classroom.

There are, however, some areas of common ground. All now agree with the need to meet each student where he or she is academically; nobody should work at a level that doesn't fit. All are increasingly committed to a "standards-based education" as well as to "place-based education"; more on these to follow. An important change in the island teachers' and students' world recently has been the development of collaborative efforts among the islands, including a formal mechanism for teacher peer support, a structured curriculum alignment option, and a series of informal social connections which never used to exist. Much of this is made possible by the recent advances in telecommunication technology, but even before the Internet, island teachers saw the value in at least occasional inter-island socializing. It just hasn't always been possible.

Differentiation

"Differentiation" is the recent in-style expression for an old concept. From an article in the *Bangor Daily News,* January 14, 2008, entitled "Clarifying jargon in education":

> Differentiated instruction: This is just good-old effective teaching. It is adapting and modifying curriculum and instruction so that every student is a successful learner. One-room schoolhouse teachers are the real experts at differentiation.

A veteran researcher, historian, and writer about American education who served as assistant secretary of education in the 1990s, Diane Ravitch defines differentiated instruction as follows:

> A form of instruction that seeks to maximize each student's growth by recognizing that students have different ways of learning, different interests, and different ways of responding to education. In practice, it involves offering several different learning experiences in response to students' varied needs. . . . Advocates of differentiated instruction say that it helps students progress by meeting their diverse, individual needs. Critics say that planning multiple learning experiences is time-consuming and that it requires extensive training. . . ." (*EdSpeak*, p. 75)

I offer Ravitch's definition, as the word "differentiation" is current educational terminology for the sort of instructional practice these one-room- and two-room-school teachers, at least to a certain extent, find they cannot help but implement. With lecture-style classes viewed increasingly as "one-size-fits-few," differentiation now describes a mainstream and widely accepted pedagogical practice. The skeptics whom Ravitch mentions are absolutely correct, however; it takes a lot of work to set up such a program. One school year will never be a carbon copy of the year before, and a teacher's routines cannot become too deeply entrenched and comfortable.

Our island teachers are acutely aware of these issues. Now that communication between island teachers is readily available and frequent, they can plan strategies to avoid these pitfalls. The discussion is open, the subject is acknowledged, and the improvements to our programs come rapidly. No one-room-school teacher in Maine has to "figure out how to do this alone" or "from scratch" any more.

In her book *How to Differentiate Instruction in Mixed-Ability Classrooms,* Carol Ann Tomlinson, associate professor of Educational Leadership, Foundations and Policy at the University of Virginia, offers some helpful description of this style of pedagogy for those who envision "school" as, by definition, simply a place where teachers stand up in front and tell students the facts, with successful students those who can repeat the same back:

> Most teachers (as well as students and parents) have clear mental images of classrooms. After experiencing undifferentiated instruction over many years, it is often difficult to imagine what a differentiated classroom would look like and feel like.
>
> Differentiated instruction is *not* the "individualized instruction" of the 1970s. . . . At least we understood that students have different learning profiles and that there is merit in meeting students where they are and helping them move on from there. One flaw in the 1970s approach was that we tried doing something different for each of the 30-plus students in a single classroom. . . . It didn't take long for teachers to become exhausted.
>
> Differentiation is probably more reminiscent of the one-room schoolhouse than of individualization. That model of instruction recognized that the teacher needed to work sometimes with the whole class, sometimes with small groups, and sometimes with individuals. . . .
>
> Differentiated instruction is rooted in assessment. A teacher who understands the need for teaching and learning to be a good match for students looks for every opportunity to know her students better.

Of course, on the islands, the teachers are not only spending every moment of most school days with the students, but are their full-time neighbors as well.

> [The teacher] sees conversations with individuals, classroom discussions, student work, observation, and formal assessment each

as a way to gather just a little more insight about what works for each student. . . .

In a differentiated classroom, just as in a large family, everyone has to take extra responsibility both for their own well-being and for the well-being of others. In this sort of setting, while the teacher is clearly the leader of the group, students can help develop routines for the classroom, make major contributions toward solving problems and refining routines, help one another, keep track of their work, and so on. Different students will be ready for differing amounts of responsibility at any given time, but all students need to be guided in assuming a growing degree of responsibility and independence as a learner and member of a community. . . .

This describes our island schoolrooms very well. Students, to the degree that they are mature enough or interested or able, lead meetings, maintain records, assist other students, design projects, and express concern when somebody is having a problem. A classroom that fits Tomlinson's description is not the result of a new discovery or a sudden flash of educational insight; it is what can happen naturally when the group is very small, quite diverse, and open to informal, relaxed, personal communication.

Standards-Based Education

As I write, the commissioner of education for the State of Maine is working toward implementing what is called "standards-based" (or "proficiency-based") education statewide. This means, in a nutshell, that Maine intends to move to a system where students must demonstrate competence in each skill or specific instructional goal that has been identified as a core standard. The *age* of the student would have far less to do with what work he or she does, and which student groupings he or she is part of, than with his or her actual academic level, his or her actual accomplishment of the required work. "Grades" become pretty meaningless. Don Siviski, superintendent of instruction for the Maine Department of Education (and assistant to Commissioner Stephen Bowen), said in his comments to a group of island teachers in 2011, "My description of the school of the future: Take the word 'grade' out of our vocabulary. You're not in a 'grade' and we don't give 'grades.' You might be in a proficiency group. . . . You demonstrate proficiency in every single skill. Then you go on."

In such a configuration, a fifth-grade student could easily be working in seventh-grade math, if math is her particular forté, but in so doing would not skip any other material, as that would result in large educational gaps. The intention is to graduate a high-school senior who has done everything identified as important—no gaps, and no averaging strengths with unaddressed weaknesses to attain a "passing grade"—and who spends school time working at the appropriate level in every subject no matter his or her age. Ideally, the student would never be either "lost" or truly bored in school, doing work too hard or too easy. Superintendent Siviski advocates for "mass customization," meaning, essentially, an individual education program for everyone. This term, and standards-based teaching in a general sense, is described in the book *Inevitable: Mass Customized Learning* by Charles Schwahn and Beatrice McGarvey, a book which was required reading for every Maine Department of Education staffer and every Maine district superintendent in 2011.

This is not, again, quite the same as the "individualized instruction" that was all the rage a couple of decades ago, because the current system is based on a set of published standards; the teacher and student do not have to make it up as they go along, and the already busy teacher is not expected to develop and manage a unique curriculum for each student.

It doesn't require a big intellectual reach to see that student age is not the only or best way to determine academic level. Few students remain precisely at their age-based grade level in everything all through their school years anyway. There are lots of ways to demonstrate real learning beyond filling out some sort of paperwork. The historic (intentional or tacit) "tracking" of older students based on their performance as elementary students (or worse, based on their behavior despite demonstrated intelligence) is pretty close to criminal, and colleges and businesses beg us to accept that mere attendance—"seat time"—is hardly an accurate measurement of qualification for a diploma. Woody Allen may get a chuckle out of us when he quips that "80 percent of life is just showing up," but school should not be about "just showing up."

The current thinking around using a standards-based (rather than age-based) process also makes room for mastery to be proved using all sorts of mechanisms—including real-world interactions, large and small projects, and technology platforms that are constantly changing—not just pencil-and-paper worksheets and examinations. That sounds a lot like how many one-room-school teachers have been working for years, and it is definitely how our current group of island teachers designs lessons. I suspect our nation's smallest schools have something to teach the experts. What we have always thought of as the "luxury of smallness," the ability for teachers and school administrators to let each student work at his or her own speed, to offer extra help when needed, to allow a highly interested student to advance quickly in a subject, and to assess a student's progress based on what he or she actually demonstrates—often without need of a written test, because the teacher knows the student well—is recognized as best practice for all, and not just a perk for a fortunate few.

Donna Isaacs, Islesford, comments on planning instruction:

We don't present a lesson where we hand the student a workbook. That's not part of our philosophy. This a moving target, and every time we teach a unit we tweak it. Part of our process is to "debrief the process." Anyway, we'll start with the topic from our curriculum guideline, look at the standards that address that topic, look at the standards we want to use. We start with middle grades and adjust our work both up and down; most of our standards tend to be pretty well expressed in the middle grades, so we expand on things for older students, and whittle them down to essentials for youngers. We use the expression "unpacking the standard," which means really trying to understand what the component parts are, what it actually means for the student. These Common Core or state standards tend to be written in complex or abstract language or to be pretty nonspecific, so we as teachers have to make them understandable and break them down into usable expectations and tangible activities. Then we do some backwards planning, developing the assessment first, because we have to figure out what indicates mastery of the standard.

We look at four levels of increasing complexity, using Marzano's Taxonomy, from retrieval through comprehension and analysis to knowledge utilization. We create a "capacity matrix," where we look at the standard from the student's perspective: what does the student need to be able to do to meet the standard? This also involves four levels: emerging, partially proficient, proficient, and advanced. Developing the capacity matrix and the rubric are part of "unpacking the standard." Then the teachers (from several islands, who are collaborating on lessons) together start brainstorming the activities we want to do. That's the fun part. So far we have limited experience; I would say anecdotally that we've had the most creative results when we can do that face to face, with all of us getting off our islands and getting together for a day. That works better than video-conferencing. We think about what are some of the activities that we can design, including trips. A lot of the social studies and science curriculum can involve field trips now, where student and teachers from several islands get together.

Frenchboro teachers Doug and Michelle Finn are spokespersons for a nationwide educational association, the Reinventing Schools Coalition. RISC, as it is known, is a nonprofit foundation that supports the implementation of standards-based education, which just happens to dovetail nicely with current one-room-school–style classroom practices, and which suits small, multi-age groups especially well. Students demonstrate competence in something determined to be a required skill, a "standard," and then move on. It means children all work at their own level in each subject—nothing new to our island teachers, but now suddenly given the credibility of being an idea adopted by large mainland districts in a growing list of places. Rather than looking like a historic relic, our one- and two-room schools found themselves on the "cutting edge."

Doug and Michelle speak publicly about standards-based education and about the Reinventing Schools Coalition. When they speak in other parts of the country, the subject of their one-room-school job invariably comes up.

When we do presentations around the country, people always want to know about Frenchboro, Maine. We explain that we're currently teaching and applying what we're describing to a kindergarten-through-eighth classroom. They want to know where, and soon it's "Oh, my gosh, a one-room schoolhouse," and "Isn't that just magical?" and I say, well, yes. . . .

When we were hired to teach in Alaska, ours was a RISC district. They were fully implemented, which meant that students were leveled according to their abilities, not their age. This is not tracking, because everybody has to pass the same standards, and they have to get an 80 percent or better on every single standard in order to pass through to the next level. There might be levels in science that could take two years to get through. Basically kids would be changing classes like they would in high school, but being taught more like the way they often are in elementary school, with big units, cross-curricular stuff, a lot of hands-on–type stuff instead of just direct instruction like you often get in high school.

Everybody is kind of on an individual learning plan. If you finish the standards in high school, you can go on and get college credits or advanced credit, or you can say, "Okay, I'm done with math or whatever, I'll just focus on my reading." Children are encouraged to take complete responsibility for their learning. They know what is expected of them, they know what proficiency is going to look like, and they slowly gain more and more control over their learning. If you get a child who is a real mover and shaker, he or she could come up to the teacher and say, "Hey, I see that I need this for science and this for social studies and this for math. I was thinking I could do this kind of project, I'm going to incorporate this with this, and do this in these ways, and that's going to show my proficiency. Do you agree? Would that be a decent project?" So students can actually choose how they are assessed. It's not that there are no paper-and-pencil tests, but they are less prevalent.

If they need the direct instruction piece, that's there, but it's a lot less of "I'm in front of the classroom and I'm talking all day." It's more of a team effort. It might be that "all of you guys need the same standard, so I'll do the direct instruction for a bit." They (both students and teachers) can choose different ways to be assessed at different times, so you don't get, for example, auditory learners always being assessed with a written exam. They get some hands-on pieces, maybe some theater pieces, some text pieces, and so on.

This takes a lot more time for the teachers. Each year I'd keep adding things that worked [to my repertoire]. With experience comes some streamlining.

Michelle and I had four years of training in Alaska in teaching multi-age classrooms. We were trained to say, "You're a student, let's look at your needs, lets fit everyone's needs into a unit." Our superintendent from Alaska was in Maine, and he told the RISC organization that we were in Maine, and they asked us to come do demonstrations. We had actually taught in this model, so we became sort of demonstration teachers. We would show what we actually do in our classroom. That kind of developed into more than just demonstrating stuff in the classroom; it became, "Can you go talk to teachers who want to learn about this style of teaching, and help them implement it into their schools and school districts?" We are contracted by the RISC Foundation to go do this. Michelle and I have been sent down to South Carolina, I've been all over Maine, I've been to California to do training, Michelle's been to Colorado, and so on. They're happy to have teachers who have had experience training in this model in the lower forty-eight.

We don't have a lot of bureaucratic constraints here on Frenchboro. If we were in a regular school on the mainland, we would be forced to do everything certain ways. Here, our school board is so supportive. One-room schools fit the RISC model so nicely. There are six or seven school districts right now in the state of Maine that are trying to implement this school-wide—huge middle schools with six hundred kids—and they want to talk to a teacher who has done it. They don't want theory. You have much more credibility when you're actually teaching this way.

A few teachers want to sit back and say, "Hey, I taught the chapters, the students just didn't get it!" This model throws that attitude on its head. You have to have confidence in yourself as a teacher. If there is a subject you're not very good at, you aren't going to be very good at presenting it to your students. Working with these standards, you show the proof that the students have covered the standards: "Here is the actual work that the students have done to show that they're proficient at it," whereas before you'd just pull out a stack of tests and say, "Here, these students passed, and these students failed."

You don't say, "You're a dumb fifth-grader because you're doing third-grade math." We don't say, "You need to get through third-grade math by the end of the year." We're saying, "You need to get through third-grade math as quickly as you can, because you need to get through fourth grade, and do that as quickly as you can because we need to get to fifth grade." We're looking for what the student specifically needs.

One place where teachers make mistakes when they try to implement this is when they think they need to toss out everything they've ever done before. No! Keep doing what you're doing that works, the things you're good at, and change the things where you aren't having much success. This takes time. You also have to train the students. Kids will say, "What? You actually want my opinion?" It takes a while for students to accept that. Actually, students who are doing really well in school sometimes have the hardest time with this. They know how to score the game! They take time to adjust.

Some Observations from Other Island Teachers

June Pemberton, who taught on Matinicus in the late 1990s before an established curriculum or any formal collaboration between the islands existed, reminded us that behavior issues can interfere with the best of intentions:

I was fine with the multi-age group, except that if there were little kids that needed to be taught to read, they needed the teacher's attention. One year I found it impossible to be the only teacher in a group of rowdy kids, most of them older, *and* teach little kids to read at the same time. Those kids [she laughs], of course they all refused to do anything at school, they would be horrible to me all day, and then at 2:30 they would be just as nice as they could be, and we would do a science activity after school was officially over for the day.

In February I would sometimes end up with just one or two or three kids, because the other families would go to Florida, but they didn't all go at the same time; they certainly didn't worry about the school calendar. So it was neat—when the group got so small, you could find out what they really liked, and then work that into every subject. Once, two kids were into the Iditarod sled dog race (they would have been first and second grade but good readers), so I said, "Let's see if we can do every single subject around the Iditarod." It was easy to do the math, and it was fairly easy to tie in science—the cold temperatures and how they had to care for the dogs. Of course for English you can just write about it, and we had a whole spelling list of Iditarod words, and we had the newspapers. We put a big map in the middle of the table and we would trace the Iditarod, so we were cartographers for that week. It was wonderful. I really remember that time; every subject got covered, they learned a lot, I learned a lot, and we all enjoyed it—but I doubt I could have done it with fifteen kids in there.

We did reptiles another week, when I had these two little kids, David and Emilia. They loved what they called "going snakin'," which meant picking up every stone or board or piece of tar paper to find those little green snakes. They loved reptiles. The funniest thing is, I'm sort of terrified of snakes. I don't actually mind those little tiny green ones, but they were trying to find out if I was afraid of snakes. I said to myself, "June, if you let them know, your life here will be hell." So that evening there's a knock on the screen door and there's little Dave and Emilia. "Look, we know you like snakes so we brought you a whole bucket full," all smiling, and I'm trying not to pass out.

Pat Walchli spent part of a year teaching just one seventh-grade boy before more students came back to Matinicus Island. She didn't start the 2002-2003 school year until November, as no students were enrolled in the Matinicus school until then.

There was a year's worth of school mail piled up. There was just Stevie, a seventh-grade boy, and me; he turned thirteen that April. There was no curriculum, and no direction from either the superintendent or the school board.

Some of my favorite memories: Stevie would bring his snack to school, which would be salted cod. He would sometimes go home with me for lunch. One day he got deeply involved in the book he was reading, I think it was *The Last Book in the Universe;* anyway, he started reading that book in the morning, and when I said, "How about some math?" he said, "Let me finish this chapter." He was right into it. There was no world out there, he was in the book. I said, "Stevie, it's time for lunch." He said, "Can I go to your house, Teach?" He read the book walking down the road, he read the book eating a sandwich, he read going back to the school. So I said, "Okay, we'll read this book today." He still remembers that day. That was one of the beauties of teaching that way.

There were old computers stored in the crawl space under the floor. I figured if they were stored that way, they weren't any good and we didn't have to worry about them, so we took them apart. Who knows about the health hazards,; I don't know. Now he knows what the insides of a computer look like. Lots of tiny little screws!

I'd haul people into the school from anywhere, ask them, "Tell us where you're from, what it's like where you live?" because everybody has a story.

We had some big boys the next year—David, Christian, Devon, and Nick—and there were the two little girls, Isabella and Hannah. You know how rambunctious our boys could be. We had a morning meeting and always went around, "Do you have anything to share?" and the boys would grunt and posture and whatever. One day Hannah announced at morning meeting, "I read a chapter in *Frog and Toad* last night!" Hannah was in first grade, and this was the first time she'd gotten through it herself. I asked her if she'd like to read a little of it for us. Those boys—they hadn't really mastered the art of not interrupting too well—but when little Hannah started reading *Frog and Toad,* they didn't move, they sat there like statues while this little first-grade girl read. The boys knew this was a big deal. I didn't have to say anything. It was a magical moment, it really was. You'd have thought *Frog and Toad* was the best story those boys had ever heard. This was a big deal for Hannah. I love how these kids take care of each other.

I got David a manual for the engine on his boat. He was motivated to read that. That was a lot of his educational program. The boys also built that little building beside the school [similar to a garden shed]. That was motivation to get their work done; they'd ask, "Can we go out and work on our camp?" (or whatever they called it), and I'd say, "Finish your math first."

Dave Duncan, Matinicus, 2011, describes his use of the computer in the classroom:

One thing that helps is technology. I think it is much easier today to find materials. You can usually find something online to help, instead of trying to look through old textbooks. A new thing that has really helped my older students is the use of wikis [a wiki is an interactive website, a personalized site which can easily be edited or added to by a group of people]. I give them specific directions for their independent work, their work to complete for the day, their assigned reading for the day. Isabella, for example [the lone middle-schooler at Matinicus that year], can look at current events, watch a news clip online, and react to it, while for the other students that might not be appropriate because it's above their level. I don't have to sit right there with her. Later, I can see how she has reacted to it. I put in links to websites, links to videos, links to other documents. If Zeke and Emma [middle-elementary-age students] are doing the weather blog, they can post that. I give them specific instructions when they work online.

I got excited when I heard about the technology involved with this job. Coming into it, I guess I thought that Matinicus would not have the Internet!

Lindsay Eysnogle, Islesford, 2011, talks about working with a wide variety of ages:

So much of the adaptation and differentiation for each student happens in the moment and child-by-child. I always begin the year by establishing a routine that students learn during the first couple of weeks of school and then depend on for the rest of the year. I work with them to set expectations for behavior during each part of the routine, and soon they know how loud they can speak to each other, when they can interrupt me for help, and when they need to work together for support. Once that basic structure is in place, it frees me to work with students in small groups or one-on-one as needed. Most of the time, there is more than one student working on the same concept in math, so I will begin a unit with some pretty intense direct instruction with a small group followed by individual guided practice, followed by independent practice until I'm positive each student has met the standard. I use a combination of self-developed lessons and materials, web-based materials, and commercially available curriculum materials. So far, the islands have not collaborated around the math curriculum, but I hope that that comes in the future.

In science, our school breaks the kids into the age spans that are highlighted in the National Standards for Science Education: kindergarten–four and five–eight. Students in kindergarten–four all enjoy the same class and they work toward the same standard, but with different expectations for what it looks like to meet the standard. In my class, all of the students in grades one through three are learning about plants, experimenting with growing plants, and learning about plants from around the world, but I have different expectations for the level of understanding and action that students take at the different grade levels. For instance, students in first grade draw pictures of what they observe from their plant experiments in their science journal, while students in grades two and three collect growth data about each plant by measuring each plant in centimeters, and they make graphs to show the plants' growth over time. The whole group has discussions together and they work on similar projects to show me their understanding of the concepts we're working on, but again, my expectations are higher for older students. Just like in math, my lessons and materials are a combination of self-made, web-based, and book-based, but I have the added support of the inter-island collaboration around the science curriculum.

Jessie Campbell, Monhegan, describes the sort of scrambled organizing required when the students represent a wide range of ages and needs:

One year, we had a student who needed one-on-one and we've kind of overcompensated. Donna [a part-time ed tech] comes in for algebra; she was the tech for a couple of years before I came, and then for different reasons she couldn't do last year, so then we had Tara. We wanted to keep all these people who had added to our school, and we now also have an Island Institute fellow this year, and then Susan was hired a week before school started to be the one-on-one ed tech for this particular student. We had to make sure we always had two adults in school. It's really hard to find people, nobody can do full-time. This year's not normal!

In science, I have four of my students all working together. That's the most I ever have doing the same content. One of them works with the ed tech. This year we're doing chemistry. I'm lucky that I know my students well enough so that I know the best way they all learn. For instance, my third-grader is super visual, so if I put something on a board or on PowerPoint, I know he's going to look at it, he's going to read it, even if it includes hard words.

He may not listen to a word I say, but he will read it, so if I'm doing visuals I think of him and think of what he's going to read. Then, where my older guys are more able to hear what I'm saying, and listen and follow directions and stay with me, I can put something on the projector and then have a conversation with the older boys and the check-in with the third-grader. Part of it is just in knowing the kids well enough, making it exciting enough for the third-grader but also challenging enough to make sure the eighth-grader is being asked the right questions. By the middle of the chemistry unit, this third-grader could balance equations, and he understood protons and neutrons and stuff. I think he learns more being with the older guys than if I just sat him in another room and made him do a third-grade curriculum.

It's really important to give them opportunities to show me everything they know, not so much everything they don't know. My fifth-grader might know more than my eighth-grader in a certain subject because it just clicks for him. I try to do a lot of project-based assessment so they can give me everything they've got [as opposed to a lot of tests].

I asked Jessie what kind of material they were using in reading and English.

The two seventh- and eighth-graders just read *Night* by Elie Wiesel, and Dalton just finished *Hatchet* by Gary Paulsen. They also have to read at least fifteen books on their own; Quinn (in third grade) is enjoying these stories called *Classic Starts* where it's classic literature like *Huck Finn* and *Twenty Thousand Leagues Under the Sea* and stuff like that, but rewritten for younger kids. Those are fun. I write my own questions for reading comprehension. I don't really like workbooks.

More recently, Jessie wrote a note about teaching a multi-age, multi-school social studies unit about explorers:

It was interesting teaching a kindergartner about Christopher Columbus at the same time I was teaching my sixth- and eighth-graders about how Columbus massacred millions of Taino "Indians" because they were not able to "produce" enough gold for him. I left that part of the story out for the kindergartner.

Exchange Trips and the Inter-Island Event

Collaboration—what you lose in control, you gain in momentum.

In the mid-1970s, Monhegan teachers Bobby and Ruth Ives initiated a pen-pal correspondence between their students and the similarly aged group of schoolchildren on Matinicus. Those two islands are at once alike and different: in some ways close, in other ways seeming a world apart from each other. Although they about the same size, Monhegan is a well-known icon, an artist's colony and beloved vacation spot, while Matinicus cultivates a reputation for wildness. You can just see Monhegan on the horizon if you stand on the west side of Matinicus; directly, over water, the islands are roughly eighteen nautical miles apart. To travel between them, however, unless you make the trip in your own boat, is a bit of a production. When I visit Monhegan I have to fly or take a boat to Rockland, stay overnight in the area, drive down the peninsula to the small harbor town of Port Clyde, and take the *Elizabeth Ann* or *Laura B* to Monhegan—a trip which, in the winter, only runs three times a week.

The Iveses had become aware that the Monhegan children thought of their Matinicus neighbors over there on the horizon as somehow a bit foreign, maybe a bit odd. Several people who were children at the time mentioned a standing joke on both islands about inhabitants of the other being "coneheads." Recalling those days, as second-grader on Matinicus Kristy Rogers says, "We definitely wondered if they were going to look different, which made no sense, but we were just kids." The joke ran both ways; Monhegan student Jeff Rollins wrote that, "All the children in the school in 1973–1974 always thought of Matinicus inhabitants as having cone-shaped heads." Sure.

Monhegan lobster-catcher Zoe Zanidakis reflects on her younger days on the island:

> I had a wonderful one-room-school experience, as did my son Ron, now twenty-six, and my mother and her mother and so on quite a ways back. Growing up on Monhegan and attending school there made for some of the most memorable and positive learning experiences in my life. We had about thirteen kids, kindergarten through eighth grade, in school at the time. We went on school trips, had Spanish lessons from one of the parents, walked the woods together exploring the island for science projects, and wrote and performed plays on our small stage—we were

Reverend Bobby Ives at The Carpenter's Boatshop, Pemaquid, Maine, a school he founded. Ives, along with his wife Ruth, taught on Monhegan in the 1970s and organized a series of student exchange trips between Monhegan and Matinicus. EVA MURRAY

a big family. Actually we did have siblings and cousins in school at the time. After school we played war, hiding and scouring the island. We raced our bikes, we played hockey when the meadow or ice pond froze over, we rowed our skiffs and fished, we sang and colored and danced at Sunday school. One student had a pony, Sammy, and another girl had a full-size horse, so we had "pony club" and learned all sorts of things about horses. We fought, we cried, we played—without our one-room school and wonderful teachers like Bobby and Ruth Ives and others, it would never have been possible.

When my mother, my grandmum, and my great-grandmum attended school, there were even more students on Monhegan. When my son was in school on the island, attendance was rather low, but school was still a quality experience.

So, about visiting Matinicus: Kristy and Maureen were my pen pals; it was a fantastic experience to visit another island school, though I thought Matinicus was so different from Monhegan. It had long beaches and more roads. The harbor was very different, too. The boat ride was always a "puker," something about the old *Sunbeam*. She rolled like a bowling ball!

The pen-pal letters were a start; soon trips were arranged both ways on the Maine Sea Coast Mission vessel *Sunbeam,* allowing the students to visit the other island and visit the school and homes of their pen pals. Monhegan native Donna Cundy recalls:

I remember staying with Catherine Bunker the first time, and her whole room was purple. She even had a purple motorcycle helmet, which surprised me because Monhegan did not allow motorcycles or four-wheelers. I didn't like Matinicus because it was flat, there was no town, people used cars to drive everywhere, and most places you couldn't see the water. It felt like the mainland. I hated being away from home.

The second time we went, Catherine was off-island—I think it was appendicitis—so I believe I stayed at Kristy's. I don't recall anything about that except arriving there and being disappointed that I had to stay with a kid younger than me. Kristy and I were later roommates at Gould Academy in high school. It took me a while to get my bearings at Gould and make other friends, but Kristy was great and I learned a lot from her about what a good friend is.

On one of those *Sunbeam* trips, either when they came to Monhegan or we went there, I gave all the Matinicus kids chicken pox. I got them from a kid in Port Clyde. The Matinicus families had been alerted, and in those days you wanted your kid to have chicken pox early rather than later.

I don't recall having any misconceptions about Matinicus [people] other than adults joking they all had pointed heads, but we knew it wasn't true.

When I taught on Matinicus in 1987 there was no mechanism in place for my students to meet children from other islands, but a few years later, by the time my own son and daughter were students in the Matinicus school, at least one annual gathering had become part of the routine. The "Inter-Island Event," so-called, took hold as a regular, annual part of the school experience in the late 1980s, and is something akin to the island schools' version of a Boy Scout jamboree. A great deal of organizing, logistics management, sandwich making, activity planning, toddler wrangling, casserole soliciting, and weather watching goes into this annual field day. Students, teachers, and a few others from as many of the small islands as can manage the trip come together on one island to sleep in tents or fire halls or church basements or on schoolhouse floors, to play endless games of Capture the Flag and Frisbee and softball, to sing, to make crafts, to look for sea glass on somebody else's beaches and walk somebody else's dirt roads, to eat somebody else's lasagna at community potluck suppers, and, above all, to make friends with kids who live on other islands.

Until recently, some of these friendships were literally based upon the once-a-year visits, rekindled at each Inter-Island Event. Before the Internet became common (or affordable) on the islands, the children would sometimes be surprised at how much their friends had changed over a year's time. Sometimes these long-distance buddies from childhood would later find themselves at the same boarding high school, and their island background would bring them together again.

A little bit of explanation may be in order as to why this is all such a big deal. People who have never attempted the trip (or who navigate at a leisurely pace between islands once each summer in their sailboat, keeping no particular schedule and at no small expense) frequently assume that it is easy to travel between Maine's islands, that "the islands" are some sort of cultural entity, and that island residents ought logically to work or socialize together regularly. It has even been suggested that they should become one county or one school district, or could somehow (inexplicably) share physical things like truckloads of heating oil. In reality, the transportation options serving each island are entirely different and do not mesh together well, and it is often easier to get to the nearest mainland hub than to the nearest inhabited "sister island."

If you look at a map of the coast of Maine and find, for example, Stonington, into which harbor the Isle au Haut mail boat steams, you will notice that the road distance from there to Owls Head, from where you would catch the plane to Matinicus, is no short hop. It's sometimes a far shorter trip island-to-island by water, but there are no passenger boats connecting most of these islands because there wouldn't be enough paid business to support them. Another common assumption is that the local fishermen can always carry schoolchildren or anybody else who wishes to travel between islands, but consider: When the weather is fit to be on the water, the fishermen are busy making their living. Their "spare time" is often during bad, sometimes dangerous weather. Also, two trips would be required, of course, were somebody to visit another island for more than a brief period of time and have any hope of getting home; if you have any awareness of the cost of operating a fishing vessel, you'll realize that two trips starts to run into real money. Such a favor may be offered once in a while, but it's nothing the non-boat-owning islander can count on.

So all social visits, all efforts toward bringing island teachers together for professional development, and all collaborative learning activities among island students are of necessity complicated, expensive, dependent on the weather, and time-consuming—and therefore, infrequent.

In 2011 the Matinicus school hosted the Inter-Island Event for the first time. The *Working Waterfront* newspaper in Rockland reported:

On September 28–30 the people of Matinicus Island hosted students and teachers from every one-room school in the state to our good food, starry skies, sandy beaches, music and art, and beautifully renovated K–8 schoolhouse. By the way, yes—we would like more people to think of those things when they consider Matinicus.

Children from Frenchboro, Isle au Haut, Monhegan, Cliff Island, and the Cranberries, along with teachers and a few parents, rose in the wee dark hours of Tuesday morning on their respective islands to catch Casco Bay Lines ferries, local mail boats, and the Maine Sea Coast Mission vessel *Sunbeam* for the potentially arduous trip to Matinicus. Those coming from Cliff and Monhegan drove from their particular mainland landing points to Rockland and then boarded Captain Jim Kalloch's *Jackie Renee* for the 23-mile trip to Matinicus. The *Sunbeam* collected the folks from the Cranberries, Frenchboro, and Isle au Haut—and admittedly, it was a bit rough out there. By time they all arrived at noon on Tuesday, it had already seemed like a long day, but the fun was just beginning.

For something like twenty years, the students and teachers of

Maine's one-room island schools have come together for an annual field day. We call this combined camp-out, potluck, reunion, arts festival, ruckus, and jamboree "the Inter-Island Event."

Island artists, hobbyists, and ballplayers led workshops and breakout groups so that the students could select from a menu of activities. Music teacher and drummer Tom Ulichny held a drumming and rhythm-band session that included lots of empty five-gallon oil buckets. There was plenty of art, including Maury Colton's mural painting on the side of the school's storage shed. Some went to the beach to build sand castles, and I had ten people in my kitchen at one point each baking his or her own blueberry cake for the potluck supper (we found ourselves eating blueberry cake for every meal thereafter, too. Probably some of Maine's islanders can go a long time now without seeing another piece of blueberry cake). The scheduled kickball game, to be led by, among others, Jessie the Monhegan teacher (kickball being a major Monhegan tradition) devolved into another round of Capture the Flag, I heard, for the lack of a decent ball.

After the potluck supper in the church basement, it was time for the talent show upstairs. The audience enjoyed some great singing and dance acts, a couple of hilarious skits such as "Death-Defying Waltz," a fire-safety talk from the smallest participant— a three-year-old from Cliff Island—and then Matinicus's own little Max brought the house down with his hula-hoop act. We could only come up with three hoops for him at showtime, but he assured us later, "I can do five while drinking a glass of water."

High-school senior Vicki MacDonald, who grew up on Isle au Haut, remembers the Inter-Island Events of her childhood:

I met Sam from Islesford, who goes to Gould now, and Jack from Monhegan who goes to North Haven [High School]. We went to a couple of Inter-Island Events together. Sam would spot me right away and then we'd go hunting for Jack, and attack him [she laughs]. The three of us hung around all the time together when we were at the Inter-Island Events. That time that I spent with them—I'd laugh so hard the sides of my face would hurt. I haven't seen Jack in about two years, and I still feel like he's a really good friend. I ended up sort of being Sam's "big sister" when she came to Gould.

I didn't look forward to the traveling, usually, but it was so worth it because I made some extremely good friends, even though I didn't get to see them very much. We'd write letters, exchange e-mails—I had pen pals, I had e-mail buddies—it made friendships that I'm going to remember for a long time. We had fond memories we could share.

The Island Teachers' Conference, the Critical Friends Group, and the Outer Islands Teaching and Learning Collaborative
Your practice and my practice.

The Rockland, Maine-based nonprofit Island Institute (more about this later) began hosting an occasional conference in the late 1980s intended to gather teachers from island schools for networking and a series of workshops. Now a regular biennial event, the Island Teachers' Conference is two busy days of learning from one another, sharing experiences, resource exchanges, informal advocacy, and moral support. Who better understands what an isolated teacher's job is like or what would be a useful addition to the classroom or what the real concerns are? Most mainland teachers work within a large system with layers of administration and a specialist for everything. In the smallest schools, the island teacher may have to be the secretary, the drama director, the soccer coach, the nurse, the librarian, and the janitor at once, in addition to teaching multiple grades and, now, staying on top of the ever-changing technology. With workshops and discussion groups led by teachers and other experts, a few keynote speakers, and plenty of time for making social connections, these conferences have become a much-anticipated opportunity to recharge.

A few years ago, the teachers of the truly one-room schools found that even at the Island Teachers' Conference they were a minority among the participants, and that their job was still a subspecialty. Educational experts who came to lead sessions, and even some of the teachers from larger Maine islands, spoke a different language and normally experienced a completely different sort of workday than those who truly worked in isolation. Mention was made of this to Rob Benson, the minister on the *Sunbeam*, and he organized the first "Island Teachers' Retreat" in 2006, specifically for the teachers in the smallest schools. For a couple of days before the start of each year, these half-dozen or so educators could come together in a very informal setting, get to know each other, and share experiences.

After a couple of years of the retreat being largely a social occasion, something happened that would probably forever change the one-room island schools of Maine—all of them. Teacher Lindsay Eysnogle of Islesford (the Cranberry Isles) was really feeling the lack of any professional peer group. She'd had a hard year or two, and as much as she loved her new island home, the *professional* isolation was becoming a real burden. She did not see teaching on Islesford as a lark, as if it were a "posting" or just an adventure; she was a dedicated educator, in it for the long term, and wished to continually grow as such. Lindsay brought to the teachers' retreat the idea that a real, serious professional peer group for the one-room school teachers would be genuinely helpful—at least as she saw it. Others agreed. (It should be remembered also that in a tiny community, there is rarely anyone with whom a teacher can discuss workplace stresses or worries without breaking some sort of confidentiality, being perceived by the neighborhood as unhappy or unstable, or just coming across as a gossip.)

So the question was presented: "How can we get together more, and support each other more, and grow as professionals while working on our separate islands?" Teacher Donna Isaacs had an answer, or at least a suggestion. Isaacs, who had spent many summers on Little Cranberry but had been an educator for many years in Vermont, was a trained facilitator for something called a Critical Friends Group. "Lindsay confided in me that she was eager for some professional support," recalled Donna. "I said, 'I know a little something about that,' and I told Lindsay about the CFG. She asked, 'Would you mind talking to the group about it?'"

Donna Isaacs explains:

A Critical Friends Group is a professional learning community that usually consists of between eight and twelve educators. Group members are absolutely committed to improving their practice through collaborative learning and collaborative work. People get together, usually once a month, voluntarily—and that's important. School districts that mandate a CFG find that it rarely works. By the way, we mean "critical" as in "very important," not as in "we criticize."

The group spends a fair amount of time setting norms, similar to ground rules. They can be agreements about communicating, from showing up on time to things that are a lot more crucial to the emotional aspects of the process, like assuming best intentions. One thing that is essential in a CFG meeting is active listening. People have an equal voice, people are heard; you don't talk over other people's talk.

Meetings make use of protocols. There are protocols for setting goals, examining work, team-building, identifying what roles individuals want to take on in a collaborative group, identifying when there is a dissonance, and for addressing how to keep it from becoming an interpersonal conflict. For example, a detail person and a need-to-move-on person might annoy each other in a meeting without a mechanism for handling this reality.

Lindsay Eysnogle added:

The majority of our preparation for the meeting will be via e-mail. We schedule our meetings and discuss what will be on the agenda by e-mail. At each CFG meeting, one person will present a dilemma or something that he or she needs help with in his or her professional practice. Once that person has volunteered to present, another person volunteers to facilitate that discussion. Those decisions are made by way of e-mail. For the actual CFG meeting we always use a technology that allows us to speak to one another.

Back to experienced CFG coach Donna Isaacs:

An important part of being a member of a CFG is getting trained in how to offer and receive feedback. A big part of the role of the facilitator is to monitor the dialogue. This is not like a study group. There is a much higher level of commitment to the structure and to the other members.

There is efficiency and effectiveness in this organized communication, but also a level of discomfort sometimes with an artificial structure. But you get valuable input from people who might not otherwise talk in a meeting. A Critical Friends Group is different from just a facilitated meeting because the relationship is already there. The shared commitment is real and is already established.

Monhegan teacher Jessie Campbell adds:

The Critical Friends Group is part of a bigger organization called the School Reform Initiative that includes education professionals who believe in excellence and equity. Since our CFG is made up of teachers from different island schools, we use many different forms of technology to conduct these meetings. We have met through phone conferences, Skype conference, and by using the Tandberg (videoconferencing) units, and we have shared documents through Google docs. There are some glitches as we learn to use this technology, so we've learned to add fifteen minutes to the beginning of our meetings to get all the technology pieces set up.

One of the big ideas behind the CFG is making the commitment to one another that we care about each other's practice and students just as much as we care about our own. This is especially important to us island teachers because the isolation we face in our practice is extreme. We need each other's feedback, ideas, resources, and most of all, support. Through the CFG we get exactly that.

Lindsay Eysnogle feels very strongly about the value of the process. She uses the word "professional" a great deal when she talks, and this is for a reason: there is still a misconception out there that island teachers are somehow not quite "real teachers," but are somehow just eager young temporary volunteers or the like. Lindsay says:

> Personally, I cannot begin to describe the impact the CFG practice has had on me professionally. It is simply the most profound professional development experience I have had since beginning my career. The CFG work has forced me to question my assumptions about teaching and about learning, and to make changes to my practice. It has made me acutely aware of my students, and it has given me the courage to ask for help when I see things happening in my classroom that I cannot understand by myself before those things turn into big issues. It has taught me to value professional collaboration—and I have grown as a teacher because of it.

Donna Isaacs also emphasizes the usefulness of the CFG for real problem-solving:

> If another teacher brings a student's work or a problem to the CFG, I adopt that student like he's my own, all the members take on that problem as if it were their own. They don't sit there and make recommendations as if it were a simple matter. One founder of the movement is known for saying, "I can't tell you what to do, but what you do is *not* none of my business." Another important expression is, "Your practice is as important to me as my practice,

and your students are as important to me as my students."

Before too long it became obvious that if isolated teachers benefited from working together with peers who truly understood their work situation, then the isolated students would benefit as well. For a few of the schools, facing a year or two with extremely small student groups, connecting with students in other places was the only alternative to a serious loneliness. Thankfully, technology was beginning to make this affordable and almost (almost!) easy.

Angela Iannicelli of Monhegan, mother of the two boys who comprised the Monhegan school student body in 2010–2011, had been concerned about what school would be like for her sons.

Knowing that school would only be my two the next year, I asked the school board and Jessie to consider having more field trips so the boys could have more peer interactions. There had already been some talk between Jessie and some of the teachers on other islands about doing things together.

Monhegan Teacher Jessie Campbell comments on how telecommunications changed everything about school for the lone pair of brothers she taught:

When I started teaching on Monhegan, almost five years ago now, I came into the school as a lone teacher, right out of college, without the slightest idea of what I was doing. I had no curriculum and really no support in terms of my teaching. I quickly became very isolated. All of that has changed now because of something called the Outer Islands Teaching and Learning Collaborative.

To put it simply, this project has kind of saved our school this year by giving two brothers who would have had no other interaction with other students their age a peer group, not only academically but also socially. It gives them something to be excited about when they come to school in the morning. They ask, "Who are we meeting with today?" They are able to have different teachers and learn from different people. We've also been able to travel a lot and see different schools and have had experiences we wouldn't have had without the Teaching and Learning Collaborative. Really, it's been the highlight of our year. Our best memories this year will be because of the TLC.

A number of things were taking place simultaneously within the island schools that contributed to the formation of the Outer Islands

Teaching and Learning Collaborative, known as the TLC, in 2010. The nonprofit Island Institute, historically eager to put their staff and resources to work on projects geared toward island community sustainability, was very supportive of the idea. In 2009 a grant from the USDA Rural Utilities Service Distance Learning and Telemedicine Program facilitated by the Institute made sure that every small island school that didn't already have a Polycom or Tandberg videoconferencing unit got one. In the spring of 2010, Donna Isaacs applied for and got some grant funding through the Institute which helped the TLC get on its feet, paying for teachers to attend the annual winter meeting of the School Reform Initiative, the national organization at the heart of the Critical Friends Groups. Says Donna, "I applied for a grant from the Maine Community Foundation to pay for us to go to the winter meeting of the National CFG and for one of our members to go through the coach training. We needed to build some sustainability here. Lindsay and Jessie both did the leadership training, and took over the coordination of the project. I wrote another grant in the spring of 2010 for help with technology support."

The TLC was formed by the island teachers for the purpose of beating back the sense of isolation and tackling some of the problems that come with dwindling student populations. Using newly available (and rapidly evolving) telecommunications technology, making every effort to get together from time to time by whatever means possible, and by developing curricula, teaching methodologies, and assessment tools together that can be used within a combined group from multiple schools, the TLC allows both teachers and students to feel a part of a larger integrated community. Jessie Campbell writes, "My students have inter-island classmates and I have colleagues. I cannot really imagine what my time on Monhegan would have been like if the TLC did not form. I wonder if I would have lasted as long. All I know for sure is that what the TLC has brought to me and to my school is immeasurable. For me personally, it has allowed me to learn how to collaborate with others, grow as an educator, gain confidence in myself as a teacher and as a leader, and work with people I truly admire and respect."

Islands schools were also beginning to look at their academic programs differently around this time. Some of the schools never had any sort of curriculum guidelines until recently. Each new teacher was expected to just know what the students ought to study. Sometimes topics would be repeated annually, as bored children rolled their eyes, while other important or interesting topics were never mentioned, purely by accident. Historically, some teachers did a better job than others leaving records for their replacements. Without a building principal, and often without any "institutional memory" or any overlapping staff member, without a complete set of textbooks to which anybody felt any loyalty, and with school boards changing frequently, it would be easy for no adult to have much awareness of what sequence of topics had been studied for science (for example) in any given block of years.

Encouraged by school board member Natalie Ames, Matinicus Island Fellow Lana Cannon dedicated a large portion of her work in 2009 and 2010 to developing Matinicus's first real curriculum template for science and social studies. This project, begun the year before by fellow Anne Bardaglio and teacher Dorothy Carter, started with a four-year repeating outline of topics; Lana assembled a substantial collection of supporting resource materials to go with them. The curriculum was not a strict script for a teacher to read, but a way to ensure that, should a student stay on the island for his or her entire elementary school experience, he or she would be exposed to each topic twice—once as a younger student by way of introduction, and once while older, where more in-depth study would be expected—and not eight times!

This curriculum would eventually serve as the starting point for an aligned curriculum in these subjects that would help students on separate islands work on projects and learn together. Total curriculum alignment among the schools is not practical, nor would it probably be desirable, but in many cases a partial curriculum alignment, or the option of working with an aligned curriculum, allows students from various islands to collaborate on their studies. This works best (so far) with science and social studies, where broad topics, rather than specifics, are in play so that children of many ages can work on the same thing. The study of astronomy—as an example of a huge subject—leaves room for everyone from the kindergartner to the advanced, science-loving eighth-grader to study at his or her own level yet collaborate on presentations, enjoy the same field trips, stargazing activities, videos, or projects, and learn from one another.

Anne Bardaglio adds, "The whole goal for this is not just to create this peer group for the students, but to help the students exceed the level of work that they could do academically working alone. The project ideally will be able to be adjusted to respond to student needs as they come up." We are reminded that there is a lot more to working together than fun social interaction. Some worthwhile school activities and lessons simply aren't going to happen if there is only one student of an age to be interested in the topic.

It had not been part of the original plan to attempt to align English/Language Arts studies between the schools, but one of the most popular collaborations turned out to be an experiment with age-based reading groups using Skype. Five teachers each led a reading group consisting of kids within a couple of years of the same age who were reading the same assigned book. A student on one island might have a reading teacher on another island and be discussing plot and characters with three or four children on islands up and down the coast. The kids are given assignments, questions to answer, or ideas to respond to, and are expected to present their input to the others at weekly meetings held for the most part through their laptops. (Most of the island students have use of a Macintosh laptop computer.) While discussing the book, they also get to know each other a bit, sharing tales of their pet dogs and runaway chickens, birthday parties and sick days. Book-group partners quickly become real friends.

Sometimes, two schools will engage in a partnership for a certain academic project, making use of either videoconferencing or real-world visits, even if the work does not include the rest of the TLC community. For example, the Frenchboro school, which did not play a regular role in the TLC that year, worked along with Monhegan on a poetry unit in 2010, and recently students on North Haven, a slightly larger island, held "literature circle" gatherings (much like a book club) with the three students on Isle au Haut using the Tandbergs. Some teachers are more involved in the collaborative efforts than are others; this has to do with the particular students the teacher has in any given year, his or her own personality, and how much other support he or she may have from on-island sources (a married couple, both teachers, may feel the isolation less). A considerable degree of independence is still an important part of teaching one-room school.

The teachers of the 2011–2012 Outer Islands Teaching and Learning Collaborative enjoy a break from the serious work of developing a multi-grade curriculum. Top step, left to right, Jessie Campbell, Donna Isaacs, Island Fellow Anne Bardaglio, Lisa Rogers; lower step, Paula Greatorex, Heidi Holloway with Cove Henry Holloway; doing the back bend is Josh Holloway. (Not pictured: Lindsay Eysnogle.) SARAH AGAN

There have also been collaborations between, and group activities among, schools that were not part of the teacher-designed TLC, and yet fit nicely into this structure. Through the 2010–2011 academic year, students on many of the islands, including several which have not been part of the TLC, participated in a weather and climate study called Students and Teachers Observing and Recording Meteorological Systems (STORMS!—clearly somebody thought up the acronym before the rest of the wording). Students made daily observations, often using weather stations provided by the program. They posted data and photographs to a website, did research projects that they presented to each other at a spring gathering at the University of Maine—sort of like an inter-island science fair—and worked the weather study into their own curriculum as it fit best. As the winter of 2010–2011 was snowier than usual on the coast of Maine, excellent opportunities for artful photography were present as well.

Anne Bardaglio observed that "What was interesting about the STORMS project was the extent to which it ended up intersecting with the community. For Frenchboro it really was about the fishing. At other schools, they would interview residents and get stories about storms that had hit the island in the past. Isle au Haut did a lot with the blog, and charting and graphing their findings; that's a younger group of students, so an activity like graphing their data was really age-appropriate." Frenchboro students got on the VHF marine radio each morning and broadcast a brief weather report to the area fishermen, who shared observations of sea conditions with the kids. "We wanted to have a VHF in the school anyway," explained the teachers, "because if anything ever happened (like a fire), that's the fastest way to get hold of everybody. In our community, everybody has a VHF (even if it isn't licensed). We have this wonderful weather station from the STORMS program, plus the kids were looking up the NOAA forecast, and the CoCoRaHS [Community Collaborative Rain, Hail, and Snow Network], which is people reporting in from all over, and they would download the marine forecast. They would get on the VHF, read the marine forecast and data from the Frenchboro weather station, and then they'd tell a joke. It was hilarious. Our little first-grader announces, 'Here's the joke of the day. . . . '"

However, the STORMS project originated outside the island school community, with the National Science Foundation, and was offered to the teachers by the Island Institute. The teachers believe strongly in the importance of distinguishing projects like STORMS—valuable and interesting but designed elsewhere—from the work of the TLC, which is, to quote Donna Isaacs, "grass roots, envisioned by us, created by us, implemented by us, and reviewed by us. It comes entirely from us, born of necessity, and is absolutely bottom-up, not top-down."

Now that the connections have been made, all kinds of things could happen in the future. It is easy now to propose an idea or a trip or an activity among the island schools, as the structures are in place. The Outer Islands Teaching and Learning Collaborative will evolve, and exactly what collaboration means could look different in the future. It is fair to say that there will be no going back to the same degree of isolation for either students or teachers.

In 2005 outer islands pastor Rob Benson organized the first Island Middle-Schoolers' Retreat, a team-building, ice-breaking, no-little-kids event in recognition of the need for teens to find some peer support for the transition to high school off-island. This offshoot of the Inter-Island Event has the capability of being more than just a social event; some island teenagers live with considerably more upheaval, independence, and responsibility than do their mainland friends who sleep in their own beds every night. Activities during the retreat are geared toward building trust, gaining confidence, and helping teens understand where to access information, resources, and assistance that may not be available on their island. Largely, it is about moving away from home for high school, although that subject may never even be mentioned outright. The island middle-schoolers learn that they are not going through this strange experience alone.

In 2011 the Island Institute made Anne Bardaglio's position permanent, and the island schools now have a full-time inter-island project coordinator: the Island Schools Collaborative Senior Fellow. Teachers and others had indicated that all the organizing and logistics planning required to make things like six-island field trips actually happen was far more than any full-time teacher could manage in his or her "spare time." Multi-island educational field trips became the norm (thanks largely to Anne, who organizes them), and in November of 2011 the first Outer Island Student Council slate of officers was elected—the president an eighth-grader from Monhegan, the vice-president a sixth-grader from Matinicus, the treasurer an eighth-grader from the Cranberry Isles, etc.

Skype conferencing improved over time, and multi-user video connections began to work better. Skype conferencing also served another unexpected and happy purpose for these students when one island boy was required to spend a considerable amount of time in the hospital on the mainland. His classmates, actual and virtual, were able to see that he was doing all right while receiving medical treatment, and he was able to participate to a certain extent in the activities of the group. He could join his reading group from his hospital bed in Portland, and from there discuss the book with his friends on Cliff Island and the Cranberry Isles.

One other factor not to be overlooked is that most of the island school boards (Matinicus being the exception) had by 2010 given up their tradition of "term limiting" teachers. Whereas for decades the island schools had been largely staffed by transient young idealists with no plans for the long term, and likely minimal experience with multi-age teaching techniques, we now saw the formation of a group of true masters of the art of teaching at a one-room school. Teachers with four, five, six, or more years of experience found that their issues differed from those of the newcomer. "How to teach all those different grades" wasn't the issue; how to continue to grow as an educator while working "in a vacuum" began to arise as a common concern. The needs of the adults began to receive some attention. As a platform for professional growth and development, peer support, and respectful, confidential discussion, the TLC and the CFG have been tremendously helpful. As a mechanism for mentoring new teachers, there is hope that the TLC will also prove valuable.

Term limits for island teachers are a "that's good/that's bad" quandary. Most agree that is takes a while to learn the skills needed to do this very complex job well. On the other hand, where students could potentially have the same teacher for their entire elementary careers, we must admit that nobody specializes in everything, and a variety of teachers means a variety of exposures. Monhegan parent and school board member Jackie Boegel recalls her daughter's teachers:

> She had a teacher for first and second grades who was a very nurturing young woman, who was a great fit for her at that age, as a shy little kid. For third and fourth, she had a young man, all of her classmates were boys, and she learned how to make snowshoes and model airplanes and battleships and had a whole different kind of teaching. For the fifth and sixth grades, she had another teacher who was a young athlete who was very proud of being a fast runner, very into encouraging young women, and for the seventh and eighth grades, she had a terrific young writer who took her to writers' conferences and got writing groups together. My daughter drew from the strengths of each of the four teachers. They all nurtured different parts of her.

Technology cannot and should not replace human contact. The island teachers closely involved in the collaborative work meet several times a year to plan activities and plot strategies together, to cement their relationships, and to "take the pulse" of the project. Students eagerly anticipate the next field trip—and those trips are getting to be amazing experiences, with loads of activities packed into several days of traveling. Students return home exhausted but sure of their friendships with kids from other islands, and island adults know that the students do not risk being "island-bound" like some were years ago—meaning that they didn't know what a traffic light was for and so on. The Inter-Island Event and its offshoot, the annual Island Middle-Schoolers' Retreat sponsored by the Maine Sea Coast Mission, the Island Institute-sponsored Island Teachers' Conferences, and the *Sunbeam*'s one-room-school Teachers' Retreat still exist, and participants look forward to them eagerly.

Needless to say, power outages and Internet failures occur from time to time, and it would be truly unfortunate if any child's school experience were entirely dependent upon this technology. Nobody intends for that to happen. Island students are still privileged to spend a good deal of their time outdoors, interacting with their community, observing their environment, studying their biome, and supporting their neighborhood.

As Principal Scott McFarland of Mount Desert (whose district includes Frenchboro, Swan's, and the Cranberries) points out, "There is an illusion that our small remote outer islands have schools that are antiquated and lack the sophistication of mainland schools. The reality is . . . their remoteness necessitates pushing the technology envelope . . . and a commitment to the digital age of learning." As teacher Donna Isaacs observes, "We're not old-fashioned—we're cutting edge!"

On the morning of December 14, 2011, the students from the Cliff Island, Monhegan, Matinicus, Isle au Haut, and the Cranberry Isles schools got together for a Christmas party—on their Tandberg units. As each small cluster of students (including the preschoolers on Cliff Island), teachers, ed techs, and a few others gathered in the respective classrooms in front of their video cameras, each in turn opened a "Secret Santa" box prepared by another school and sent across the water in the mail. Others cheered as the four Matinicus students opened a large carton which contained a beautiful handmade Christmas wreath, a box of cookies, and individual gifts for each student:

large mugs painted with their names and stuffed with hot chocolate mix and mini-marshmallows. Tiny lobster-buoy and miniature knitted-mitten tree ornaments completed the package. The students figured out that their Secret Santa was the Isle au Haut school. As the Cliff Island students opened their box next—which happened to be packed by the Matinicus kids—they received a mobile made of origami cranes, flip books, alphabet books, handmade counting games, and similar things suitable for smaller children. In turn, each of the participating schools opened its box, each finding something different; then, after a few "Christmas riddles" and some silly dancing in front of the camera, each small group shut off the teleconferencing equipment and went back to being just that, a small group within the confines of their island (although most were munching on homemade Christmas cookies at that point!).

Mission and Institute
Auxiliary islanders!

Two organizations have historically played a very large part in helping to overcome the very real isolation, including the peculiar separation from each other, that islanders experience (to the extent that such "overcoming" is desired). Staff members from these two nonprofits have become true friends, reliable helpers, and regular members of the island school communities, as familiar to the students as are their teachers. These respected, and if I may say, sometimes beloved "auxiliary islanders" work for the Maine Sea Coast Mission as the crew of the vessel *Sunbeam,* and for the Island Institute as island fellows, education staff members, and other specialists.

It is truly the individuals associated with the Sea Coast Mission and the Island Institute who have made such a difference in the lives of island adults and children. "Visions" and "strategic plans" and "mission statements" and carefully worded descriptions of lofty ideals are helpful for building websites (not to mention endowments), but the human beings who interact with island residents at work, who just happen to be employed by either of these two multifaceted organizations, are why we hold them in such high esteem. Islanders who do not choose to ever set foot in a church like to hang around aboard the *Sunbeam,* drink coffee, and enjoy some informal fellowship with the captain and the engineer.

The Maine Sea Coast Mission has served the islands and some other remote down east towns of Maine for over a century, and despite the religious sound to the name, the Mission provides a variety of services and benefits, some far more important to the islanders than the connection to a religious institution.

The Island Institute, founded in 1983, brings together skilled staff members, funding from a wide variety of sources, and an expertise concerning island issues learned by working with scientists, educators, businesspeople including seafood harvesters, and community activists to address the very real problems that confront year-round, working-island residents.

The Maine Sea Coast Mission

The seventy-five-foot steel-hulled vessel *Sunbeam V* makes regular rounds of the more isolated islands, bringing a nurse's office including a Telemedicine videoconferencing unit (and, of course, Sharon Daley, RN), a large galley and main deck "saloon" where island community suppers, art lessons, meetings, and game nights can be held (and, of course, Pat Dutille, the cook/steward), and is built tough enough to serve as an icebreaker if necessary (with Captain Mike Johnson and Captain Storey King, the young captain and engineer, equal to whatever task is required of the boat). The history of the Mission and the vessel can easily be found; a few years ago Maine filmmaker Jeff Dobbs produced a full-length documentary film called *A Century of Hope on a Sea of Change* about the history of the Mission's work with Maine's islands and remote coastal communities.

The Mission was, to quote the documentary, "from its inception entirely nondenominational in character." From its earliest days at the beginning of the twentieth century, a priority has been to "provide or facilitate medical care to island and coastal communities" because of recognition from the start that "health and general welfare were completely inseparable from spiritual welfare."

Of primary importance is "the continued sustainability of life in these small island communities." The Mission is not really all that "missionary" in its technique; saving souls, if such a thing happens, takes place subtly, as examples are set, underserved people are assisted, cultural and educational bonds are formed, and friendships are cemented. No crewmember aboard the *Sunbeam* pays any attention to

The *Sunbeam* at the Matinicus wharf. Low tide leaves the vessel "high and dry," but when the *Sunbeam* makes an overnight visit to Matinicus, "grounding out" is just part of the routine. EVA MURRAY

whether any given islander attends church. They do notice, however, if somebody seems down or lonely or ill, or if, on the other hand, there seems to be local cause for celebration. The boat crew are our good friends, and we smile when we see them coming into the harbor (old-timer's gossip about the *Sunbeam* traditionally bringing bad weather notwithstanding!). The organization is and has ever been "always inclusive, responding in crisis, supporting a better life."

The Maine Sea Coast Missionary Society (later renamed the Maine Sea Coast Mission) was formally organized in 1905, with its first vessel, the *Hope,* and shortly thereafter the thirty-eight-foot *Morning Star.* In 1911 a Colby College sorority wrapped up some toys for Christmas presents for island children, this act becoming the start of the Mission's Christmas program. These days, hundreds of children, elders, and others receive Christmas packages from the Mission—for the needy, something substantial, and for all the island children, the customary hand-knit mittens and candy wrapped in white butcher paper tied with red string. The first boat named *Sunbeam* was launched in 1912; in 1941, the *Sunbeam* got the nation's first "seabound" radiotelephone equipment. The boat currently in service, *Sunbeam V*, was launched in 1995.

The *Sunbeam*'s island "mission" is not specifically school-related, but assisting with the needs of isolated children has always been a significant part of their vision. Decades ago they brought schoolbooks to lightkeepers' children (as well as Christmas presents and, I heard somewhere, the occasional dentist). The "boat minister," nurse, and other crew can offer island funerals, weddings, biweekly telemedicine trips, informal church services somewhere around major holidays, and they occasionally help in connecting people (discreetly and confidentially) with needed off-island counselors, doctors, support groups, and social services.

"The EdGE," or Ed Greaves Education, is a gentle at-risk youth program sponsored by the Mission which does not involve the islands and the *Sunbeam,* but which does have an impact on many of Maine's schoolchildren. According to the Mission: EdGE is an innovative youth development program of the Maine Sea Coast Mission for students in grades four–eight in coastal Washington County, Maine. It is designed to encourage youth to stay engaged in school, aspire toward and attain higher levels of achievement, and develop the personal skills that will enable them to achieve success. These goals are pursued using a wide range of interdisciplinary and experiential curricula. EdGE provides after-school and summer programs that include visual and performing arts projects, leadership training, innovative science and technology workshops, skill-building in math and language arts, and outdoor pursuits. Elements of an arts and humanities program have been part of the core strategies used to meet our goals since the program's inception in 2002. In 2006, EdGE was recognized as the outstanding Twenty-First-Century Community Learning Center Afterschool program by the Maine Afterschool Network.

Since 2006 the Mission has also sponsored the *Island Reader,* a small annual literary magazine which includes poetry, short stories, and other writing, photography, and art submitted by island residents of all ages.

In recent years, some amazing men have served as the "pastor to the outer islands," or so-called boat minister. Stan Haskell was a friend to fishermen and others who normally had little patience for clergy. Tony Burkhart was the minister when I first came to Matinicus, and made sure my students and I were always welcomed aboard the *Sunbeam* for refreshments and arts and crafts with steward Betty Allen. Ted Hoskins is a former Isle au Haut schoolteacher, lobster fisherman, and Yale-educated theologian with a booming voice and a commanding public presence. Retired from the Mission, having served as the *Sunbeam* minister for a number of years, Ted still lives in Maine, though once in a while he makes service trips to Belize to work on construction projects and to organize local fishermen. (For several years, Maine islanders participated in these trips as well, for some, substituting for a "winter vacation," for others perhaps the farthest they'd ever been from home.) He now holds the unique job title of "pastor to the coastal communities and fisheries," a description written for him, working not on sermons but on meetings between commercial fishermen and regulators, scientists, politicians, and—hardest of all—other commercial fishermen. Protecting this lifestyle means protecting this resource, but "protecting" does not mean stopping the harvest. There is a tricky balance that must be negotiated, and there is a long history of distrust among the various players. Ted, with his informality, his sensitivity, and his absolute credibility hopes to assist in opening the lines of communication for the benefit of the commercial fishing communities.

The current boat minister, the Reverend Rob Benson, known to all simply as Rob, is a long-distance swimmer who used to coach swimming, a former middle-school and high school English teacher, and the father of two young sons. Rob's interest in supporting the island schools—and in particular the isolated teachers and the island adolescents—is perhaps informed by his own experiences before he took the position with the Mission. His official title is "pastor to the outer islands," but *pastor* is not a word we normally associate with Rob. His world is not the pulpit. His expertise is not in centuries-old ritual or fiery preaching, and I have never heard him quote the Bible outside of church except in fun. He is quite expert, however, in listening, in sorting out the fixable problems from the psychology and the drama, and in organizing to get something done. He is tactful and diplomatic, exceptionally hardworking, sensitive to small-town politics, acutely tuned in to the complexities of human nature, and knows better than to be too aggressive in his desire to "improve" people's lives. He is absolutely unconcerned with whether or not people attend services, but he offers such church services for those who appreciate the tradition and the gathering. He is humble, quiet, very well educated, and surprisingly aware of everybody's "back story."

I spoke with Rob Benson about his perception of the Mission's responsibility to the island children, and, more specifically, about recent activities he has organized such as the annual Island Middle-Schoolers' Retreat:

Ted [the previous boat minister] ran field trips where he took some of the older students to New York and Washington, D.C. [This was another example of an activity where middle-school students from several different islands, who likely had never met before, were able to begin friendships.] There is also the legacy of the Inter-Island Event, from which the Middle-Schoolers' Retreat branched. Getting fifty people to some central point is most expediently done with the *Sunbeam*. It is incumbent upon us to do logistics—that's how we can help.

About six or so years ago, Lorna Stuart, the teacher on Frenchboro, voiced the observation at another teacher workshop that the teachers of the little schools were sensing that "probably about 70 percent of this stuff doesn't even apply to us; we don't have a principal or an arts director and all this." The teachers at the smallest schools were saying, "You know, what we need is this same sort of meeting, but specifically for the really small island schools."

I said, "That I can help with. The boat is yours—for two nights—right before school starts. You just get your schedules cleared with whomever."

For the first few years it was pretty unstructured, but from that a few significant things arose: the teachers got to know each other, began seeing each other as colleagues, identifying with one another. Secondly, it folded Monhegan back into the group.

Monhegan had not been participating regularly in the Inter-Island Event because of scheduling and travel problems, so they were less connected as schools began to get to know each other through that annual event. The other major thing that came from the Island Teachers' Retreats on the *Sunbeam* was that three years ago, a new teacher arrived who had experience with this thing called the Critical Friends Group. That actually resulted in a transition in the retreat itself from a less structured social event to a more highly structured working meeting.

Cliff Island's participation in the Teachers' Retreat has been a big addition. They're in Casco Bay; I think everybody up here just figured, "Hey, they're Casco Bay, they're Portland, they're probably a lot more like Peaks," when in fact they're a lot more like Isle au Haut [meaning despite the legal connection with Maine's largest city, the real community on Cliff Island more closely resembles those on the "outer islands" farther east].

So about the Middle-Schoolers' Retreat—I was talking to one of the educational technicians, who said, "What I'd really like is something for our middle-schoolers to help them get ready for high school, because I know how hard that is." We had also been hearing from the Frenchboro teenagers about how they feel "out of their element" when they go to Mount Desert Island High School. There was a bit of prejudice: "You're from an island." A lot of these kids had grown up in their lobster boats, they were making a good living, they were a part of their community, and suddenly they move from a nurturing, familiar setting to "You're out in the big world; lots of luck." Some of these confident, self-possessed kids absolutely wilted when they got to high school.

There was a work group, teenagers from the Bar Harbor Congregational Church, where some of the Frenchboro teenagers were hosting some Mount Desert Island kids, and the Frenchboro kids said, "Let's take them out in our boats," and only one of the MDI kids in the group, Marya Spurling, whose dad is a lobsterman, had ever been out in a lobster boat!

It should be mentioned that an offshoot of the Island Middle-Schoolers' Retreat is the collection of letters "back" to the island eighth-graders from high-school students who have recently made that transition. This collection, called "I 2 I" or "Eye 2 Eye," offers advice and reassurance not from parents, teachers, pastors, or authorities, but from kids only a couple of years older, former classmates who have journeyed across the water to a mainland high school (public or private) and have survived the transition. (There are samples in a later chapter.)

As it happens, I was along as a chaperone for the first Middle-Schoolers' Retreat. The event was held in Rockland and was scheduled for a weekend that turned out to be the worst blizzard we'd had in the area in a very long time. Everything was closed. It was mid-January, bitterly cold, blowing a screeching gale, with deep snow and plows having a hard time keeping up with it. We were all staying in what you might call an "economical" motel. I was camped out on the floor in my sleeping bag so the middle-school girls in the room could have the two beds. The room was full of ants. I mean *ants,* and not just a few, in this blizzard in January in Maine. One of the kids had a box of Cheez-Its but we couldn't eat them because it was full of ants.

Rob Benson, the teachers, and a few of us parents from each school, and probably fifteen or twenty island-raised sixth-, seventh-, and eighth-grade students put on every bit of winter clothing we had packed and went out to find some supper. Nothing was open except Burger King. These particular teachers were not normally folks who would feed their students "fast food," but under the circumstances, they said "What the heck" so we walked into the deserted Burger King in Rockland, Maine, and ordered up a couple of hundred dollars worth of food. Rob Benson and Lindsay Eysnogle, the teacher from the Cranberries, started contra-dancing in the Burger King.

The whole event went on for a day longer than planned because nobody could get back to their islands because of the storm. Mail boats, vehicle ferries, and airplanes were all canceled. Kids got to know each other a bit, and realized that they had a peer group made up of kids from other islands—kids who shared the experience of having grown up at the mercy of the weather, too! This was before all the teleconferencing and online communications options that exist today. Eating burgers in that blizzard was fun, but the experience of getting stuck in Rockland was also exactly what the retreat was all about: bringing those kids together in a real way, breaking the ice, assuring each one that he or she was not alone in a strange island experience getting ready for high school. All the structured team-building exercises and circle talks in the world couldn't have done a better job.

The Island Institute

From the Island Institute's website: "More than a century ago, there were 300 year-round island communities; today there are 15. If that kind of decline had occurred to a population of wildlife, there would be an endangered species program to reverse it."

The Island Institute, founded in 1983 by Philip Conkling and

Peter Ralston, has grown to be a widely recognized advocate for island causes, a starting point for many mainland people who want to know more about Maine's inhabited islands, and a highly respected non-profit organization within philanthropic and social service circles. The purpose of the Island Institute is broad, and its role with respect to the island communities continues to evolve over time, but the Institute has always taken a keen interest in the islands' small schools, and has always been more than supportive of school-related initiatives. From the first Island Teachers' Conference in the late 1980s, the Island Institute has worked to facilitate conversations among those who work within the island schools. The Institute cannot make school policy or provide teachers or make the transportation easier or solve specific island problems, but there are some things it can do, and do well. It can organize meetings and conferences, bringing people together to network and to educate each other (and this means everything from providing the venue to organizing speakers and workshops to ordering lunch for a hundred). It can help put talented young people together with promising local enterprises and agencies, help financial donors and deserving programs find each other, and help minimize administrative complexity for smaller local organizations. It serves as a central clearinghouse for scholarships and charitable giving, it finds and writes applications for grants, and it employs experts who can assist with research. It can support islanders' efforts to lobby or present issues and facts to policy makers and legislators. It can act as a go-between to help connect those who can offer enrichment projects to island teachers and interested community members. It publishes two high-quality publications, a monthly newspaper called *Working Waterfront* and the handsome glossy annual, *Island Journal.*

These days, the Institute does a lot more with the island schools than just host an occasional meeting. With ongoing "Education Initiatives" and a full-time education director, the Institute's place in the life of the island schools is undeniable. It supports the recent collaborative efforts, assists with keeping the islands on the "forefront of the technology," and offers to connect students with educational opportunities such as the National Science Foundation's STORMS project described earlier.

Island Institute Education Director Ruth Kermish-Allen describes her role this way:

In short, my job is to listen very carefully to what teachers, students, parents—the community as a whole—are saying about their schools and education in their community. Once I understand the needs that are out there, I try to develop programming to meet those goals. I always partner with islanders to develop programming, and I also try to reach out to other organizations that may have done similar work so that we can all learn from each other. Then, of course, comes the grant writing.

My job is also to help facilitate discussions between island groups, between island communities and their mainland counterparts, and between island communities and policy makers. I am always on the lookout for new communication methods or facilitation tools to help this process along.

In its strategic planning for the next few years, the Island Institute intends to work with island educators to "promote the strengths of island schools for the purpose of retaining and attracting young families; leverage new distance-learning technology; strengthen curricular offerings by supporting K12 education in the areas of energy, marine resources, climate change, and island culture and history." The Institute's plans for the future also mention "classrooms without walls," using videoconferencing and many other emerging technology tools to open new doors for the rural student.

Perhaps the mechanism by which the Island Institute has provided the greatest impact to island communities, though, has been through the Island Fellows program. "Fellows" are recent college graduates, trained by the Institute, who are sent to islands after a request has been made for somebody to assist with a specific project. The island communities tend to be short on young, eager, educated people; most "native" young islanders are either involved full-time in commercial fishing or must work off-island much of the time. Island Fellows, funded through a variety of sources including, until recently, some AmeriCorps monies, help with community projects where the island is shorthanded. According to the Institute's website, since 1999 over seventy fellows in about fifteen communities have assisted with "comprehensive planning, Geographic Information Systems (GIS) mapping, sustainable agriculture, affordable housing, economic development, technology support, curriculum development, historical preservation, library sciences, public health outreach, fire safety, nonprofit management, volunteer recruitment and management, and theater and arts programming." An Island Fellow usually stays for two years, becoming a year-round, if often temporary, part of the community. I say "often" temporary because several have put down deep roots in their assigned island homes.

The two Island Fellows who have worked at Matinicus, Anne Bardaglio and Lana Cannon, in addition to working very hard at their appointed tasks and enduring everything from unheatable homes, fuel shortages, and the stresses of living alone to the very real burden of having an ever-increasing to-do list with no end in sight, became good friends to us all. These women were each, in turn, the very best of neighbors—asking little and demanding nothing, contributing much, and remaining sane in the face of some admittedly peculiar circumstances. I was initially skeptical of the Island Fellows program, at least as it might apply to Matinicus, fearing it might be "busywork" for the idealistic but clueless, and wondering just where the Island Institute thought these young do-gooders were going to live. My fears were unfounded. These hardworking new friends speak volumes for what can be accomplished when a program is run well and the right people are placed in the right positions.

Lana Cannon served as the Matinicus School and Historical Preservation Fellow from 2008–2010. Says Lana, a native of Peaks Island who went to college in Pennsylvania:

I always thought I would go into the Peace Corps, but I wanted to come back to Maine. A Peaks Island family friend saw the notice—probably in the *Working Waterfront* newspaper—about the position [as an Island Fellow] and e-mailed me about it; I frantically e-mailed Chris Wolff [Community Service Director, and essentially in charge of the Fellows, at the Island Institute] to ask if I could apply late.

I grew up sailing to different islands in Casco Bay, bombing around to islands. I love islands. The idea of living on an island by myself sounded exciting. The chart of Matinicus showed a tiny bit of land and mostly water.

I didn't really understand what my responsibilities would be. The interview process and coming out here was really cool, but I still didn't know what I would be doing. It felt right, though; kind of electric.

I took so much from my experience here that I hope I was able to give back something even close to as much. I got attached, very comfortable here, very quickly. I am so thankful and happy that I was able to do it. I wish I lived here.

Place-Based Education
Squid lab and exquisite cider.

Visitors to the islands immediately recognize what abundant educational resources are at hand. For science, the children have easy access to undeveloped beaches, tide pools, and easily observed marine environments; forest, salt marsh, and other ecosystems; dark skies, gardens, and lots of people who work on engines, and sometimes tiny island electricity companies or other hands-on mechanics and physical-science "labs." For social studies, the children have easy access to local municipal governance and community agencies; to nascent historical societies eager for help collecting artifacts, photographs, and oral history; to neighbors who grew up when times were different; and to real problems that need to be solved by committed "civilians"— community members such as themselves. Little is behind lock and key; little is handled by professionals who wouldn't welcome the interest of students. The real world is unusually accessible to these kids.

Sometimes educators need to be reminded that it is okay for students to get away from the books, off the computer, and go outside to take a look at the world. "Taking a look" will very likely result in caring, in wanting to help, and in feeling a sense of connection to one's home. This is place-based education, and island teachers are very good at it.

From the *Promise of Place* website: "Place-based education (PBE) immerses students in local heritage, cultures, landscapes, opportunities, and experiences, using these as a foundation for the study of language arts, mathematics, social studies, science, and other subjects across the curriculum. PBE emphasizes learning through participation in service projects for the local school and/or community." Among the "principles of successful place-based education" the site notes:

> Learning focuses on local themes, systems, and content; learning is supported by strong and varied partnerships with local organizations, agencies, businesses, and government; learning is interdisci-

plinary; learning experiences are tailored to the local audience. . . .
[and perhaps most significantly] Learning is grounded in and supports the development of a love for one's place.

The findings are clear: place-based education fosters students'
connection to place and creates vibrant partnerships between
schools and communities. It boosts student achievement and
improves environmental, social, and economic vitality.

The Island Institute tells us:

Place-based education is a strategy that encourages students to
connect with their communities and public lands through hands-on, real-world learning experiences on community-based projects.
It's especially effective in the context of Maine's small, rural,
marine resource–based islands and coastal towns.

Ruth Kermish-Allen adds:

Islands offer a perfect opportunity for place-based learning; in an
environment where tight communities are formed, it is no surprise
that island schools are using a form of learning that teaches their
students about the community.

While place-based and project-based learning may be gaining
popularity with educational reformers around the nation, it is simply the way island schools have functioned for many years. When
you do not have computer labs, a different teacher for each grade
and discipline, or a science lab, you are forced to get creative. . . .
Using place-based pedagogy has worked extremely well for island
teachers who don't have access to the same resources their mainland counterparts sometimes take for granted.

Place-based education need not only refer to environmental science topics. Superintendent Jerry White observes that:

Placed-based education promotes students' understanding of their
community through study of history, personal anecdotal stories,
and assisting in various community projects. The result is that students gain a greater appreciation for their community and the
world around them and their role in continuing to support and
add to the community. Often, students are amazed to learn what
life experiences community members have had and what those
members can tell about their families, going back several generations.

From Michelle Finn:

> We have a form that all the parents have signed that says the island is our classroom. We leave a note on the door whenever we go outside saying things like, "We're on the trails behind the library" or "We're at the community garden." The freedom we have to roam and enjoy our island is one of the best aspects of teaching on Frenchboro.

How does a new teacher from Minnesota instruct a bunch of Maine lobstermen's kids about marine biology?

When Matinicus teacher Dave Duncan first considered a saltwater aquarium for his classroom, he was initially looking for donations of old fish-tank equipment. Duncan contacted the Maine State Aquarium, a branch of the Department of Marine Resources, to discuss the necessary permit required to possess an undersized lobster. The DMR's education director thought a field trip to Matinicus sounded like a good idea. She brought a DMR intern and natural science educator, and a DMR-employed retired elementary teacher to visit the island school. To Mr. Duncan's surprise they offered to bring the whole works: aquarium, supplies, information and print resources, even live specimens. That was just the beginning.

A marine biology lab was planned for Monday. "We're going to dissect squids!" The Marine Resources educators had brought along a bin full of small squid, with lab activities suitable for even the youngest students (the Matinicus school that year, 2010–2011, included students from kindergarten through the seventh grade). As the department director took Mr. Duncan through the research-permitting paperwork and explained why a few marine species should not be kept in the aquarium, the others conducted the squid lab.

Each of the seven students was presented with a fresh (although quite dead) squid on a paper plate. It was tempting to laugh when these kids, most of whom have spent much of their lives aboard a lobster boat and think nothing of handling the messiest of half-rotten bait, still made faces and joked, "Eww! It's slimy!" Nobody took that too seriously. They took measurements, discussed squid body parts, and learned some proper terminology. They examined the delicate skin, with its chromatophores that enable it to change color for camouflage. Students were shown how to remove their squid's "pen," a stiffening internal structure with a texture similar to fingernail. They examined the eyes and removed the hard lens that provides the squid with uncommonly good eyesight. They examined the squid's eight legs (or arms) and two tentacles, seeing those to be quite different structures. They looked at mouth parts and removed the animal's bird-like beak. Finally, the young biologists carefully opened up the animal, looked over the internal organs, and found the ink sac. Then, dipping the "pen" into the squid ink, they wrote their names on their lab reports.

After squid science, the students enjoyed some squid art. Each child made a colorful squid print on a fabric flag using paint and their specimen (thankfully still whole enough to look like a squid!).

The DMR educators recommended against tossing remains of deceased aquarium animals overboard, and they didn't want to toss the squid either, as that would set the wrong example. The subject of dead specimens arose because predation became an issue before the classroom aquarium was even fully operational. Most of the crabs were evicted almost immediately when it was discovered that they'd eaten the first juvenile lobster right in the shipping cooler (tiny lobsters need to be able to retreat to shelter). Something had also chomped the little skate. A second lobster was dispatched by DMR to Matinicus on the airplane, a fact that drew a few chuckles from the adults: "Who ships lobsters TO Matinicus?" When one of the local fishermen appeared at the schoolroom door with a bucket containing a selection of small critters from his day's haul, the children loudly informed him, "No crabs welcome!"

A list of aquarium chores posted in the classroom reminds the students to do more than just clean the tank. This is real science; salinity, temperature, pH, and other variables must be measured, and other tests of water quality must be done periodically. "Do collect some mussels," the DMR director reminded the class, "because those sea stars were really after that moon snail."

Says Dave Duncan, "I never would have had a chance to do this in the Midwest."

Doug Finn remembers a service-learning project that had results right at home:

Two years ago Michelle and I wanted to do "service learning" with some of the standards that we had in the Maine Learning Results. We had the kids walk around the school with cameras, in small groups, and take pictures of things they wanted to change. We looked at all the pictures and made this big list of all the things they wanted to change about the Frenchboro school—the physical school—everything from changing a lightbulb to fixing an old broken door. The ideas were coming from them. We prioritized the list by voting, then drew up "costs money" and "doesn't cost money" lists. We had two interior doors that were in really rough shape, so for a math project we fixed those. We put in new doors. We had a special source of school funds to buy the materials; it was a math service-learning project, and the kids did the measurements and the demolition. You look at the trim and it's got hammer dings all over it because some of the kids were learning how to use a hammer. I can look at each ding and say, "I know which kid put that nail in."

They also wanted to add to the playground. There was a wooden tower already, and they wanted to add more to it. We'd been saving up for two years for that, and finally we finished it. They put the mulch in, they built it, they dug the holes, they put the cement down, they painted it—they have a very strong feeling of accomplishment, and it was a very long-term goal.

Teachers Josh and Heidi Holloway and the students at Cliff Island School offer "subscribers" an excellent online school newsletter from time to time. Although much of the newsletter consists of still photography, scanned artwork, and video clips, some of the short text pieces offer a peek into the activities and special projects that the Cliff students undertake. Should anybody still think that these students sit in their little classroom all day doing seatwork, and by virtue of their isolation are missing out on the wider world, these short posts written by students (the oldest in fifth grade) should convince us otherwise:

Aquaponics

The Cliff Island School students teamed up to write a successful grant for an aquaponics system. Are you wondering what aquaponics is? Aquaponics is a smart and efficient way to plant, combining hydroponics (growing plants in water without soil) with aquaculture (fish farming). The system contains a fish tank with fish like tilapia, and a grow bed for plants like spinach. The water gets pumped up to where you put the plants, bringing fish waste up, and that is what feeds the plants. The plants remove the waste and the water becomes aerated. We feed the fish (tilapia) worms from our vermicomposter, scum from the side of the tank, and plant waste from the greenhouse. We feed the worms some of the leftover plant parts and newspaper.

We will be keeping the aquaponics system in the classroom. The Cliff Island School will have it operating all next school year, so come and check it out!

Electric Usage Cutbacks

Every day we check the electric usage. First we read the number of KWH (kilowatt hours) on the electric meter—a circular meter on the side of the building. Then we go inside and write the date and the number of KWHs on a whiteboard. After that we subtract the number from the day before from the new number to find out the electric usage for the 24-hr. period.

We have cut down on our electric usage by turning off our lights, unplugging the water cooler and fridge, using less electric heat, turning off unused appliances, and we are thinking of changing the lights for the exit signs to LED or fluorescent bulbs. We have already lowered our usage by 50 percent, but we're looking for ways to reduce it further.

STORMS

This year the Cliff Island School participated in STORMS (Students and Teachers Observing and Recording Meteorological Systems). One of the many things we did with the other island schools (Long, Monhegan, Matinicus, and Frenchboro) as part of the project was post daily weather data and pictures to a weather blog. Every day one of us would record the barometric pressure, temperature, relative humidity, precipitation, wind, and take a picture of the weather outside. We would combine all of that into a post, so we could compare our weather data with the other schools.

Barry Dana

Barry Dana was the Native American chief of the Penobscot tribe. We visited him at his camp in Solon, Maine. During our time there we made fire, shelter, and we practiced stalking deer.

When we were stalking, we got the choice to either go bare-foot or not, and if you brought a blindfold, you could wear it. We followed a string winding around trees through the woods.

We also made fire with no matches, lighters, or any of that. We did it by using friction.

We made shelter by taking two Y sticks and using them to hold up one ridgepole (long stick). We filled in the sides of the shelter with lots of branches and leaves.

Greenhouse Temperature Study

Every hour, on the hour, we took measurements of the temperature in different locations around the greenhouse and "quick hoops." We had thermometers in the snow outside the greenhouse, in the quick hoops, in the dirt inside the greenhouse, under the vent of the greenhouse, and at the top of the greenhouse. At the first reading (9:00 A.M.) everything was pretty cold. At 11:00 A.M. it was 70°F at the top of the greenhouse. In the afternoon it was so warm we could water the garden for the first time in two months!

Sugar Season 2011!

This year we [the Cliff Island School] tapped maple trees around our school, just like all the other years, but this year we tapped the trees in February so we would get more sap. Guess what! It WORKED. Mr. McVane came into school to teach us more about tapping maple trees for sap. It has become a great yearly tradition.

We made spiles (a.k.a. taps) from hollowed-out staghorn sumac (not poison sumac) because we did not have fancy metal taps, and we reused milk containers for buckets.

Even after extensive daily sampling, we still got over a liter of maple syrup. What happened to the burnt stuff? We made it into maple candy.

A few days ago we had a pancake breakfast, and we only used our own maple syrup!

Storm Trackers

"We will be tracking the big snowstorm that is coming," Mr. Holloway announced. "We will need to write down the time, wind speed, wind direction, pressure, distance from the edge of the storm to us, barometric pressure, humidity, temperature, and cloud type. Can you make a chart?" Mr. Holloway asked.

"Sure," we said.

"When do we have to write it down, Mr. Holloway?" I asked.
"Every hour when we are here," he replied.

Testing Our Soil's pH

We are testing our soil's pH level. You might think that I spelled pH wrong, but it actually is spelled with a little p and a big H. The p stands for a mathematical function. The H is the symbol for hydrogen. Testing the soil is part scientific method project, part garden project, and part garlic project, as you will see in the video below.

Cliff School Agriculture

As part of our Island Institute Four Season Agriculture Grant for the school greenhouse, we are writing a report on our progress. We just finished the construction of our greenhouse on the 10th of November. The kids did all the reading of instructions, assembling, and measuring, and Mr. Holloway and Uncle Sean used the power tools and caulking gun.

The planting space of our old garden was 143 sq ft, and our new one is 192 sq ft; so our new garden has much more growing capacity. We have two 8 ft x 3 ft raised beds under our greenhouse. In one, we are growing leeks, onions, Swiss chard, and spinach. In the other, we are growing Bull's Blood beets, Nelson carrots, and Mokum carrots. Because of the greenhouse, we are able to have a much longer growing season for those beds.

100 percent of the Cliff Island year-round community is aware of the garden project. We held an island harvest dinner for everyone to come to. At the harvest dinner, all the food was from our garden. We had pumpkin, squash, salad, fennel, tomatoes, and so much more. During the building of the garden and greenhouse, people from the community have often stopped by to see what we are up to. Community members helped supply materials for the new garden. Eric A. supplied all our wood, and Bobby H. supplied all the dirt.

Cider Season!—Picking Apples

"Look out!" Mr Holloway warned. We all cleared out and he shook the apple-laden branch. It was raining apples—seriously! When the bonk, be-bump bump dwindled down to just bonk—bump—we all converged to gather the apples.

"That was awesome!" Eliza exclaimed. We all agreed.

I found an immaculate apple and bit into it. It was crunchy and nectarous. "Yum," I thought, "these apples will make exquisite cider."

Technology use among the island schools does not go unnoticed. Maine State Senator Christopher Rector (R-Thomaston) observed in 2011 that "What you are all doing with the island schools and distance learning is really incredible. We're actually using that as a model for the 'Many Flags, One Campus' project (a new vision for high school in the Rockland, Maine, area), which incorporates both traditional academic learning with career and technical education, community college and university instruction and industry-based 'centers of excellence,' allowing for vocational training that is industry directed. Your incorporation of distance learning in the instructional framework, and the success that you are demonstrating can help to serve as a model for a distance-learning component in the Many Flags initiative. You all set a great example and a really good model for the rest of the state to look at."

While not necessarily a mechanism for studying their hometown, these students also benefit from the fact that many adults with much to teach enjoy visiting the islands. Through a non-profit organization called Island Readers and Writers, based in Bar Harbor, Maine, an Island Book and Author Program brings writers and illustrators such as Lynne Plourde, Mary Beth Owens, Ashley Bryan, Lois Lowry, Rebekah Raye, Scott Nash, Gary Schmidt, Paul Janeczko, Toni Buzzeo, Cynthia Lord, and Chris Van Dusen, among others, to visit island schools. These special visitors offer arts workshops for the students, discuss what is involved in writing, illustrating, and publishing a book, encourage aspiring young writers, poets, and painters, and meet and sign books for islanders. Visits are integrated into the local teacher's wider lesson planning so that history, science, or other topics relevant to each visiting author's books can be addressed.

THIS *IS* THE REAL WORLD

Visiting the Monhegan School

It's twenty degrees below zero and you want organic spinach?

One of my visits to Monhegan was planned for a few days in January that turned out to fall in the middle of a severe cold snap. Island custom, and the lack of year-round grocery stores, suggested a call to my Monhegan host and the island teacher the evening before the trip: "I'm in Rockland; what do you want from the store?" What they both really wanted was vegetables. I loaded up my basket with the requested broccoli and other produce (I do not recall whether I was able to round up any organic spinach at that hour) and asked the bagger to load my purchases into triple paper bags. Even the fifty yards from the store's exit to my car would freeze and ruin any unprotected vegetables.

I buried the leafy greens in several insulating layers of luggage. The next morning I stopped at the feed store on the way to the boat to collect the fifty-pound bag of chicken feed my hostess had requested. I also loaded in some wine, Oreo cookies, and peanut butter.

I called the Monhegan Boat Lines number in Port Clyde to make sure the scheduled boat would be running. They told me there was no reason why it wouldn't be. The radio happened to mention that the warmest place in Maine that morning was Matinicus Rock, at one-half a degree. Surrounded by sea.

As I arrived at the wharf in Port Clyde, somebody was shoveling snow off the deck of the nearby fishing vessel *Reliance*. It was tempting to think of all the summer visitors who come here, their only image of this place a tourist's paradise. The surface of the ocean was obscured by sea smoke, and the faces of the boat crewmembers were obscured by more balaclavas, ski masks, parka hoods, and mufflers than I think I have ever seen on human beings. I couldn't recognize anybody.

They didn't recognize me, either (not that they should have),

View from the deck of the *Laura B,* the Monhegan mail boat. With neither state vehicle ferry service nor an airstrip, passenger boats like this are the only way to and from Monhegan—aside from the fishing boats, of course. Eva Murray

because as I stepped aboard the *Elizabeth Ann* one of the guys was muttering to himself about this strange woman who was obviously not a regular. I think he feared I was going to be what they call "high-maintenance." An old notice posted on a bulletin board in the passenger cabin struck me as comical in this January deep freeze: the Carina store on Monhegan announced it was offering the "quiche of the day." I doubt it.

Walking along the road on Monhegan, I meet Jessie Campbell, the teacher, who is called by her first name as this is the tradition here, and seventh-grader Dalton and his mother, Angela, headed toward the school. Fifth-grader Quinn is still not feeling well; everybody has been sick in turn recently. Three dogs tag along, and Millie, the teacher's puppy, is welcomed inside.

Jessie and Dalton begin the day with a few yoga stretches, and I join in. So does the puppy, which makes morning exercise more silly than serious.

Dalton works on his business plan, part of an economics unit for social studies. He will soon show his work to other middle-schoolers on a couple of other islands at a planned get-together (if the weather doesn't interfere!). He has chosen his sample business based on a perceived real island need—a mechanic and tool retailer.

The Internet is down, and Jessie is sure the problem is not on the Monhegan end of the link. "We can't watch the cell video today [planned later for science] unless the Internet comes back on."

Sounds are muffled by the uncommonly deep snow, and the island seems especially quiet. Everybody notices that it's nice to have no wind for a change.

Jessie wears jeans and a colorful hand-knitted wool hat. Dalton and Quinn each have small "offices" set up within the classroom, little work areas that are distinctly their own. Being brothers as well as classmates, they appreciate some individual territory. Dalton works on a series of tasks, all the while making quiet, unstructured conversation

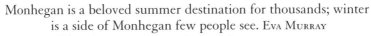

Monhegan is a beloved summer destination for thousands; winter is a side of Monhegan few people see. Eva Murray

with Jessie, occasionally patting the puppy and checking the Internet, which eventually comes back. At that point, Dalton posts weather findings to the blog, another collaboration with other island schools, and mentions the extreme cold-weather phenomenon of sea smoke.

Dalton makes good use of his time, and he is fortunate to have such an enviable workspace. The room is warm, bright, colorful, and quiet, with hot drinks made on the kitchen stove in the back, a puppy, and, in Jessie, someone who can help but will also let him work at his own speed. There is a large student-made time line around the top of the walls in the room, from the Precambrian to the Quaternary periods. The length of each section is proportional to the length of each era, so three and a half walls are Precambrian.

A list on a whiteboard itemizes today's plan: stretching and weather reporting; work on the business plan; Language Arts with a "writer in residence" (me!); work on persuasive pieces if there is time; plant cell in the microscope (this will actually wait until Quinn comes back); lunch; free reading time; math; art with Donna. Scheduling is not extremely rigid, but Jessie keeps the day moving so that Dalton

Monhegan teacher Jessie Cambell. Eva Murray

works on a variety of subjects. He has just finished reading *Museum of Thieves* by Lian Tanner; his Skype reading-group instructor is Dave Duncan, the teacher on Matinicus.

There is a single bathroom, a kitchenette with a gas stove, and library shelves almost all the way to the high ceiling. The presence of the Tandberg videoconferencing unit contrasts with the old-fashioned style of the schoolroom. Jessie describes how the telecommunications options really make an enormous difference, with just the two brothers in school. Island artist Donna Cundy comes in at the end of the day and works on linoleum block prints with Dalton and Jessie. Sometimes she does Lego robotics with them. There is homework. I am reminded that this is not a typical day, but rather strangely quiet, with only one student, no Internet, and the usual winter gale at rest for a change. It has been lovely.

The Monhegan school board met during one of my visits. Discussion was about officially altering the school week to better fit the boat schedule. Superintendent Martha Witham, who had chartered a lobster boat to come out to attend the meeting and to observe the classroom a bit, told the board that if they moved the hours around but still held a little bit of school on Monday and Friday, they would not have to ask permission of the state for the change and risk getting bogged down in administrative procedures. So the Monhegan school schedule will likely be as follows, at least in the winter: Monday, school in the afternoon, following the boat's arrival at the island; Tuesday to Thursday, have the school day go a bit longer than before; Friday, open school for a couple of hours in the morning, and end in time to catch the boat. With only three boats a week, this is the only way students or teachers can do things on the mainland over the weekends and not miss school. It will make life a lot easier for everybody involved.

Monhegan student Gabe Church, now in high school, recalls how older students do still help out the younger ones in school:

Back when I was in first grade, I remember a day when I was working on some math and I was going through the problems quickly. At some point I came to a problem that I couldn't do no matter how hard I tried. So I decided to skip it and come back to it. I soon finished the other problems, so I went back to the hard one and sat there looking at the problem. One of the older students who was in the middle of a lesson asked the teacher if he could take a break. The teacher told him yes and he walked over to me, sat down, and asked if I needed help; he sat with me and went through the steps of the problem again and again until he was sure that I would be able to do it by myself. He then wrote down a few problems for me to practice with. After he helped me, I never had any problems with similar math problems again.

Then, when I was in eighth grade, I was finishing up some work and I looked over at another student. He was doing subtraction for the first time. I could tell he was having trouble because he was looking at his worksheet like it was in another language, and I remembered being in the same place, so I dropped what I was doing to go see if he needed help. He said yes, so I sat down and stayed there until I was sure he could go on without me.

School Is in Session
We are not Old Sturbridge Village!
A number of the island teachers relate some variation of the following story:

It is a fine spring or autumn day, the weather is pleasant, and a few tourists and visitors are in evidence on the island, even though the busy season hasn't quite started (or has ended) for the year. Today is a school day, and the teacher and students are busy at whatever work may be at hand. An older child may type on a laptop or be curled up in a corner with a thick novel; a cluster of youngers may circle a teacher who reads to them from a picture book or demonstrates how to measure in both inches and centimeters or helps them with arithmetic practice. An ed tech works one-on-one with a student at a table in the corner or is on the telephone with tech support solving a computer problem. Children's jackets hang on the hooks near the entry, and a scattering of boots and muddy shoes are in a heap near the doorway. It's pretty obvious to even the casual observer that school is in session.

Or it should be.

Into the room stroll a couple of strangers, with neither a knock nor a polite inquiry first. They smile broadly as they look around, as though viewing a staged display or volunteer docents in a living history museum. They walk into the room without invitation and neither introduce themselves nor ask any specific question. They appear to approve heartily of everything they see, but they do not address the teacher.

"Can I help you with something?" asks the teacher.

"No, thanks; we're just looking around."

Imagine that. Imagine something like that happening at your local school. Out of the question.

"Well, school is in session right now," says the teacher, as the children begin to look up from their work; older kids who have seen this routine before might cock a cynical eyebrow at the tourists. "Is there something we can help you with?" Again, the teacher is trying to find out whether the visitors have a reason to be there, a message, any reasonable question, some legitimate errand. Are they perhaps a student's grandparent or some long-ago invited guest who finally made the trip out to the island, or maybe a local journalist working on a regional article?

Nope, just tourists. "We saw your quaint little schoolhouse and we just thought we'd like to look around."

"The children are busy working right now," says the island teacher, a bit more sternly than before and hoping that they'll take the hint.

"Oh, that's okay," the oblivious inspector replies. It is? Sometimes they'll even add, "I'm a retired teacher myself." (Inexplicably, teachers and former teachers are among the worst culprits in this rude exercise; somehow they do not put themselves in their island colleague's shoes or recognize their own unexplained presence as an interruption.)

Yes, it happens, at least once a year, somewhere. If they don't walk right into the school, they press their noses up against a window and stare through cupped hands into the room. Our tiny rural schools do not have security guards or front-desk school offices, although at least one island teacher has decided that this behavior presents a security risk, and the doors are now normally locked when children are present. Some schools have guest logbooks, but nobody has time to guard the entrance. Gabe Church, at the time a seventh-grader on Monhegan, told me:

> They've walked into the school, and we've had to explain to them it's like any other school—"Would you walk into any other school?"—and they say, "No, but this is a *cute, little* school!" So we explain to them again that this is school, it functions normally, and

they can't just walk in and interrupt.

In the words of teacher Donna Isaacs of Islesford, "They look at us like zoo animals." Michelle Finn of Frenchboro reminds such drop-ins, "We are not some kind of exhibit!"

These well-meaning, harmless visitors seem completely unaware that the tiny school they are so interested in observing is, in fact, a regular public elementary school—not an exhibit.

Another teacher adds, "It's not just strangers. Community members come by also, to drop off paperwork for their car registration or call about their taxes because a town employee works at school. There is an incredibly laid-back attitude about keeping schedules and business as usual here. Sometimes I do feel like we are in a fishbowl, and everyone feels completely comfortable tapping on the glass."

A Frenchboro teacher relates how, when people gaze into the schoolroom from outside, faces up against the windows in June, her students remark, "Guess the tourists are back!" Another teacher offered the following:

I have a story about tourists photographing island children in the summer when they thought there were no adults around.

Last summer, my husband and I saw a small group of photographers, all young women, taking photos of island kids at a lemonade stand. Their leader, slightly older than the rest, sported a badge indicating a well-known national magazine.

A little further up the road, we found a few of the photographers in a huddle, asking one of my students to roll and jump on the grass for them in funny and cute poses, while they click-click-clicked away, pointing their giant lenses at her.

I politely introduced myself as the child's teacher and asked them if they had permission from the child's parents to photograph her (on this particular island, many people are very sensitive to uninvited attention). The leader pointed to her badge and told me that she was from this national magazine. She was training these people, doing her job, and I should mind my own business.

Besides, she said, the child had said it was fine with her.

I pointed out that the child was six years old.

It turned out, they were really a photojournalism class (affiliated with a travel group from out of state), and their instructor was actually a freelance photographer who had done some work for this widely recognized magazine at some point in the past. When we found out their true identities, my husband, a former college art professor, went out to find the instructor. His intention was to engage her in a discussion regarding the importance of teaching her students about the need for sensitivity when entering a community and approaching people as potential subjects for a story.

"There are ethics involved," he told her.

Her response was indignant: "Are you kidding? I'm trying to teach these people how to deal with F-stops! I don't have time for ethics!"

Sometimes you just can't win.

Myths and Misconceptions
Do you even have electricity?

Lindsay Eysnogle tells this story: "We attended a meeting about small schools at Northern Illinois University and ended up being the keynote speakers about one-room schools. We'd made a movie, the people could see the inside of the school, all that we do, and the questions we were asked were still, 'Do you have electricity?' even after seeing that movie! Unbelievable!"

There are a few common myths and misconceptions about these schools and their island communities that I'd like to address right away. Keep in mind that each of the eight one-, two-, and three-room island schools (Monhegan, Isle au Haut, Frenchboro, Matinicus, Cliff Island, Islesford, Long Island, and Chebeague) have as many differences between them as they have commonalities.

I have heard each of the following items expressed as "fact"; herewith, a dose of reality (and we will explore most of these topics in more detail later).

Myth: The islanders are a tight, strange, even inbred group of people who neither leave their island nor allow new people in; they view all outsiders with hostility and their wild, old-fashioned youngsters are almost foreigners on mainland soil.

Some of the islands truly enjoy their reputation for being a bit wild; Matinicus fishermen certainly don't go out of their way to diffuse that impression. However, the notion of islanders as dangerously isolated is nonsense. Years ago it was more common for people to remain on their islands for longer periods of time, but keep in mind that years ago the island communities were very different. Some of the islands had multiple schoolhouses, and most had far larger populations. These small, isolated but complete towns offered many more services (stores, resident nurses, community organizations, etc.) and opportunities for socializing (clubs and associations of all kinds) than they do today. We should not imagine the "old days" as being "just like now only without electricity and the Internet." That's not an accurate image.

On islands where a commute is possible, plenty of people go back and forth to work each day. On the outer islands, even expensive and complex travel arrangements don't really prevent people from going to the mainland for business and for pleasure from time to time. The expense is significant, and this does stop people from making unnecessary trips—islanders are careful about accomplishing as much as possible during each mainland visit, and we joke that you never go to Rockland just to get a quart of milk—but children are not raised in true isolation unless the parents wish to do that, and then it is not the fault of the island.

Myth: Teachers are sent, dispatched, or posted to the remote islands by the state, and islanders take whomever they are sent. Who they get for a teacher is out of their hands.

The State of Maine Department of Education actually has relatively little to do with the routine operation of these schools. Each school is part of a local school district, administrative unit, municipality, or other organizational structure; these each have a superintendent and one or more school boards. Several of the islands are their own school district; others are part of AOS 91 (Mt. Desert) or the City of Portland. Those school boards and superintendents work out budgets, answer to taxpayers, advertise for and hire teachers, and, increasingly, share resources and knowledge with each other. In any event, teachers are carefully interviewed by islanders before being engaged.

Myth: The island schools must obviously be impoverished, antiquated, and extremely short of everything (especially technology), and they will gladly take any hand-me-downs people send.

The island schools are now extremely technologically advanced! If anything, they are more likely to provide a computer for each student (or close to it) than are larger schools. They use a wealth of online tools and advanced telecommunications for instructional purposes daily. The schools are not wealthy, but neither are they impoverished, and a few of them enjoy the generous support of summer property owners and well-to-do taxpayers. They have everything they need. (Well-intentioned folks have, in the past, sent cartons of musty, culled-out library books and old computers that won't take up-to-date software. With all gratitude and humility: please don't.)

Myth: These children are all going to be fishermen anyway, so they don't need to be prepared for higher education.

Every recent graduate of the Isle au Haut school has gone to college. On Monhegan, none of the current students is planning on a career in commercial fishing. Matinicus, Chebeague, and Frenchboro have some of each; some students who plan to fish, others who don't, but fishing is no longer a guaranteed lifelong occupation, and even those who are already piling up their lobster traps may decide some further education is wise. That island stereotype is simply not accurate, even though islanders hold a higher ratio of lobster licenses than anybody else in Maine (figured town by town).

Some islanders look forward to high school and will enjoy advanced work; some will only endure it and will do the minimum, but that is the same anywhere. The islands have sent students to prestigious colleges and universities and to jail. That is also the same as it is anywhere. There is no island pattern, and it certainly has nothing to do with having attended a one-room school.

Myth: There exists somewhere in statute a minimum number of students required for a school to be allowed to be open, and the island schools are always threatened with the state hoping to close them down for being too small.

This misconception is based on the assumption that the funding and administration of the school comes directly from the state. In truth, very little comes from the state (more on the Matinicus budget as an example later). For island schools that are not part of larger districts, the decision rests at home: if local taxpayers wish to support the school, they will do so, no matter the number of students. Schools that are part of larger districts are potentially more at risk than those that are truly independent, and schools where a commute is possible are of course likely to have people suggest that option, but the state itself has nothing to gain by closing these island schools. The administrative costs, by the way, are miniscule. Part-time superintendents, who often have responsibility for several small schools around the state, are already "consolidating" their tasks. For example, Chebeague and Long Islands share a superintendent with Acton, a small mainland district in southwestern Maine.

Islands that are under the auspices of larger districts may or may not have concerns in this area. Truly remote islands with school-age children aren't being threatened with school closure as I write; the superintendents involved (at least right now) realize that a commute is not possible, especially for small children. The fear is that this could change as administrators change. For islands with regular daily ferry service, that risk is real. Long Island and Chebeague Island, both in Casco Bay, seceded from Portland and Cumberland, respectively, largely over worries that their pre-K-through-fifth-grade schools would be closed. Older students can and do commute, but the nineteen students on Long and the twenty-two on Chebeague who are in the early elementary grades are not going to be sent on the ferry each day. Islanders would much rather have the young children educated on the island, and they have provided excellent facilities toward that end.

Myth: Teachers don't really need to be certified to work in those schools.

Of course they do. The days of teachers hired "in a pinch" just because they seemed reliable and intelligent, despite lack of an education background or qualification, are over. These are taxpayer-funded public schools and subject to the same rules and regulations as any other. Island school boards and superintendents scrutinize résumés, academic records, and credentials when examining applicants, looking for a high level of qualification. Even a teacher hired on short notice, if necessary, must at least be eligible for Maine certification.

Myth: The students are being shortchanged a significant part of their childhood because of the lack of team sports.

The topic of sports seems to come up whenever somebody who doesn't like an island for reasons of his own tries to make the case that it is not a fit place to raise a child. That is simply nonsense. Experience has shown that students with an interest in sports are able to participate in high-school sports even if they have not grown up with Little League baseball or pee-wee anything. Teachers and parents do their best to support a child's athletic interests, although, to be sure, being "on the team" simply is not possible where there aren't many children of the same age or size in the community. One Matinicus middle-schooler spent part of each year in Rockland playing football to make certain that he'd be ready to make the team when he got there for high school. Another, who attended boarding school, became one of the fastest bicycle racers in New England. Students from several of the islands take weekly swim lessons on the mainland or compete on a YMCA swim team even when they cannot attend many of the practices. Frenchboro students are specifically taught to play hockey, softball, and other sports as part of their curriculum, by popular request. We do the best we can.

The argument can also be made that island children are among the privileged few, these days, who still have unstructured childhood playtime, and that an excess of coached activities at a very young age is overrated as a lifestyle choice.

Myth: The state tells the teachers what to teach; the curriculum is standardized, and the books are sent by the state.

Curriculum is a big subject—and we shall investigate that further—but suffice it to say that Maine does not have a statewide curriculum or required textbooks. There is a set of standards (Maine has adopted the Common Core Standards), and all the island teachers make use of this (and the Maine Learning Results before that), but specifics of curriculum—in fact, whether or not there *is* a set curriculum—differs from island to island.

Some of the islands are currently developing a collaborative mechanism and shared curricula for science and social studies; they hope to align their activities and units more and more, to allow students to have academic peers on other islands. This is especially helpful for student in the tiniest schools, those with very few kids. The Outer Islands Teaching and Learning Collaborative, formed recently by island teachers in part to address this need, includes efforts to align some of the academic activities so that groups of students can work together. A few years ago, Matinicus Island created its first detailed set of curriculum guidelines, and that has served as a catalyst for subsequent curriculum design and refinement in several of the schools.

Myth: The state pays for island students to go to expensive prep schools if they choose to do so.

The local district (not the state) pays a state-averaged tuition amount to enable students from a district that does not have a high school to attend public high school in another district. This amount of money is set annually by the state (not the island) and is not negotiable. The same thing takes place on the mainland for students from small towns without a high school. Thus, a Matinicus student may attend any public high school at no cost to his family, although which school he attends will depend upon where he can board—essentially, where he knows someone with whom he can live. The household where the island student boards may also be given a stipend to assist with living expenses, and this can range from small to generous. Unlike the secondary-school tuition payment, this "room-and-board subsidy" amount is determined by the island.

Some students attend private boarding schools instead (often because they do not have a friend or relative who lives near a high school and has a spare bed, or because they wish to pursue a particular interest). In these cases, the private school is paid that state-average public-school "out-of-town student" tuition amount—which is nowhere near enough to cover private school tuition—and the student's family is responsible for the remaining cost or for applying for financial aid. The taxpayers do not pay the cost of expensive private schools.

You may have noticed that many of these assumptions include the same phrase—that being "the state." In Maine there is very little interaction between the classroom teacher and the State Board of Education. It is the superintendent's duty to manage the bureaucratic responsibilities. It may be different in other states. In Maine, "the state" does not directly call the shots, either with regard to lessons taught or whether or not a school remains open or who the teacher is or where a student goes next. All of that is decided locally.

Thoughts on a Childhood Without Soccer
It's a heck of a place to raise a kid!

To paraphrase Shakespeare's unctuous Malvolio in *Twelfth Night*, "Some are born to island life, some achieve island life, and some have island life thrust upon them." Where some of the children who attend the island schools have generations of ancestors who have done the same, others are here because their parents thought it would be a good idea. For certain people, it is a good idea, but it may not be for everybody.

Moving to an island is not just a change of address. Everything about one's life changes. What you do for a living changes, how you deal with emergencies, and holidays, and all sorts of things you never used to think about have to change. How you get heating oil into your tank may well change. You won't be attending a pilates class or going to the movies or sending important documents out by next-day air. You won't need a good haircut, your high heels, your roller skates, or in some cases even your cell phone. You may well need a pickup truck, a portable fuel pump, or a marine VHF radio. If you're wise, you will have a fat-tired bicycle, a large freezer, reliable rubber boots, spare milk, and a big set of wrenches. And a thick skin.

What your children do with their time will definitely change.

Those who bring children to an island may or may not give any thought to whether that child thinks it's a great idea. Obviously babies and preschoolers do not worry about such things, but for some school-aged children, the move can be quite an upheaval. Friends cannot be visited easily, organized activities such as extracurriculars must usually be sacrificed, and what the child will be doing for fun will likely seem somehow old-fashioned. Before too long, as a general rule, the child is proudly motoring around in the harbor with his own outboard or driving her uncle's pickup truck, but it may take a while before the appeal is obvious. There may be an adjustment period before the freedom of island life is really appreciated. On the other hand, some children will tell you that they like a very small town where there are few strangers, where friendly dogs wander the roads and kids have few worries, where there are beaches to play on and woods where you can build "camps" and "forts," and where school is relatively informal. One can "never say never," but there is absolutely less bullying, less peer pressure, less body-image consciousness, less violence, and less "teaching to the test" in the island schools. Some children appreciate island life but if pressed couldn't really tell you why; they "just like it here."

The first person I interviewed for this project was Charlotte Strong Ames, probably ten years old at the time. Charlotte had gone to school both on Matinicus and on the mainland, and she explained

Various sports and the rules of the games are taught at the
Frenchboro school. COURTESY OF MICHELLE FINN

that on the island, life as a kid was easier. Nobody cared what you
wore or who you hung around with. There was no pressure to be styl-
ish; there was simply less stress.

For children born on the island, who cannot compare this lifestyle
with any other in their experience, having only one or two year-round
friends, getting their schooling in a multi-age classroom, and being
part of the working community along with the adults from an early
age just seem normal (as do sledding down the middle of the road in
winter, jumping into the harbor in the wake of the state ferry in the
summer, and completely ignoring the finer points of motor vehicle
regulations any time of year). Not many children are in a position to
compare and contrast the pros and cons of this versus another lifestyle;
it is adults who ruminate on "is it worth it to give up piano lessons for
long walks under the stars?"

For those who have decided to raise children pretty far off the
beaten track (as my husband and I did), the opinions of the rest of the
world will not always be positive. "How can you think of keeping
your children on that island?" "What would you do if they got sick—
there's no doctor!" "But that means they can't play sports!" and my
personal favorite, "How are they going to handle it when they have to

face the *real world?*" The assertion is always that the island is some-how not the real world. If you think about it, a place where, when something needs to be done, you usually have to do it yourself may be more "real" than a cushy suburb where an effortless smart-phone call brings the plumber, the pizza delivery, the fire department, or an orderly little adult-supervised playdate for junior.

But we do hear criticism, usually from well-intentioned relatives who do not really know what life on the island involves. The issues of team sports and medical care seem to be the big subjects when people who have never lived here express their concerns.

For everything that an isolated child cannot access, something else of intrinsic value seems to rise to take its place. Our children and their friends camped on the beach during the summer, studied the night sky, learned to bag bait and drive the truck and read meters, and helped older folks set up their new computers. They flew many hun-dreds of times in a small Cessna airplane, went up in the electric com-pany's bucket truck, learned to kayak, played in a very high tree house, and set up small businesses each summer as young teenagers. They also learned a few of the "real world's" lessons: they cared for younger children while those kids' parents went through crises, they worked on a wildfire, cleaned and bandaged minor wounds, rescued an overwhelmed swimmer from a dangerous current, helped dig a grave, towed a dead car with another vehicle, and again and again watched the adults around them drop everything to respond when a mariner was lost, when the power went out, when a storm did some damage, when somebody got sick, when there was a wedding or a funeral or any sort of public event, when anybody was in trouble or needed a hand or even just deserved a celebration. Whether it was grab the oxygen and run or grab the chainsaw and walk or bake a cake and carry it over, the kids saw this sort of response modeled all through their childhood. What better education for "real life" could a child receive?

If there is truth in the slogan, "It takes a village to raise a child," then a very small town such as one of these islands, each truly a village, shines when its children succeed. The meaning of success is not uni-versally agreed upon. To those who think that a "successful" young person is necessarily one who got good grades in school and went on to college, allow me to describe a common "success story" around here.

My kids' friend Dave is an independent small businessperson in his community, doing something he enjoys and has hoped to do since he was very young. He makes good money, far more than his teachers, and has no boss except the weather. He is considered one of the adults, or nearly so, for even in his youth he has proven himself one of the working community. He has skills not everybody has, and which cannot be learned from a book. Such is the young lobster fisherman of Maine.

Plenty of island kids do go on to college. As I write, a young woman who grew up on Little Cranberry and with whom I correspond, is about to graduate from college and has just been accepted into her master's program. However, higher education must not be viewed as the only arbiter of success—not when job satisfaction, general happiness, prosperity, and independence are all attainable, for some, right on these nearby waters. We all know that the lobster fishery is hardly guaranteed for life, but our younger community members also know that a college degree doesn't guarantee satisfaction or financial stability either, these days.

Whether an island child has a rich, well-rounded, skill-building, character-building childhood or is a bored brat who just plays video games all day has a lot more to do with his or her parents than with the geography of his hometown. Parents can isolate their children here, but so can they on the mainland. Island parents are all different, just like parents in any other community are all individuals. There is no "typical island parent." Some let their kids run completely wild, and others demand that permission be asked for every trip out the door. Some feed them unlimited junk food, and some won't let a crumb of white sugar cross their threshold. One will buy his second-grader the worst of violent computer games, while another won't allow his child in the same room with a wireless device because of potential health risks. Most, of course—on the islands just like anywhere—find something in the middle that suits everybody better. Here, like anywhere else, everybody does as he or she thinks best. Whether or not a child gets into Harvard Law School (Avery Day, Vinalhaven) or the Knox County lockup (it's happened plenty of times; just look in the papers) cannot be laid to where he grew up.

Budgeting for a One-Room School
Who pays for all this?

The words of a teacher from Colorado are a chilling reminder of how tenuous the existence of our tiniest schools can be—and how fortunate we are on isolated Matinicus Island! That teacher, one of my western-states one-room-school correspondents, mentioned that the student population of her school was expected to shrink to twelve next year, and "the district says they have to have eleven students to make expenses."

In small towns all over Maine, up in the woods and over in the mountains and way down east, tiny rural schools—one-room and somewhat larger—have been consolidated and closed. Somebody at the Mount Desert Island Regional School System has been compiling a list as schools in Maine close, year after year—Allagash, Abbot, Bremen—alphabetically, frighteningly, it goes on. In 2009 not only Shirley and Rockwood (the last two Maine one-room schools inland) were closed, but at least seven others closed, most in small rural towns. Once in a while, the local authorities or the townspeople cite a non-financial reason for closing the school, such as making the case that the children will get a better education at a larger school (which is undoubtedly true sometimes, but is hardly established fact across the board). Perhaps they just can't justify the repairs and upgrades that might be needed. Most of the arguments are economic. As Bill Folsom, the last teaching principal at Rockwood Elementary told the *Bangor Daily News,* "It's just the numbers," in an article with a headline that read, "Rockwood School Not Viable Economically." As a rule, nobody wants to be the bad guy and bring down the ax, but school board members and district leaders cite the "bottom line," blame the "bean counters," and insist they are "just doing the math."

The Island Institute, in its publication *Island Indicators,* a collection of statistical information about many aspects of island life based on data gathered in 2009, reports that the islands of Maine fund 78 percent of their school costs locally with the remaining 22 percent coming from the state. The statewide average for such local funding is 53 percent. However, even this out-of-balance number is inaccurate for some of the smallest island communities, as it includes the larger islands of Vinalhaven, North Haven, and Islesboro (which support high schools). Matinicus, because of—in the words of our superintendent of schools—the huge gap between our state-set property valuation and our enrollment numbers, receives almost no ordinary state education-subsidy monies.

During the nine years I served as the school-district bookkeeper, I received and deposited the state subsidy checks on behalf of the Matinicus Isle School Department. The largest monthly state payment we received in the first decade of this century was about $1,000; the lowest was exactly $22.66 per month. Each time we of this island are asked whether we fear that "the state" will discontinue our school due to low enrollment, some of us are tempted to smile and ask, "What, you mean they might take away that $22.66 a month? Whatever shall we do? I guess we'll be terribly short of paper clips that year!"

Let me tell you a little about the math.

Most discussions of public school expenses eventually work back to "per-pupil costs." Ours do not. On Matinicus (and I will use this district as the example, although details will vary among islands), we know that the fixed costs change little whether we have one or six or fifteen students. We know that the per-pupil cost will be off the charts compared with that at larger mainland schools. We also understand that our total cost is both reasonable and worthwhile considering the alternative.

The reason Matinicus is so fortunate is that no matter how much the school costs, at least the decision about whether or not that is "too much" is our decision to make. We have no fears of what "the district" (or, as in the case of Peaks and Cliff, "the city") will require of us or do to us, because we are the district in its entirety. So what does it actually cost to run a one-room school? Not much, actually.

In the 2008 newspaper article about Rockwood mentioned above, the school's annual operating cost was stated as being "about $150,000.00." For two or three students, yes, that is a lot. For the operation of a school in your town, with all of the community-related advantages that potentially brings, 150K is not a great deal of money. It's a matter of perspective. With what are we comparing this number? More important, how final is the decision? Once a school is closed, unless it could boast a nearly brand-new physical plant with every up-to-date feature, it is extremely unlikely to ever be opened again. (Rockwood, as it happens, had an exceptional and relatively new facility, making the closure even sadder for the few locals.) As of this writing there are no students enrolled in the school at Great Cranberry Isle, but the local board is not hurrying to formally close it. The building needs maintenance and there are issues to be resolved locally regarding small children commuting from either of the Cranberries to the other, but it would be far more costly to open a new school at some time in the future; certainly too costly for a community as small as the Cranberry Isles. "No students enrolled this year" is not the same thing as "closed."

The budget for Regional School Unit 65, Matinicus Isle School Department for FY 2010–2011 (as I write) was just under $157,000. Of this total, about $10,500 was balance carried forward, about $3,000 came in as state subsidy, and roughly $1,200 was expected from the American Recovery and Reinvestment Act ("federal stimulus" program). The remaining $142,000 was raised from local property taxes (please note the 47:1 ratio of local to state money!). Matinicus is not one of those islands where the shoreline is a ring of summer "cottages" surrounded by acres of lawns diligently mowed by locals on retainer. This island community, middle-class to the point of being almost statistically invisible, can pay for what it needs simply because it doesn't need much.

The elementary school is the only expensive portion of this community's municipal budget. Matinicus maintains a few miles of primitive gravel road and employs part-time or nearly volunteer town officials; even the airstrip so essential now to year-round living is on private property. We spend but a few thousand a year on the volunteer fire department, EMS, solid waste, and town office expenses. There is no town water, sewer, street lighting, harbor committee, or public works department. The town has a dirt-floor truck garage containing a snowplow, the power company's elderly bucket truck, and some firefighting equipment. We have several hand-me-down fire trucks, rarely any debt, no healthcare facility, and no law enforcement whatsoever.

We do have a school.

Curious visitors often ask islanders what the minimum number of students is for a school to remain open. There is no minimum here. Matinicus has seen budgets recommended by the school board and passed by the voters to run the school for one or two students (we have seven as I write). We pay our superintendent $4,000 per year, barely more than the bookkeeper. As should be evident, the recent argument in Maine for school consolidation, that being high administrative costs, is not our particular problem.

Taxpayers do notice that the school budget often goes up. In fact, it had tripled in the past couple of decades. The costs of a special-education consulting teacher who visits regularly and a required full-time educational technician, increases in insurance rates, and enormous increases in the cost of heating oil and electricity have forced the budget up considerably. Matinicus and Monhegan have what may be the highest electricity rates in the country (on Matinicus, the rate ss approximately seventy cents a kilowatt hour). The costs above are obligatory. The old town-meeting rant about how " We didn't have that in my day, so why do we need it now?" doesn't work anymore. Special-education services carry the weight of law, and they should. We have spent a significant amount of money on the school building itself, and intend to protect and maintain our school building because the cost of not doing so, down the line, would be far higher.

Anybody familiar with a large school's budget is probably in for a chuckle now. I offer, in its entirety, the Maine Regional School Unit #65, Matinicus Isle Plantation Elementary School FY 2010–2011 budget:

Teacher salary	$40,000
Teacher health insurance	$16,500
Teacher Medicare match	$660
Teacher housing stipend	$4,000
Nurse	$700
School equipment repair	0
Instructional supplies	$1,350
Instructional books	$1,800
Travel and conferences	$2,500
Tuition to another district	$9,000
Room-and-board subsidy	$3,325
Educational technician	$17,800
Ed tech FICA	$1,361
Purchased professional services	$4,500

Contracted services	$21,875
Director stipends	$860
Audit	$4,000
Advertising	$225
Liability insurance	$4,500
Maine School Board Assoc. dues	$97
Superintendent salary	$4,000
Superintendent FICA	$306
Bookkeeper salary	$3,500
Bookkeeper FICA	$268
Communications	$900
Office supplies	$600
Custodial services	$1,200
Custodial FICA	$93
Building insurance	$3,570
Electricity	$3,000
Heating oil	$3,000
Building maintenance	$1,000
Custodial supplies	$400
Total	$156,890

By way of explanation: the "teacher housing stipend" of $4,000 is a bit of housing or heating assistance. "Tuition to another district" is the out-of-town student tuition for our one current high-school student; this amount is determined by the state, not by us, and would cover the cost of tuition to any Maine public high school. "Room-and-board subsidy" is the $95 per week we traditionally provide to help with that high-school student's upkeep; it isn't much, and some island communities offer much more. "Purchased professional services" means things like computer tech help and guidance; "contract professional services" is the visiting special-education teacher. "FICA," of course, is Social Security and Medicare withholding matches paid by the employer for non-teacher employees (teachers have a different arrangement through the Maine Public Employees Retirement System). In discussion of the budget for the next year, we will be raising the amounts for insurances and utilities, we will plan to tackle repair expenses, and we will keep in mind that one never knows who will show up on the doorstep as students.

Very little of the money that supports Matinicus Elementary comes from a source other than Matinicus taxpayers. We do get a couple of hundred dollars a month from the State of Maine in school subsidy payments, and there is one other source of funding that is large enough to actually be useful: the Rural Education Achievement Program funds, or REAP.

In the words of our Superintendent, Jerry White, REAP "complements and is indispensable to our educational program for our students." According to the U.S. Department of Education's website:

> Part B of Title VI of the reauthorized Elementary and Secondary Education Act contains Rural Education Achievement Program (REAP) initiatives that are designed to help rural districts that may lack the personnel and resources to compete effectively for Federal competitive grants and that often receive grant allocations in amounts that are too small to be effective in meeting their intended purposes. The . . . initiatives include the Small Rural School Grant Program (CFDA no. 84.358A) [which] authorizes the Secretary to award formula grants directly to eligible Local Educational Agencies. . . .

Superintendent White, who was closely involved in the creation of the program, reminds us that "REAP was passed in the late 1990s to assist rural schools with the extraordinary costs of educating students in rural settings. The wording is broad enough to include all manner of expenses for student achievement. The upper student count limit is 600. Funds are awarded on a sliding scale. For instance, a school with fewer than 50 students gets $20,000 minus any federal program money, such as Title I and so on."

Tiny schools like ours spend an astronomical percentage of their budgets on fixed or obligatory costs such as teacher salaries, insurance, and utilities. We who support these small isolated schools understand perfectly well how economies of scale do not work, and that per-pupil costs will, of necessity, be very high. That's fine; the alternative (having no school) is not an acceptable choice. A few thousand dollars can make a big difference to a half-dozen students, though. An amount of money that a large school district might expend on just the costs of *applying* for a grant could be, for us, enough money to bring isolated students from all over Maine together several times through the year. It can and does send the students to cultural events, allow them to interact with age-mates from other islands, and teach them lifelong skills not available in their remote communities. For a school like ours, $15,000, plus or minus, is a lot of money, and every dime of it is used on real things and real activities for students—not a penny for administration, none for blue-ribbon panels of experts, nothing for anything intangible.

Matinicus has used REAP funds to purchase science instruction equipment and supplies, to pay for the (always expensive) transportation off the island so the students can participate in cultural and enrichment activities to which they've been invited, and to expand our library. It has helped teachers attend conferences to work with other island educators, and it has allowed us to bring special guests to Matinicus to hold elementary-age workshops in dance, Spanish, theater, and other "specials." Each winter for the past few years, our students have spent time at Sugarloaf during "kids ski free week," participating all day in serious skiing and snowboarding lessons (other fundraising or in-kind assistance helps pay for this trip as well). Says our superintendent of the Sugarloaf trip, "It's absolutely hilarious but it's [a lot of] our physical education program. I can defend that one until the cows come home!"

Some readers will say to themselves, "This country can't afford to tax people so that a few island kids can go skiing." Ordinarily, I'd probably say the same thing, all else being equal. All else isn't equal, though. I urge you to think of it this way: most schools spend truckloads of taxpayer money on bureaucracy and things a student never sees. Most schools couldn't even pay for their office supplies with the few thousand dollars we get from the government and spend on student enrichment. Most students have plenty of opportunity to interact with children outside their handful of immediate neighbors without the school's help. Most children are the indirect beneficiaries of a great deal more tax money than this. Finally, the tiniest schools in America are fighting to exist, and I feel strongly that we need to remain on the larger government's radar. We are still "real schools."

Just because we're small, we don't need much, and we are fairly self-sufficient, does that mean we shouldn't be part of the larger taxpayer obligation to the nation's children?

Teaching on an Island Is Not for the Faint of Heart
Circular, moral, and impotent.

I have seen teachers cry. Readers need not think this job is always easy, nor should we be in denial about the realities of any teacher's workday. Teaching in a tiny remote community isn't always a picnic, but I can say with absolute certainty that it is a far better situation today than it used to be. I also do not wish to add fuel to the fire of anybody who already looks to criticize our island communities. A collection of sunny stories alone would lack authenticity; there certainly are hard parts to the job.

Keep in mind: these students have no need to pass through metal detectors or have their backpacks searched; there are no "no hat" rules, gang colors, or required uniforms to prevent theft of clothing. They do not fear being shunned and insulted for wearing out-of-style sneakers, they can walk or ride their bikes to school safely, and they aren't going to get cut from some team because they missed one Saturday. So no matter how much the ignorance or boorishness of some single adult on occasion may shock the outside observer, remember that, in general, the school experience on these islands is hands down safer, less stressful, and more nurturing than what many children get.

Historically, a young single female teacher would from time to time have to put up with a bit more attention than was desirable. Nowadays, when every intrusion could easily be considered inappropriate, professionally intolerable, or even dangerous, many will take issue with my "making light" of this activity, but the fact is that teachers have had to deal with something that is not really either bumbling friendliness or sexual harassment, but is something somewhere in between.

"I dare you," says one well-oiled young fisherman to another at an hour well beyond suppertime, "to go knock on that new teacher's door!" Yes, it is as childish as it sounds, and the teachers as a rule would be filled with uncertainly (the first time) about whether the hapless visitor's intentions were benign or otherwise, or even if he'd remember the visit the next morning. But, as a rule, it would be no more than the knuckle-headed adolescent foolishness it sounds like. Sari Ryder Bunker relates her example of this common experience:

I remember my "initiation visit." I was doing my paperwork in my bathrobe, my hair's up in a towel, and there's a knock on the door. I open the door and there stand two men, both grinning sheepishly.

"Hi. What are you doing?"

"Schoolwork."

"Got anything to drink?"

All the guys had eaten supper together and the others had kind of dared these two to go introduce themselves to the new teacher.

If a teacher is too prone to anxiety to handle the situation by simply locking the kitchen door and shutting off the lights, she might be in for a scary night, because there is nobody to whom the teacher can go to "rectify the situation." There are no police on Matinicus or on many of the other islands, and the bigger, brawnier neighbors who generally might act as public-safety personnel will most likely write the whole complaint off as meaningless. "Oh, he's harmless. Just steer him back to the road and tell him his mommy is calling him." Once the teacher has been in the community long enough to get to know people, she can either call on some of her own friends to come over and offer the reassurance of numbers, or perhaps she might call the "visitor's" parents or lobster-boat captain to come and collect the sorry bum (by then very likely passed out on the porch). Carefully chosen words and a somewhat tough attitude are usually the best way to avoid becoming the brunt of any future shenanigans.

The islands of Maine are not charming fragments of the "olden days," preserved under glass and innocent of all trouble. Drugs, domestic violence, adult illiteracy, drunk driving, vandalism, and psychological disorders are all potentially island realities, just as they are mainland realities. Every stressor, every problem, every weakness that exists among people on the mainland can exist on an island as well. Islands should not be held to a higher standard of behavior (or of stability or sanity or contentment). In the late winter, cabin fever, economics, and unremitting mud conspire to exacerbate bad moods and negative attitudes. Fishermen are territorial, occasionally violently so. People with serious emotional problems sometimes move to isolated communities because they can't handle "adult responsibility." Thankfully, those very real issues are not the whole picture. Islands are communities where neighborhood really matters, where everybody rushes to the aid of anybody in trouble (friend or supposed "foe"), and where a true emergency is universally recognized as reason for at least a temporary peace treaty.

Sometimes an island teacher will have to deal with parents and others who are less than easy to befriend. Educators in larger schools have the same responsibility, of course, but they can leave work at the end of the day and, at least physically, be away from the source of the stress. There have been cases of teachers being bullied, insulted, and harassed by parents or other adult community members—generally people with long lists of their own troubles who do not have access to support services, counseling, or whatever else they may require. There is almost no "going home from work" when you live in a community of fewer than 100 people and work in the public eye. One island teacher, not all that many years ago, experienced a parent stomping into the classroom and screaming in his face—about what, he did not know—and using the coarsest of make-a-sailor-blush language, right in front of the children. The teacher was left standing there, confused, humiliated, silently angry, and determined to rise above it. There was, of course, no security officer or principal to call.

One respondent who wishes not to be named described some of the harsher realities of island life, with this memory from over a decade ago:

We had a situation here, a period of time for about ten years, when the island was probably at its most, well, dysfunctional. People were dropping kids off at school, anytime, without registering them or providing any background information. The school was supposed to just serve as a free day care center in a way, and the teacher didn't know from day to day who might show up. These kids were sometimes sadly neglected children—I mean violent, angry, resentful children. The family situations were ugly. These poor kids were not getting much of the "warm, nurturing island childhood." They weren't for the most part kids from island families, either. Their parents had so many troubles of their own that they weren't really able to parent well. They were people running from things, who thought they could come out here and get away from responsibility, get away from their bills, and also get away from the law. I think they were running from themselves and that never works, does it? I know this probably sounds judgmental, and I shouldn't talk like that—like I know how to be a better parent than somebody else—but a lot of alcohol, a lot of substance abuse, and living like an overgrown teenager can't do a little kid much good. I think the parents themselves were sort of "kids in crisis." So we had these kids in school who had never been read to in their lives. You'd feel terrible for those children. Those kids didn't have island roots; they got moved around all the time. Who was thinking about those kids' feelings?

School boards in these tiny communities are not necessarily made up of professionals or, as in many larger municipalities, people with aspirations to higher office who see the board as a political starting point. Island school-board members can be anybody. A former teacher recalls having once written a letter to the school board following the end of her academic year. She described a few concerns that she felt ought to be addressed by the community. In the letter, she happened to make use of the words "curricular," "morale," and "impetus," all quite logically part of a memo having to do with educational issues. The school board member who read the letter to the assembled meeting of islanders read those words as "circular, moral, and impotent." That four-word expression became a comic one-liner among a few on that island for a little while.

By far the worst Matinicus teacher story: Not terribly many years ago, the teacher discovered that a feral cat had taken up residence in the crawl space below the school, a storage area which could be reached through a hatch in the school's back room. The one middle-school student volunteered that his grandfather, a well-known island native, owned a Havahart trap, which might prove helpful in this situation. The teacher contacted the man, assuming he would deliver the trap. Instead, he showed up with a gun, shot the cat in front of the teacher and two students, and carried it out of the building dripping blood on the floor.

A lot has changed since then.

HOW DID YOU GET HERE?

Most of the islands are shrinking in terms of year-round population. Some of them are trying to do something about it. Teachers are often the community's newcomers, but several of Maine's islands are actively welcoming young families, businesspeople, and others who will participate in the local economy and civic life. Before we hear from teachers about how they chose to move to their respective islands, we'll visit Isle au Haut, where the community has recently decided to encourage "immigration."

A Visit to the Isle au Haut School
A hundred years and counting.

I arrived at the Isle au Haut school in the middle of the weekly art lesson, having stopped first to chat with islanders at the library, which is housed in an interesting stone building a few steps from the school. "Library hour" is a social time, and while some people select books or use the Internet, talking is not only allowed, it's the main reason to be there. Brenda Clark, the librarian, makes sure that the coffee pot is on and the snacks are ready. On the table were cheese and crackers and somebody's homemade banana bread; with no other local gathering place during the winter, a visit to the library becomes a fun chance to catch up with neighbors.

At the school, the four Isle au Haut students—all boys, all in fourth or fifth grade—are downstairs drawing and painting elaborate Chinese dragons with Anne-Claude Cotty, the visiting art teacher. Anne-Claude has been coming to Isle au Haut on a regular basis as art instructor for fifteen years, taking the mail boat from Stonington in the morning and returning on the afternoon run the same day. As Chinese New Year falls around the time of my visit, and this will be the Year of the Dragon, dragons are an obvious idea for an art project. Anne-Claude and the students have discussed the difference between traditional Chinese dragons in art—symbolic of power, high esteem, and good fortune—and the more threatening medieval European dragons, which generally require slaying in the folklore. All four boys are immersed in their work, although it is clear that they come to it with different interests and different artistic sensibilities. Anne-Claude keeps their minds on their work; this is not free time for idle chatter. When I, as a visitor, ask one the boys an unrelated question, she reminds me gently that this is time for thinking about the art work. By doing this she affirms to her students that art deserves respect as a serious activity: this is not playtime or a break from school.

The basement of what is properly called the Isle au Haut Rural School is a neat multipurpose room with a couple of large tables in the middle set up for the art lesson. On shelves, in the joists overhead, and in corners are art supplies, sports equipment, musical instruments, and science materials. I notice a French horn, various drums, carefully stored craft supplies, microscopes, snowshoes—and each of the students has a ukulele and a recorder, which they learn to play when the much-beloved music teacher visits on Fridays. "Mr. Mike always brings a new musical instrument for the kids to see and hear," I am told. "He also has them singing, a little chorus."

Earlier that morning the boys had Skyped with their reading groups from some of the other island schools. Of all the new technology platforms being tried out to expand the student peer group among the islands, the Skype book groups seem to be the favorite.

Lunchtime in the Isle au Haut school brings adults and children together around a large table in the schoolroom: teacher Paula Greatorex, long-time ed tech and Isle au Haut native Lisa Turner, visiting art teacher Anne-Claude Cotty, the four boys, and I all eat whatever we've brought. A small kitchenette in the back of the room offers a microwave for warming lunches and hot water for tea.

After lunch, the boys have a short outdoor playtime when they can run around; the day of my visit happens to be a pleasant (if snowless) winter day, without the harsh winds so often characteristic of Maine island weather. Returning to the classroom, the boys cluster on a rug in the library area as Paula reads aloud from *Tom Sawyer*.

The Isle au Haut Rural School turned 100 years old in 2012. The old-fashioned, classic schoolhouse architecture, with the working school bell, high ceiling and windows, traditional entryway with coat hooks, hardwood floor, and antique woodwork has been lovingly pre-

The Isle au Haut Rural School staff still uses the old school bell, rung by a pull rope, to call students in from recess. ROB BENSON

served. Like all of the island schools, the telecommunications hardware indicating a thoroughly modern schoolroom is also present—the Tandberg videoconferencing unit, desktop computers, and student laptops get heavy use. The teacher, whom the kids call "Ms. G," asks me to assist one of the boys with editing an article he is preparing on his laptop for the school newsletter.

A handmade model solar system is strung across the middle of the classroom overhead, with the nearer planets clustered on one end and Neptune, alone, far on the other side of the schoolhouse. On the walls we see plenty of art and lots of Dr. Martin Luther King, Jr., quotes, pictures, and facts (the MLK holiday having just been observed as I visited). Tissue-paper "stained-glass" stars decorate windows, these a gift from the students on the Cranberry Isles.

Ms. G announces that it is time for a special lesson. The Tandberg unit is turned on, and the classrooms on Monhegan and Cliff Island appear. The students on several islands are working together on social studies, and today, art teacher Anne-Claude has brought materials and a discussion of her coming to this country as a baby. She explains why and how her parents emigrated from Switzerland in the 1940s, and shows their passports (her own photo, as an infant, appears in her mother's passport), the naturalization papers, and other interesting documents, as well as pictures of the Swiss town where she was born. Students on the other islands ask Anne-Claude questions over the Tandberg.

After the videoconference experience, Ms. G and Lisa lead the Isle au Haut boys in a discussion of family trees and ancestry. Andrew and Michael are descended from Peletiah Barter, the first European to settle on Isle au Haut, who arrived in 1792.

After school ends for the day, Anne-Claude and I still have to wait for the afternoon mail boat, so we stick around school for a few extra minutes. This is Paula Greatorex's fifth year teaching at Isle au Haut, although she had been visiting the island for many years before that while she worked as a special-education teacher in a nearby district. She talks about how the Isle au Haut students have been given a lot over the years, how generous summer homeowners and friends have donated to make sure the students lack for nothing. Paula and Lisa joke about the school field trip to Florida a few years back, before Paula was the teacher. Lisa laughs. "That was the one good thing about when I broke my leg—I didn't have to go to Disney World!"

"When I had some older students [a couple of years ago]," remarked Paula, "we did one year all about giving. Everybody gives to them, because they're island kids. I said, 'It's time for you to give back, to give of yourself.' We did a lot of fundraisers that year."

We chatted a bit about Isle au Haut's recent efforts to invite newcomers to the island—in particular, newcomers with children, and small businesses, who would plan to live here year-round. "It makes me sad to see all the empty houses—not just here, but up and down the coast of Maine," says Paula. She makes an excellent point. With valuations in coastal communities rising and property taxes escalating constantly, more and more homes in coastal Maine towns are sold by year-round working families only to be purchased by seasonal vacationers. This has a direct impact on schools as well as other public-service agencies that rely on volunteers, such as small town libraries, fire departments, and emergency medical services. In the winter, on some roads, you can walk a mile without passing a house with the lights on.

Isle au Haut Invites People to Move to the Island
We need families.

"The winters drive you crazy/And the fishin's hard and slow/ You're a damn fool if you stay/But there's no better place to go." (From the song, "The Hills of Isle au Haut," by Gordon Bok.) Do you have a small business, craft enterprise, or other form of employment that would allow you to operate from the island? Are you licensed to lobster? Many people daydream about moving to a remote island village like ours: for those readers who can answer yes to the above question, it that daydream could very well become a reality. To sustain a vibrant year-round community, we readily welcome new year-round residents. We particularly sound the call for families with children to attend our school; to people who can work remotely; to commercial fishermen; who would add to our fleet; to people who care about building community. Life on the island requires a certain amount of self-sufficiency, creativity, and practicality. While life here doesn't always qualify as easy, it certainly qualifies as unique. Though it's not everyone's cup of tea, it's ours. And who knows, it may very well be yours.

This is taken from the Isle au Haut Community Development Corporation's website, and it is a big step. For a very small, somewhat isolated community that includes schoolchildren who are descendants of—and still carry the last name of—the first European settler, to open its communal arms and welcome new people flies in the face of clichéd impressions of islands. Contrary to a common stereotype of islanders as hostile to "outsiders," stuck in a "time-warp," insular in attitude as well as geography, or just plain weird, these islanders are taking the long view and doing what they see as best for their beloved small town.

The year-round populations of most of Maine's smallest island towns have been shrinking in recent years. Matinicus, Monhegan, Cliff Island, and Isle au Haut have all recently experienced the lowest midwinter head count in anybody's memory. When you can count your schoolchildren on one hand, people obviously begin to worry about the future of the community. Sometimes proactive steps need to be taken, and Isle au Haut is doing just that. Through the use of a well-designed website, headlines in Maine newspapers, and other media attention, Isle au Haut has announced that several homes are being built with the intention of renting to newcomers. Ideally, these would be newcomers with young children, portable small businesses, or telecommuting jobs, and a willingness to try year-round island life with an open mind.

This is not the first time that Isle au Haut has been through this process. Steve and Kate Shaffer operate a very successful gourmet chocolate business called Black Dinah Chocolatiers from Isle au Haut (with all products handmade on—and shipped off—the island on the same twice-daily mail boat that carries the art teacher, high-school students, carpenters, and nearly all freight). Kate Shaffer first came to Isle au Haut as the cook for a high-end inn. When the owners retired, Kate and Steve had to figure how to make a living or they would have to leave Isle au Haut. The chocolate company, named for a nearby mountain, has grown from a tiny kitchen business to a specialty food producer with nationwide recognition. As earlier participants in a similar ICDC housing program, the Shaffers are now helping to welcome new residents to their beloved island.

Island communities shrink because people have good reason for leaving. Island librarian Brenda Clark, who, with her husband Bill also chose to move to Isle au Haut, makes the observation that "You can't begrudge anybody leaving." She mentions families who move off when their children reach high-school age or who have health issues or are offered better employment on the mainland. "For most people the big thing is making sure there are kids in school. I think the community in general wants to see more people come here." Big projects like this don't happen without some struggles, though, and getting past some local politics is inevitable. "Most of the community is really happy."

Alex Harris, Isle au Haut's newest Island Institute fellow, remarks that "Everyone who leaves is pretty substantial," meaning that each time an islander moves away, the result is a noticeable change in the community. Harris goes on to say, "After the *Bangor Daily News* article [December 19, 2011] and some other publicity, we do now have a group of potential people." I ask about the process, and whether they are simply looking to fill the two homes that are currently under construction. "It's live, it's ongoing. It's not just a pile of applications and we pick a couple and then it's over. If more people want to come, we'll find a way to help make it possible."

Sue MacDonald, who raised her two college-age daughters on Isle au Haut and is married to a lobsterman, adds, "We need families. We need to keep the school going after these kids graduate. We need a mechanic desperately! If you are able to run a business off your computer, we have the wireless. The island has a lot to offer kids. My daughter just made the President's List at her college, and I said, 'I don't know where you got that,' and she said, 'I got it from the island school, from all the one-on-one attention from the teacher.' If somebody from out here wants to go to college, they can!"

The Twenty-Four-Hour Interview
The first thing we do is try to scare the applicant away.

How do we actually hire a teacher for our island school? Short of putting each applicant through a rigorous battery of psychological tests akin to what NASA is considering for potential astronauts who think they want to sign up to go to Mars—well, actually, we'd like to do that. The ideal candidate would pass NASA's array of examinations, have lots of hobbies, not be afraid of large dogs, small airplanes, wild outlaw fishermen, or crummy TV reception—oh, and be certified in Maine to teach kindergarten through eighth grade.

Usually, the first thing we try to do is scare the applicant away. We describe neighbors armed and dangerous (though always willing to lend that cup of sugar), six-day stretches of pea-soup fog, twenty-foot seas, marginal cell phone reception, and a complete and total lack of latté. That all makes a few applicants smile. How odd.

The Matinicus teacher search process might not resemble what you were taught at the career center at your college. Never mind dressing for success; just plan on trying not to freeze to death. It's fair to assume that the wind will be blowing on the day of your interview. Don't talk to us like you're trying to sell us a new car. "I'm the one you need because. . . ." "I've never actually seen the ocean but I feel in my soul that I am an islander at heart." "Facilitating inspiration is my passion." "I've always loved the idea of living in a quaint little village." These are the wrong things to say.

Tell us how you are going to fix all of our problems, lead children to righteousness, or bring the light of learning to our forgotten speck off the edge of civilization and you will not get an interview. You might get a restraining order.

We need somebody who can admit that he or she hasn't got the foggiest idea what teaching one-room school on an isolated island is going to be like and is okay with that. An adventurous spirit helps.

Experience has taught us that there is far more to finding the right teacher than comparing qualifications on paper. Some of the things we'd like to talk about are, to be frank, a little weird. Occasionally, we've spent more time trying to ascertain whether somebody would keep an eye on how much heating oil is left than we have discussing his or her philosophy of education. So, we now invite the most promising applicants to spend the night, if their own schedule allows, and we try to make sure they are on the island long enough to find themselves alone for a while. What does it feel like? If they are going to be freaked out they may as well discover that now, before they sign on for this duty.

On a beautiful day in April, one applicant landed at the island airstrip with the mail aboard the red, white, and blue plane. This was a deceptively gorgeous day, and a deceptively easy transportation experience.

The *Sunbeam* was at the wharf that day, so I took the prospective teacher aboard for a cup of coffee with the engineer and the cook. We got her checked in at Tuckanuck Lodge, where Bill announced sternly, "We're having pork chops, unless you don't eat meat!" She assured the innkeeper that chops sounded delicious. At 3:00 P.M., the kids were turning on the Tandberg videoconferencing unit for an Outer Islands Student Council meeting; we brought her to the school to observe that unique element of an island education. After school we encouraged her to take a walk on the beach with the ed tech, who had to walk dogs Frank and Rossi anyway. Only about an hour of her visit was taken up with the formal interview. She told us that her first teaching job had been in outback Australia years ago.

The next day just happened to be "oil boat day." She observed the line of trucks on the wharf waiting with their barrels for diesel and kerosene from the little tanker, and the power company man hoping for a few thousand gallons for the generators. This part of island living can be hard to explain.

As we delivered her to the airstrip for her flight to the mainland, we assured her that the weather wasn't usually this agreeable. In fact, we tried to convince her that it was usually lousy. She smiled.

A few weeks later, she told me about the other passenger on the flight headed back to Rockland. Evidently there had been a census guy here, and as soon as the airplane engine started he began hyperventilating into a paper bag. Our teacher asked, "So, did you set that up just for my benefit?"

Ah, good—a sense of humor, too.

Talking with one of the dispatchers at Penobscot Island Air, the small air taxi company that flies passengers and freight to some of these islands, I was told that they (the flying service staff and pilots) could tell in about thirty seconds whether an applicant would do for Matinicus. The ones who seemed to be enjoying (and successfully managing) the new experience clearly stood out from the ones who were either terribly anxious or were more or less clueless about what was going on, those who didn't understand how working around the weather and staying in touch with the air service about scheduling needs worked. We considered that perhaps we should just let the air service guys tell us which teacher applicant to hire next time.

Superintendent Jerry White, who lives on the larger island of North Haven, talks about teachers for that relatively convenient island who find the ferry ride a bit too harrying for them, and school administrators of the past leaving the poor new hires to fend for themselves. "When I went to North Haven in 1983," says White, "the superintendent had never interviewed an applicant on the island." He indicated that it wasn't uncommon for teachers to quit over the trip. "Anybody who's coming out here to live and work has got to ride that ferry, they've got to come out and see the island."

I asked Jerry what sort of questions he has been asked by prospective applicants when they first respond to an advertisement for the position. Questions about Internet, telephone and cell phone, and even TV reception are logical, and inquiries about a store make sense, but when they start asking about McDonald's or where they can get their hair styled or the closest mall (and they do), you know they haven't done much homework. Sometimes it is clear that they haven't even looked at a map. "Is Matinicus an island?" Sometimes they think they understand how things work when they don't: "One ferry a month to bring the mail? That's amazing!"

It sure would be.

We are really hoping that anybody who wants this job will have done a little bit of research—and not just have read one online article, either, because there is a lot of misinformation and unfortunately inaccurate commentary on the Internet. First of all, look at a map.

When I first came to Matinicus in 1987, it was in answer to a classified print ad in the *Bangor Daily News* that read: "Teacher wanted for one-room school."

That is not how we do it anymore.

The Internet being what it is, we now get applicants for this position from all over the country. Of course, it would be perfect lunacy to hire somebody for this job and expect him or her to live happily and independently on this enigmatic island without having visited first. Obviously, that reduces the applicant pool considerably, and sometimes it's too bad, because very promising-looking people just can't get the days off to make the trip. Still, it would still be wrong to bring somebody out here who isn't going into this adventure with eyes wide open.

We explain how electricity costs seventy cents a kilowatt hour and propane is a hundred and thirty dollars for a hundred-pound cylinder and gasoline is close to five bucks if you can get it at all. Then, perhaps, some details about small aircraft and ex-Alaska bush pilots and groceries ordered by fax. We try not to tell them quite yet about wholesale lobsters and starry nights and beautiful sand beaches and the best home cooks in Maine. They have to earn the perks.

A few somehow manage to remain intrigued, and we bring several candidates out to Matinicus to visit the school, meet the children, parents, and staff, and have a real interview here. Some here are of the opinion that the best method to gauge applicants' organizational skills would be to inform them that their interview is at 11 A.M. on Thursday and see if they can figure out how to get here on their own. Most generally, a sympathetic school-board member takes pity on the prospective teachers and talks them through the complexities of "making a flight." (This means calling the air service and establishing a tentative sort of reservation, subject to the vagaries of weather, medical flights, and other random unknown interferences. Plan B might be to see if Captain Tarkleson is running a boat trip. Plan C is to call all over the place asking if anybody's heard of any possible rides on lobster boats. There is no way the newcomer to an island will know this.)

Matinicus school-board members Suzanne and Natalie talk about the school board's process of examining applicants in 2009. Suzanne begins:

> I was talking to an applicant from my son's phone once while I was visiting him in Boston; I'm calling this teacher, I'm telling her all about Matinicus, and I'm going on and on about how hard it is, and my son Alex comes into the kitchen and goes out and comes back in and goes out, and pretty soon a note is handed to me which says, "If you want her to take the job, tell her *something* positive!" But the positives take care of themselves. The negatives—you tell them something important, and they look at you and say, "Yup, yup," but they don't really hear you, they don't really get it. Once they get the job, the reality can be devastating, and we can't have a teacher leaving in the middle of the year.

I asked Suzanne for some examples of things she said to "emphasize the negatives."

> Every single thing you do, from when you get up in the morning to going to bed, depends upon the weather. You cannot get groceries, you cannot get mail, you cannot come and go at will, you cannot use the phone sometimes if the weather doesn't cooperate. Fog, rain, snow, ice, high winds, high seas—you might want to think about whether you want to come here. Just because you call Shaw's doesn't mean the groceries are going to come; it might be three days and you're out of milk. Heat costs all kinds of money. I mentioned all the negatives I could think of.

Natalie added:

> You may have what you think is the perfect week planned, you have somebody coming to teach the kids something really cool for art, and you've got your units all planned out, and—oops! Half the families went off-island that weekend and can't show up on Monday because of the weather! You're there, ready to teach, and your kids aren't there because they're stuck on the mainland. Or, your artist can't get there. You don't just need a plan B, you need plans C and D and E. One time when Mary Tetreault was the teacher and all the families were stuck on the mainland, and Mary was as well, they had school at the Rockland Public Library. We worked it out; she did a couple of hours of school at the library, then we all went over to the Rockland Recreation Center and did some gym

stuff, and we had a legal half-day. We did that for three days.

Most of the islands now can offer a year-round freestanding rental house to the teacher, but Matinicus cannot. Until recently, Monhegan was in the same position. School-board member Jackie Boegel describes a close call, by way of explaining why the "nosy" questions are so necessary:

We had an applicant once, a single mother with two kids, and she was the best candidate for the job. Of course, it's not legal to make an applicant's family or living situation part of the interview process, and in the end she was hired even though there was no housing for her. It was one of those untenable situations where you say, "We're offering you this job, and I'm sorry, there's no place for you to live here." At that time we had a tiny little efficiency apartment for the teacher; we were kind of limited to hiring young people right out of college who were single and who had the mindset that they were joining the Peace Corps, and they'd come here for a year or two and they'd move off. That's what we looked for. Historically, we were looking for someone young, cheap, and transient; we never expected to give anybody tenure or to pay anybody very much.

The teacher right before Jessie is the first one we gave a continuing contract to. That was a huge risk. It had always been "two years and you're out." Now, the town owns a home that is the teacher house. It's rented to the teacher, subsidized, at a very reasonable rate; it's a two- or three-bedroom home, a real winter place, and you could potentially come to Monhegan with a family. It actually means the teacher can be part of the community.

Jackie also offered some observations on the backgrounds of successful island teachers:

A few years ago we had a guy who had tried a number of things; he had fished offshore for a while, but he decided he liked working with kids and had gone back to school to get a teaching degree. It was like a new adventure for him. He had definitely found his calling; he was really great here. We kind of decided that young and idealistic and energetic worked well, but there's also a case for having "life experience." That's the back and forth.

If we ask the kids for their input while we're interviewing candidates, they always go for the energy and spark that come with the younger people over the ones who seem more nurturing and stable. I don't know. I keep going with the Peace Corps analogy.

We've had teacher searches where there have been a lot of applicants, and we've had them when there have been two or three people. Some of the applicants are just casting a wide net; they're pretty easy to eliminate. By the time you actually interview, they know what they're getting into. We put a lot of energy into describing the situation: "You aren't going to be able to get away on the weekends." We really try to describe the winter. A lot of people think twice; they say, "Okay, this was interesting." It's not for everybody. It's not for the faint of heart.

We make up a search committee. Every family with a child in school is invited to have somebody on the search committee; we also include a couple of community members; we try to drag in a man if it looks like it's all women or whatever; we're trying to get some balance in there. Ideally there are also a couple of people who aren't invested personally in the school, so it's a big committee. We brainstorm to get a list of the characteristics we're hoping for in a teacher. We brainstorm for the questions we want to ask the applicants, and the current teacher also does that with the students so they come up with some questions. I think a huge feature of island schools is how the kids have such ownership of their school; they know it's theirs. On interview day, we all get on a lobster boat early in the morning and go to Thomaston. We borrow an office, generally; we've been able to borrow the Thomaston school superintendent's office sometimes, on a weekend. We set up interviews every hour all day long. The applicants pretty uniformly look like they're in shock when they walk into the room and see eight or ten people waiting for them! We try to put them at ease and we explain what our relationship is to the school. Generally, we have our questions all figured out, our superintendent asks them, we sit quietly, and we try not to make the applicants nervous. Then they can ask questions of us.

The best teachers, the ones that seem to end up coming here, are the ones who, when we say "Do you have any questions for us," turn to the present teacher and ask intuitive "What is it really like" questions. "How does it work when you do . . . this?" You can tell they've been imagining themselves in the position. We look for experience or training in working with different ages at the same time, different subjects, being kind of a "Renaissance teacher." We look for a teacher who can forge a community with the kids. He or she has to be someone who is empathetic and a natural leader in an organic kind of way. You look for that stuff in their letters of recommendation.

It's hard not to scare them to death. We have an interview question that's kind of like a scenario: You've been with the same six kids all day, and you can't get off the island for a month, and it's your best friend's birthday, and you just want to go home, and a kid knocks on your door and wants you to do this or that, and you know everybody knows what you buy at the store, what kind of ice cream you like, everything. How would that feel?

That big committee participates in the first round of interviews and then they're through. They're not allowed to even observe the interviews on the island. The parents cannot micromanage the process. The applicants get interviewed again by the three-member board and the superintendent. Each one is taken on a carefully choreographed day by a community member who's been drafted. They come out on a chartered boat all together, then are taken to a house for a snack or whatever, taken to the teacher house to see it, taken to see the island highlights, the church, the store, whatever, taken to the lighthouse or the headland or whatever depending on how much time you have to kill, then taken to the school to be grilled by the schoolchildren, who have their own interview process. There, they also can ask the teacher and the kids questions, and then they are taken down to the library where their formal interview takes place. We set up a schedule so that while one applicant is at the interview, another is at the school, and one's at the teacher house, etc.

As much as we're going through all these contortions, in every free moment the applicants try to get together and compare notes. They're all bonding on the dock when they're getting ready to go.

Matinicus Was Closer
I thought I was headed for Alaska.

I wasn't an education major. Unlike some of my teacher's-college classmates, I had not spent my childhood certain that I would be a teacher. If anything, my inspiration was at least in part "what not to do," which examples I did not want to follow. I remembered very artificial-seeming, formal teachers standing up there and saying "Now, boys and girls . . ." all the time. In retrospect, to give them a chance, they were probably just nervous. I knew that whatever I did as a teacher, I was likely to be the odd one out, though, not part of the clique. I didn't want the kids to keep their distance, I didn't particularly care whether they lined up by size like we had to, and I worried about some administrator or expert telling me I had to teach page 27 on Thursday. I was also not one of those women with extremely neat hair who prefer to work with a lot of order and protocol and a chain of command.

I'd had some good examples, a few teachers who managed to do a very good job in either pretty adverse circumstances or despite a bunch of heckling or by changing their professional course mid-career and following their heart.

Anyway, along with a liberal arts degree, I found out which courses were required for certification in Maine, and although my college (Bates) didn't offer many of them, they agreed to accept the transfer credit from the University of Maine, so I went from Bates to the University of Maine and took the necessary teaching courses and then went back to Bates, where I was closer to graduation.

We had a required course, something about teaching in America we called "Itty Bitty Four," because it was numbered in the university catalog as Ed.B 4. It was taught by a blustering former military man and school-district budget director or something, the sort of guy you might think of as a typical school bureaucrat. He was a bit scary at first, but he was actually a nice guy. Some of the students in the class didn't like his attitude or his bossiness and said they didn't think they should be spoken to that way. He was rather imperious, with a military demeanor. I remember thinking, "If we're going to work in a school district, we're going to have to deal with guys like this, so this is kind of part of the training."

We had to write a long research paper for the course, and he offered the option of making an oral presentation and engaging in a Q&A discussion with him rather than typing it up. I had about six other papers to write at the same time, so I took him up on the oral report option. Nobody else did; he was too intimidating. When I got to his office, I told him exactly what I thought about his bluster and his navy chief routine, in terms of our future workplace realities as teachers. He grinned and told me I was absolutely right. That broke the ice. My research topic for that semester, by the way, was one-room schools.

So this buzz-cut professor and I talked for an hour about historic one-room schools, "schoolhouses" we probably called them, mostly with regard to the westward expansion in the late 1800s and early 1900s. I described what I had read about teachers being total public servants, where every facet of their lives could be scrutinized or commented upon by the community, young women being criticized or potentially even fired for going for wagon rides with men; how they might be boarded around at different homes, with no privacy, hardly treated like adults in some cases; and how the male teachers were typically paid a good deal more than the women. We talked about how they might have to teach "boys" who were pretty nearly full-grown men and not easy to control in a classroom; how they'd need to deal with hungry children and keeping the heat going and shortages of supplies and small kids hurrying to run to the outhouse; and how sometimes there was no one to talk to who really understood their job.

But with all the changes over the past century, most of that still exists. Well, maybe not the outhouses and hopefully not the pay differential.

I had to do my student teaching (required practicum) after I graduated, which was hard because it meant working a full-time job with no income. I was living at the time in a camp (that's what we call a small cabin in Maine) with no running water, not much for insulation, just a woodstove, but the rent was low and included electricity and telephone. I hauled water from a neighbor's home, took showers at my grandmother's a mile away, and started the woodstove each afternoon to warm the place up a bit before I went to bed. I would be all neat and dressed properly for going to work at Rockport Elementary and then have to climb under the truck and put the chains on to get out of my icy driveway. That turned out to be good background for Matinicus, but that's getting ahead of things.

My University of Maine student-teaching advisor was offering to help me find a job, maybe, and I told him I was seriously interested in looking to see if there were still one-room-school positions to be had, or at least I'd like to look at isolated rural schools.

"Alaska," he suggested. "Kotzebue, Alaska." That sounded fine to me.

Before I got around to investigating the Alaska options too closely, I took what employment I could find close to home because I wasn't ready to pull up stakes immediately. I substituted in a couple of area schools, Rockport and Appleton—and Appleton Village was pretty rural. I washed dishes and fried clams for tourists, I set tile, I worked in a lumberyard for a year and enjoyed that a lot. The office women at the lumberyard didn't believe I was really a teacher because I was always running around all sweaty in a bandanna with messy hair, or spent the days shoveling snow off the piles of two-by-fours or unloading trucks (which truly was my job). I threw snowballs with the yard gang boys and outworked most of them; not very ladylike at all. I looked a complete mess by the end of the day; they didn't think I could really be a schoolteacher.

I interviewed for an elementary teaching job in Rockland, near where I lived, and one of the members of the school board was a real force to be reckoned with. That interview was not what you'd call a "warm" experience. She asked me if I was a "team player." She said they were looking for a team player, so I lied. I am not a very good liar. I did not get the job. I will now readily admit to anybody that I am not a team player.

While I was working at the lumberyard days and frying seafood and washing dishes nights, I saw a simple classified advertisement in the *Bangor Daily News* that read: "Teacher Wanted for One-Room School." The position was for one of the islands. I knew that there were people on some of the outer islands year-round, but I thought their teachers were long-term career natives. I imagined some old lady who'd been teaching for forty years and had no intention of leaving or ever changing her ways. I had no idea that they had a regular or frequent teacher turnover. I'd also heard some rough stuff, like how the Matinicus guys were violent, because I lived near a man in Spruce Head who'd been in a big knife fight with one of the Matinicus fishermen.

I wrote to the superintendent, who was also at the time the superintendent for the Rockland area. I applied for the island job and ended up filling out an application form in the superintendent's kitchen, by hand. He asked me a bunch of questions to determine whether I had a sense of humor, could deal with some fairly demanding people, and could live alone. He never asked me whether I was a team player.

When the time came to interview on the island with the school board, I flew out on the little mail plane for the first time, and it was a windy day, lots of turbulence. I think that was my first examination. The school board was made up of three island moms. Sue Kohls was the mother of eighth-grade and sixth-grade boys and also had a preschooler. We met at her home for the interview. I don't remember much about what they asked me, but there wasn't much about educational philosophy or teaching methods. Their priority was trying to ascertain whether I'd like it and could handle life on the island. I do remember being urged not to let anybody talk me into taking on preschoolers because the babysitting would never end. It sounded like there had been some stress in the past about that. I met with the kids at the school, met the teacher, a young man named John Rankl who nobody seemed to hear from again after he left.

Sue and I went for a long walk in the wind, all over the south end of Matinicus. My hair was a rat's nest before we were back to her house. Thankfully that didn't seem to matter. They didn't judge a teacher on how neatly she presented herself, like some of the office women back at the lumberyard did!

That day, as it turned out, was what I later described to somebody as "subpoena day" on Matinicus. Almost none of the island men were around at first. I later found out they'd all be summoned to Rockland to testify in the case of some small, nonviolent lobster-fishing malfeasance and were fairly disgusted with the waste of their time, especially the ones who never got to speak in court. It is expensive to go to the mainland. Sue's husband, Rick, was one of those men. When he got home, I was in for some theater!

Rick burst into the kitchen, where I was sitting at the table. Sue introduced us. He smiled, tore off his shirt and threw it dramatically into a corner, grabbed a half-gallon of Canadian whiskey and took a swig of it from the bottle, slammed the bottle down loudly, plopped into a chair at the table and began to ask me ridiculous questions of an entirely personal and unimportant nature. The idea was to find out whether I would recoil in horror at this crude foolishness. When I just looked at him and smiled and said something about "This place is more like up in the woods than I even realized," he cut out the funny stuff and we had a normal conversation from then on. I guess I passed the second examination.

Years later, somebody told me that they'd hired me for, among other things, the fact that I'd worked in the lumberyard "lumping ninety-pound bags of cement around." They also thought I had lived in the Bronx at some point (it had been Brooklyn, but that doesn't matter), and that such a background might indicate that I was tough enough. I don't know whether that story is true or not.

So we went from "Are you a team player?" to "Are you tough enough?"

I was told I had the job in the late spring, so I still had a while to work at the lumberyard. I remember one of the hardware-store guys telling me I shouldn't go to Matinicus because, he assured me, "They kill people out there. They throw a guy overboard, and if he tries to climb back aboard the boat, they bash on his knuckles with a bait iron."

No, actually, they don't.

Doug and Michelle Finn, Frenchboro
This is not the Peace Corps.

We talk as we hike around the Frenchboro trails, finding the last hidden patches of snow in the spring woods. The Finns walk an African Basenji dog, who understands commands in Mandinka. The Peace Corps reference comes up as it has on several islands, but this time, Doug has actually been in the Peace Corps, in Gambia. "No," he assures me, "this is definitely not the Peace Corps." I tell him he describes Frenchboro as seeming very comfortable. "Yeah. Savoonga was like the Peace Corps."

Michelle comments on how they learned to teach in such a school as theirs: "Four years in Alaska, in multi-age, multi-level classrooms. They don't teach you anything about this in college." Doug and Michelle Finn met while teaching in Savoonga, Gambell Island, Alaska, where Siberia is closer than the mainland United States.

Michelle adds, "People told us it would be a hard winter here, that a lot of people won't talk to you in March. We thought, 'That's it? That's all?'"

"When we were thinking of leaving Alaska," Michelle continued, "we knew we wanted to come back to this area sometime because we already had a house in Maine. It just so happens that my mom is the curriculum coordinator of a nearby district, and she knows the principal (of this district), who is also the curriculum coordinator, and they were just chatting at a meeting once, he was joking about looking for 'people who want to live out on a remote island in Maine.' My mom called us and left us a message. We weren't planning to leave Alaska yet, but Doug got online and started looking at the whole area. He's an avid paddler, he's been kayaking since he was young, and he says, 'Oh, honey, come look at this!' I thought, oh, my gosh, beautiful, and then reading about how small the community was—the more rural the better."

Doug adds, "When we left Alaska, we took a huge pay cut. The cost of living is quite a bit higher. We went from two big paychecks to one paycheck. We've adapted, but living on the island, you remember that everybody who pays taxes pays your salary."

Michelle says, "We're very frugal, too; we're thinking, let's turn the heat down, turn the lights off. In most schools people don't think about that. We know what a struggle it's been this year (with the lobstering and the economy), and that's what we can do to help, try to keep costs down."

The school board started talking to the Finns about the isolation and Doug said, "Look, you can see the mainland from here!"

Michelle said, "In Alaska we were, like, 180 miles off the coast of Nome."

Doug added, "When we first came out, I kayaked out from Bass Harbor."

Doug: "We were the only applicants. We had a verbal agreement that we wouldn't look anywhere else and they wouldn't look for anybody else, but we didn't have a contract yet. Our contracts are signed in February in Alaska, so we actually flew here in May and had the interview, and we went from February to May not knowing whether we had a job in Maine. It turns out that it's been difficult for them to get teachers. They wanted two people but didn't have housing for two separate people. Rachel and Erica, the previous teachers, were residents [and thus did not need the teacher house], so it couldn't have worked out better for both sides."

Michelle can't help but smile about the idea of Frenchboro being so isolated. "The whole 'roughing it' thing—when he was in his hut in Africa, I was living in a hut as well, something I'd built [Michelle teaches primitive skills and survival]. The fact that you can't run down to Walmart is *not* 'roughing it!' Oh, we can't get ice cream tonight. Okay, well, get out the ice-cream maker. The fact that we have milk in our refrigerator—that is a privilege! Some of the people here feel like this is extreme, like this is the edge, living on the island is really tough; they take pride in that, so when we start talking about Alaska or Africa they sort of just tune us out."

"People don't really want to hear about Alaska," Doug smiles. "It almost kind of offends a few people if you knock down this thing about the island being extreme."

Mimi Rainford, Swan's Island
I really wouldn't want to be anywhere else.

"I don't know if I'd like it any smaller than this, this access we have to the mainland." I had asked Mimi if she thought she knew what it was going to be like to work here.

No. It was funky; all of the applicants came out on the ferry together, all six of us. I missed the first round of interviews because I was teaching in a school in New York, and I was hosting an event with my second-graders, something that had been planned for a long time, and I couldn't disappoint them and leave. I told the Swan's board, if they still needed somebody, let me know. Gary (my husband) called me and said Swan's Island was doing a second round of applications. The first time they had been looking for a math teacher, but the second time they were looking for a language arts teacher. [It used to be that the three teachers on Swan's Island taught different subjects rather than different age groups.] My fear, by the way, was being somebody's math teacher for nine years—if we didn't mesh and I've got that kid for nine years and they've got me for nine years.

I remember coming out on the boat with these six people; one woman had this whole portfolio and everything, and she asks, "What language arts do you teach?" and I thought, "What is she talking about?" I thought I was interviewing to teach a math class.

I had never been to an interview situation like that. There were board members, school people, teachers, parents—close to a

The three-classroom Swan's Island School also offers K–8 students a beautiful gymnasium and playground. Eva Murray

dozen people around the table. When it was your turn to interview, everybody else was out taking a tour of the island. That was one of the questions: "What do you think island life is like?" They were asking that of me! I said, "You know, I really don't know. I've lived in a small town, I know about 'rumor mills' and that sort of stuff about small towns, but I don't really know." That's why we rented at first. There was really no help with housing. I moved nine times in the first two years. We were winter people; we had to move off for the summer, when summer rentals were opening up. [Many of Maine's island homes can be rented at high rates to tourists.] I ended up renting a house from one of the other teachers. Now, as the years have gone by and school-board members have changed, we now pay for some of the off-island teachers to stay at the hotel, but I slept on the school floor! They finally realized that they can't really say, "Fend for yourself, and good luck!" Now we have an off-island teacher who commutes every day. They'd never had an off-island teacher before, ever. I was one of the first ones who moved here. "You're the new teacher!" I was "the new teacher" and Gary was "the new teacher's husband."

When I came out for the interview and for a day to observe,

the kids were just running around, the older kids were helping the younger kids on the swings, it was just amazing. I had just been in New York, you know, breaking up cat-fights among fifth-grade girls, so to me all these children really helping each other out was what made me want to be here. The kids out here really seem more like siblings than they do classmates. They get a little sick of each other in February and March (we really need that vacation), but I really wouldn't want to be anywhere else!

Mimi and Gary have a preschool-aged daughter. "I want my daughter to grow up here. It's a lifestyle I really enjoy. You see island people off the island and they always wave. We have some people who've had run-ins with the law or whatever, but there is not one person on this island that, if I had an emergency, I would be fearful about going to for help. I could go to absolutely anybody on this island and say, 'I need help,' and if they could do something, they would."

Josh and Heidi Holloway, Cliff Island
Fish and coconuts.

"Originally, we taught for a few years in Hawaii," explained Josh. "Heidi had been there eight years, and we bought a sailboat and decided to sail the Pacific. When we got to Australia, we heard about a job in a one-room schoolhouse in Papua New Guinea, and so we were going to cruise northwest for that. An ex-pat venture that they had set up needed someone with teaching experience from K through 5. I had the experience and was going to apply for the job, and then we realized it was a malaria zone. Heidi, we'd found out in Australia, was pregnant, and we decided that malaria wasn't a good idea. We headed south, sold the boat in Brisbane, and went back to Hawaii.

"We were going to teach there again, but our parents flew out to visit us and did a little arm-twisting. They wanted to see their grandson when he was born. Heidi's mother is on Great Diamond Island and my parents are in Pennsylvania, close enough to drive, so we flew home to have the baby in Portland [Maine]. Heidi had the baby, and this job was advertised in the paper. We had been thinking about teaching in a one-room schoolhouse, and this was the perfect opportunity if we were going to stay—it's a nice setting. So last year I applied and took the job. We were still living on Great Diamond Island. I would get up and take that 5 A.M. ferry from Portland; it would swing

Island youngsters play outside the Cliff Island School in the snow. The Cliff school now also offers a program for preschoolers. Josh Holloway

by, pick me up on Diamond every morning on their mail-boat run, and bring me to Cliff, so it was a long day. I'd get here at 6:00 A.M., so I had two hours of planning time. That's a lot of planning time! I got to know the Maine State Learning Results frontward and backward!"

Josh showed me a special item in the school's entry hall. "We've got a bell out there that's got every teacher and the dates that they taught here engraved in it."

He told me more about the sail across the Pacific. "When we were on our travels for three years, my brother-in-law set up a website. We didn't have any way of communicating with people about where we were, so when we got to a place where we could get an e-mail out—like Western Samoa, Fiji, Tonga—he'd post it on our website, and he'd upload all our pictures."

I asked Josh whether Casco Bay seemed awfully easy after that trip. "Yeah, a lot of the Pacific islands that we visited—for example, some of the islands in Kiribati [which he correctly pronounced as "Kiribosh"], one of them had forty people living on it. We were there for four months. They got a supply ship every, what, three years or so? It gives you an idea how island life works. So they've got similarities,

Josh Holloway, who along with his wife Heidi teaches on
Cliff Island. Eva Murray

but anytime we need to here we can go into Portland and get resupplied. There, it was fish and coconuts."

Then I asked Josh if he thought he and Heidi were Cliff Islanders for the long term.

In a regular school, at the end of the school year, your class moves on. Here, at the end of the school year, maybe one student graduates and that's a happy time, but your class is still here. You get attached to them.

We want to go sailing again, Heidi's an avid surfer, we're both divers, we love fishing, we like the boat life. So initially, our thoughts were, we're going to have Kai, then we'll have a boat somewhere in the Caribbean. Then this job came up. I'd had such a wonderful first year, and Heidi came out to Cliff a lot of afternoons with Kai [coming on the ferry from Diamond]. Mrs. Little was the ed tech that year, and she was ready to retire, so she encouraged Heidi to apply for that job." The community unofficially told Josh and Heidi that it would be all right for Heidi to work at school with Kai there. "That didn't necessarily come from the top, but. . . .

When I was in college there was a Teach Abroad program, and I taught in Costa Rica and then in Panama. Then, because I knew Spanish, I taught in Arizona. [Josh is teaching the Cliff kids some Spanish.] I'm also really into rock climbing. I went to Mammoth Lakes, California, and taught in Mammoth, and then moved to Hawaii. I shipped my truck over, camped out, and found a job teaching first grade in Hawaii. That's where I met Heidi; she was a teacher at the same school. We both wanted to do a little sailing, I bought a little boat to mess around with, and we ended up going really far!

Heidi Holloway adds a few details:

So we were both living on Maui and teaching. We met each other and eventually there was talk of getting a boat and sailing around the Hawaiian islands. I'd done a little 'dinghy sailing,' Josh had not, and obviously neither of us had done any serious blue-water sailing. We bought a boat that needed a lot of work. It was what we could afford. Josh ended up ripping a lot of it out, so it was basically just a shell, an open boat, not room enough in the cabin to even sleep. Josh hauled the nonfunctional engine out and we never got around to putting another one in. We just sailed. We slept out in the weather; if it rained, we got rained on. We had a camp stove and a bucket; it was rough. The seas between the islands in Hawaii are pretty rough. We bathed in salt water forever. We never went into marinas. We ended up in Kiribati on this little atoll with about forty people, stayed a while, went to places with almost no people, no stores and stuff.

I asked about food.

"We speared fish."

Kai goes to school with his parents and is part of a real preschool program with other four-year-olds Aiden and Sophie. The Holloways' second son, Cove Henry, was born in 2010.

David Duncan, Matinicus
I was afraid my wife would think I was crazy.

"How did we find our way here? The Internet!" Dave and his wife, Rachel, both laugh before continuing.

We came across the job opening online, but there was a lot that led up to it. Our honeymoon was in this area—we went to Isle au

Haut. We loved the coast of Maine, and a few years later, we decided that we wanted a change. We felt like we were really stuck. We owned our own home in Wisconsin [the Duncans are only in their mid-twenties] and had a job where everyone expected us to stay forever. With all the night meetings, we just wanted a change. I [Dave] wanted to focus on my teaching and not so much on the administrative aspects. In my previous job at a small private school, I taught grades six, seven, and eight, I was principal and athletic director for the school, and the list could go on—technology man, coach. I don't have the knowledge to solve some of the technology problems that we'd have, and that was a challenge. The meetings were endless. I didn't have the chance to focus on teaching. I did a lot of the work a secretary might do, and I'd be setting up for a basketball game after school and coaching the soccer team, when I'd really rather be working on improving assessment or planning for the next day. Everyone would tell me to prioritize, that what was most important was the teaching, but there were things I couldn't neglect. [He says the all-things-to-all-people job on Matinicus was almost less work than what he'd done the previous year in Wisconsin.]

I liked being principal, I enjoyed that, but it wasn't what I went to school to do. We had about seventy kids in pre-K to eighth grade. That job was basically an assignment—you know, 'We feel this is a good fit for you.'

We were getting ready to sell our house, so I was up late every night refinishing the floor or painting the porch, and I'd be browsing around online at around 12:30 A.M. after getting done with housework. I found this job at about 1:00 in the morning.

Rachel says, "He woke me up to tell me about it, because he was excited. He said, 'I think I might be crazy, but. . . .'"

Dave says, "I held back a little on being excited because I thought Rachel would think I was crazy."

Tom Gjelten, North Haven
That's not really a small town.

National Public Broadcasting correspondent Tom Gjelten taught on the island of North Haven in the 1970s, and in 1978 published a small book entitled *Schooling in Isolated Communities.* In comparison with

Matinicus, Monhegan, and the other "one-room-school islands" in the area, North Haven seems like a regular city, with a high school, year-round store, and many other civilizing influences, but during the winter it is still what most people would consider an extremely small town. In the mid-'70s, when Gjelten worked on the island, North Haven had about eighty-five students in grades K–12; as I write there are approximately sixty-four (two of whom have recently moved temporarily from Matinicus and at least one of whom is a high-school student from Monhegan).

Gjelten speaks for many, though, as he describes aspects of his and his wife's North Haven experience. Not that much has changed in a few decades.

> Here were people who had chosen a small community-oriented school because they believed in its features, its potential as a system of people and ideas, not administrators and paper forms. From experience we knew that such a positive attitude toward rural schooling was rare. The prevalent view seemed to be that small country schools are characterized by mediocrity and are out-classed in every way by large suburban schools.

With regard to moving to the island as a new teacher, the Gjeltens' experiences mirrored those of most of us who have done the same:

> We discovered that teaching on a little island could be as tough as teaching anywhere, with its own problems to balance its obvious blessings: teachers are in a conspicuous position in the community, and while attention is enjoyable, the lack of privacy may lead to feelings of vulnerability. . . .

Gjelten writes about the need to respect tradition, to tread lightly with community norms, and for new teachers to acknowledge that the community (not the latest in a stream of transient teachers) "owns" the school. "Teachers in a rural town need to approach their work with humility." Those are wise words.

> One day I was telling my class about the town in Iowa where I grew up, describing it as a small town. "Did it have a shoe store?" one boy interrupted. I thought for a minute and recalled that it did. "Then it wasn't a small town," the boy corrected me.

Jessie Campbell, Monhegan
Wow, I have to do this!

The interview process can be a bit unusual, as Jessie remembers:

> I never thought I would take a job like this, especially for my first teaching experience. At the interview there were ten people! In the first interview, no one really asked me about my teaching, my philosophy, or anything like that; they were asking things to see if I could 'hack it on an island,' which I thought was so weird, but at the same time, it intrigued me.
>
> Then I came out for my second interview, on the island. It was a really crappy day, foggy, a horrible boat ride over, you couldn't really see anything, the island wasn't looking so beautiful, just soggy Maine in early May. But when I walked into the school, I thought, "Wow, I have to do this!" It was vibrant and exciting, and I loved the kids, and I loved that the kids were part of the interview. Nowhere else would I get to meet the kids that I might be teaching; I thought that was excellent.
>
> The list of questions was hysterical. They went around the table—the school board, the superintendent, the ed tech, the guidance counselor, the past teacher, all the parents, and somebody who introduced herself as just a townsperson. I remember thinking, "What, did you guys have a sign-up sheet?" Other interviews are about "Do you know all the latest buzz-words in education, do you know the right thing to say, do you speak the jargon?" and they are maybe fifteen minutes with three people. Here, it was an hour with ten people, and they were asking about me as a person before anything about education. They had questions like "How do you feel about people knowing what time your lights go out, and if you buy beer or wine at the store?"
>
> I saved some of the questions because they were so funny, things about living in a fishbowl, and having the kids call you by your first name, because that's the traditional thing here.
>
> I think I've adapted pretty well. As a first-year teacher, you don't have time to do anything except school anyway. I remember people asking whether I was bored or lonely, but truthfully, I was always at school. Every part of living here the first year was about school. Staying over the summer really helped me meet people on another level, and I made friends, found the people I could talk to

about things other than their kids. I fell in love with my life here.

Rachel Bishop, Frenchboro
It must be so nice to only have five or six students!
Rachel taught on Frenchboro before the Finns. She recalls:
Three years ago, I was approached by the school board and asked to take on a half-time kindergarten position [that year's incoming kindergarten group of five students was going to double the school size]. I agreed to apply, and dutifully beefed up my résumé with all my town positions and my office-assistant experience, secured new references, and sent it to the district. Late in August, I received a call from the office inquiring whether I was available for an interview—I replied that I was rather tied up working in the local deli restaurant and I really didn't know when I could get to the mainland. Not a problem here, though—the superintendent happily hopped on his boat, sailed to the harbor, and met me for coffee on the dock for half an hour before my shift started. No power suits, no committee members, no scary interview questions. Just a rather amiable conversation that ended with "You know you've got the job; I just wanted to come out here for the afternoon."

If I had a dime for all the times I've heard variations on the phrase, "It must be so nice to only have five or six or eight students!" They're all in different grades, and even those in the same grades have differing abilities, so things are broken up even more. I now teach eight children (one K, two first-graders, and five second-graders), but I actually teach four math groups, four spelling/phonics groups, and all the reading instruction is totally individual.

I was once asked by a reporter in an interview, "Don't you get bored?" My response, after I got done telling him it was a dumb question, was something like, "Every single person living on an island who has any social conscience whatsoever fills so many jobs that there is little opportunity to have a whole lot of extra time!" In all honesty, though, the ability to occasionally do nothing other than take a walk to the shore or sit on the deck and watch the harbor is one of the perks of island living.

For years, living on Frenchboro, I was "Rachel" or maybe

"Bishop's wife," and eventually, "Lance's mother." But once I was hired, I became "the teacher," even in non-school situations.

After Being an Island Teacher
Where do we go from here?

Working on an island changes a teacher. Working alone and having final practical responsibility for everything that goes on in the school building, be it a celebration or a fistfight, an educational breakthrough or a stuck toilet, cannot help but be a transformational experience for an educator. However, for a variety of reasons ranging from local custom to personal needs to a desire for graduate education, teachers usually do move on from their island duty and seek employment on the mainland. How does a teacher who has grown used to leadership, improvisation, and a minimum of bureaucracy fare in a typical large school?

Tom McKibben (brother of writer and activist Bill McKibben) taught on Matinicus for six years in the late 1980s and early 1990s (such a long tenure itself unusual for this island). He describes his experience after he and his wife, a Matinicus native, decided it was time to leave the island:

One of the greatest joys and biggest challenges of teaching on Matinicus was the autonomy and independence. I loved being able to make decisions and create assignments and projects that I thought would benefit my students. Although it was a wide-open plan book, it was also difficult, as self-doubt would make me question my decisions. What if I made bad choices or missed something that was important? There was little opportunity to discuss my ideas and plans, and no one to check on the quality of my teaching.

When I made the decision to leave Matinicus after six challenging, wonderful years on the island, I was worried about what job I could find and if I could successfully make the transition to a larger school with all the oversight and bureaucracy that would mean. I was also curious whether I could carry over my successful ideas and practices from Matinicus.

I sent out a large load of résumés and answered many ads and was lucky to get a few interviews and several solid offers. My last interview was for an elementary position at the Mast Landing

School, which is a public elementary school in Freeport. The interview committee consisted of nine people—staff, administrators, school-committee members, and parents. It was the only interview where people asked me about teaching on the island. One teacher (who wore a flannel shirt to the interview because he had seen a *Down East* article about the school, where I was wearing a flannel shirt) asked me the question that sealed the deal for me: What could they learn from me and my experiences?

I have been teaching the third-, fourth-, and fifth-graders at Mast Landing for the last eighteen years. It is a job that I love and I have been fortunate to work with a great crew of teachers, a supportive community, and a couple of wonderful principals. Though I sometimes get frustrated at the decision-making process and the predetermined curriculum, I still find myself relying on what I learned on Matinicus Island. I teach much the same way I did on Matinicus and often use my experience on the island to help guide the decisions I make for my students and myself.

I often tell my current students of my adventures on Matinicus. They feel a bond to my former students and know of the antics of Nicky and Samantha, Crystal, Evan, and Derek. My current students and I often set up a saltwater aquarium like the one we had on Matinicus and walk on the nature trail that winds through the woods near the school, just as we did on the trail my students created on Matinicus. I have told my current students that we used to wander out of the school at snack time in the fall and find a tart apple from one of the many island apple trees. This spring, my students in Freeport dug holes, moved dirt, and planted a small apple orchard in a corner of the school's playground. It won't be quite the same, but soon students in Freeport will be able to harvest their own snack from nearby trees just like the students on Matinicus Island.

TERM LIMITS, SECESSION, AND CONSOLIDATION

Monhegan Goes to the Legislature
Small schools at risk.

In January of 2007, Maine's governor, John Baldacci, and Commissioner of Education Susan Gendron proposed, as part of the 2007–2009 biennial state budget, that Maine's many school districts be consolidated into twenty-six "regional centers," claiming that this would save the state nearly 250 million dollars in three years. According to the *Bangor Daily News* (January 9, 2007), Commissioner Gendron claimed that "savings in administrative costs would be used to expand the laptop program into the high schools, create college scholarship funds for low-income high school graduates, increase professional development for teachers, and place a full-time principal in every school." Governor Baldacci stated that the consolidation plan would result in no school closings.

It didn't take long for the sparks to fly.

Barely a month later, a headline in the *Bangor Daily News* read: "Critics say small schools at risk" (February 6, 2007). At a legislative hearing held at the Augusta Civic Center (usually the venue for things like rock concerts and boat shows), hundreds of Mainers came to make their concerns known. According to the *BDN,* "Most of the hearing participants predicted that the plans would result in unintended consequences and likely would lead to the closing of small, rural schools. 'All small schools are struggling for survival and all small schools are in danger,' testified Roger Shaw, superintendent of schools at Mars Hill [in far northern Maine]. 'Whether by chance or design, we are in the crosshairs of state policy.'"

"Deeply flawed" is how Scott Porter of the Maine Small School Coalition described the planned consolidation, and the *BDN* reported that he "warned that local school boards would be decimated by its adoption."

Monhegan's Richard Farrell, who attended the hearing at the state capital, was quoted as explaining that it "would be unworkable to relocate the management of its seven-pupil elementary school to the mainland," and that the island's overall costs would be bound to increase.

By March of 2007, the newspapers were reporting that a proposal to create eighty districts—rather than twenty-six—would be put forth, and that the hope was that no district would have fewer than 2,500 students if at all possible. According to a Rockland newspaper, "If municipalities don't cooperate, a plan will be imposed on them." Legislators representing rural parts of Maine were less than eager to support this consolidation plan. "This is a rural vs. urban issue," said then-senator John Nutting (D-Androscoggin). "The rural caucus has no trust in the Department of Education."

Among the islanders who had been watching inland rural schools being absorbed, consolidated, and closed over the years, this issue looked like it might become a make-or-break concern for the future of their communities.

The *Working Waterfront/Inter-Island News* of March 2007 reported:

[Governor Baldacci's] proposal was greeted with a firestorm of protest from parents, teachers, superintendents, and concerned citizens across the state. Nowhere was that opposition more vocal than in Maine's year-round island communities, which support fourteen multi-grade schools whose survival is closely linked to the survival of the communities themselves.

When the Maine Legislature convened a day of citizen testimony on various consolidation proposals . . . island school supporters came out in force, rallying in Augusta under a "Save Island Schools" banner, and telling legislators why island schools require unique solutions.

Chebeague Island, which had been working for quite some time to extract itself from a larger municipality and would soon become the independent town of Chebeague, was hardly enthusiastic about the idea of being absorbed into a Portland-based "mega-district." On Monhegan, a petition was circulated urging the governor to withdraw the proposal, and every single resident who was on-island at the time signed it. Students from the Monhegan school attended the hearing with their teacher, Sarah Caban, and a large contingent of other islanders.

According to the *Working Waterfront* article, Monhegan received only about 1 percent of its annual funding from the state. Having been the Matinicus school district bookkeeper myself at that time, I can attest that this number sounds about right.

There is widespread misunderstanding about who pays for the island schools, which, to be sure, have a per-pupil cost far in excess of "regular-size" schools and many times above the state's average cost. However, as noted earlier, any attempt to force economies of scale onto an isolated island community with very limited transportation options—no matter how good the intentions—will be doomed to failure. To a degree that would surprise most, islanders pay for island schools, and thus local taxpayers can best make the decisions with regard to the use of those resources.

Island taxpayers do not need to be protected from themselves. Kathie Iannicelli of Monhegan spoke for many when she told the assembled legislators, "We are being asked to sign our rights away. We are asked to give up local school boards, local control of tax dollars, and accountability to local taxpayers. We are being asked to give up ownership of our school."

In January of 2007, when I was the bookkeeper for the Matinicus Isle School Department and an occasional columnist for the *Lewiston Sun Journal,* I offered the following as I began an editorial (*LSJ,* January 14, 2007):

The subject of island students' freedom to attend the public high school of their choice was a significant concern as this topic was discussed formally in the halls of power and informally over the hoods of pickup trucks up and down the coast. As it stood then (and thankfully, still stands now), students for whom a commute is not possible or realistic may be "tuitioned out" to any public high school where their family can arrange a boarding situation, typically to a friend or relative with a spare bed. This is not necessarily the geographically closest high school, and it is certainly not necessarily one within the same school district. Matinicus, Monhegan, and Isle au Haut are not part of a larger district but are legally school units or municipal districts unto themselves. So much for a requirement that districts have no fewer than 2,500 students!

It is not even clear exactly how many school districts, as such, there are in Maine. According to the Maine School Management Association, as of January 2011, there are 93 full-time and 29 part-time superintendents in the state. That compares to 118 full-time and 30 part-time in 2006–07. The state's 122 full- and part-time superintendents oversee 622 schools, operate 179 school districts, and report to 249 school boards.

Yet the original goal of the school consolidation law passed in 2007 was to reduce the number of school boards and districts from 290 to 80.

While the state DOE reports there are 179 school districts today, the actual number would be greater if AOSs (Alternative Organizational Structures) were counted the same as Unions, but AOSs are counted as single entities whereas the state counts every town in a Union as a school administrative unit. If they were counted the same, there would be 234 districts in Maine under the direction of the same 122 full- and part-time superintendents.

No matter how you do the math, the problems the reformers seek to address are not caused by tiny districts and their very part-time superintendents. Whether it potentially saves money or not, island schools cannot share a maintenance man, a load of heating oil, or so much as a box of paper clips with a mainland district (an art teacher, yes). High-school students who cannot sleep in their own beds each night must not be issued orders about which school they will attend. Thankfully, after a good deal of hand-wringing and appearances in Augusta, the island schools (and the tribal schools) were exempted from the consolidation mandate. Now, five years later, other districts want out of their consolidation agreements. This will be a subject of disagreement for quite some time in Maine.

Teacher Term Limits and a Visit to Long Island
It takes more than a year just to find all the light switches.

On most of the islands, at least in recent decades, teacher turnover has been fairly regular and rapid. Sometimes, teachers would realize after a few years into their island "posting" that personal needs, professional development, or just readiness for a change of scenery signaled time to move on. Sometimes, teachers found the job and conditions in any given year extremely stressful and nobody could blame them for leaving after a year or two. In some communities, a tradition of "term limits" was (and on Matinicus, still is) in place to prevent an island teacher from becoming tenured, as the assumption had always been that no one adult would ever provide everything the children should ideally be exposed to over their elementary years.

Paula Johnson, who has taught in Long Island's two-room K–5 school for over thirty-five years, made a face when I mentioned to her that Matinicus customarily offered teachers contracts for only one or two years. "It takes longer than that just to find all the light switches!" she smiled.

On Long Island, in Casco Bay, nineteen students were in attendance when I visited the school. With a population of roughly 200 year-round residents, Long Island had been a part of the City of Portland until the community seceded and incorporated as an independent town in 1993. Like several of the other Casco Bay islands, much of Long had been used as a U.S. Navy base during World War II; in this case, as a fuel depot for the heavy oil used by the big ships. Prior to the war, the island community had three one-room schools serving area children (having multiple schoolhouses was very common on the islands, as in most towns, before there were many roads or motor vehi-

The Long Island School's current building was built by the military in the 1950s; Long, like other islands in Casco Bay, was a navy base during WW II. Mark Greene

cles; recall that for several generations the smallest children would, of course, have to walk to school through the snow and rain).

The current Long Island school was built by the U.S. government in the 1950s. Paula says, "The military didn't do everything right, but they sure could build things. They did a good job building this school." The large windows, narrow-board hardwood floors, and old-fashioned woodwork give it the look of the historic small schoolhouses all over New England, but replacement windows and a relatively new furnace keep it warm and comfortable. The two rooms, one for the K–2 students and one for third–fifth, are bursting with color, crowded, and busy—science equipment and art materials, bins filled with math manipulatives and children's books and pieces and parts for all sorts of activities. Models of the planets hang from the ceiling. The children sit at old-style desks just like those I remember from around 1970, but behind them, a large-screen videoconferencing unit makes it clear that we are in a modern classroom. In the entryway to the school, seedlings start in flats: various peppers, tomatoes, and several kinds of flowers, which the students will transplant outside when the weather gets warmer.

Attached to the old-style schoolhouse is the new event room with a stage (also serving as lunchroom and gym) and the beautiful new community library. School lunches are delivered to the island, actually catered from Portland—prepared by a real caterer, not the Portland school district. The sandwiches looked great, with piles of fresh sliced vegetables on each and a child's name handwritten on the rim of each plate. Beneath the school, a huge dry basement (a holdover from the navy-base days and rare on the solid rock ledges that are the Maine islands) holds supplies and equipment of every sort. As two eager students gave me the grand tour, they called the large basement storage area "the archives" (the students were also very conscientious about turning the lights out). The new, immaculate and comfortable library adjoining contained a nice collection of books and movies for children and adults. Outside, there is a new tennis court and surfaced play areas, a greenhouse for starting seedlings, a strawberry bed fenced in with chicken wire against the marauding island deer, and a beautiful new playground. On the day of my most recent visit, we could see New Hampshire's Mount Washington from the island.

I am told that on Long, as on some of the other islands, the school week works around the boat schedule. This may mean that Monday and Friday have hours adjusted to accommodate those who would like to go to the mainland for the weekend to participate in sports, family activities, etc.

I observe Paula teaching; her style reminds me of my own grade-school teachers in the 1970s. Children raise their hands, and she writes on a huge pad on an easel. She takes her students through a multi-step mathematics word problem that requires several operations to solve. There are computers, but not a laptop for each child as in some island schools. The Maine Laptop Initiative, which originally provided a MacBook for every seventh-grader, was the early impetus toward the "laptop for every student" pattern, and the K–5 schools were not eligible. There is plenty of access to technology here, just the same.

The Long students gather around and ask me about Matinicus. They are particularly interested in the small flying service that carries passengers to and from our island. They tell me about the foxes, beaver, and deer on Long, and ask about wildlife on Matinicus.

Although the Long Island school is not involved at this point with much of the collaborative work that some of the one-room schools farther east utilize, they were part of the STORMS project, where teachers received additional training and students monitored weather using equipment provided by a National Science Foundation Grant through the Island Institute, did weather and climate-change related research projects, and met in the spring at the University of Maine to share their projects, socialize, and have a sort of island "science fair." The trip to Orono was great, Paula reported, adding that the kids loved being with a larger group of students.

Lead teacher Paula has taught her own children, and now three grandchildren are enrolled in school, although they are in the other class, as all are youngers. Marci Train teaches the K–2 group; she has been part of the staff since secession (as of this writing, that is eighteen years). Marci also has one child in the elementary school, and another commutes daily on the ferry to King Middle School in Portland. Neither Paula nor Marci finds it odd to have family members among the students. Marci offers a peek into what it's like to have your daughter among your students:

Of all the children that I have taught, I think that my daughter was the only kid that didn't slip and call me "Mom." At the dinner table at home she would tell us things that "Mrs. Train said," and I would always reply that I thought "Mrs. Train" was brilliant. She was able to keep mom and teacher separate, but I was still harder on her because I knew her potential, and she was hard on me because she knew what buttons to press. I feel that some kids were harder on her because I was the teacher, yet she is turning out to be a wonderful person so I don't think it hurt her too much. I also always met with my husband at parent conferences. People always thought that was funny, but I thought it was important for him to see their work in the classroom and to dedicate that time just to their academics.

A two-room school works essentially the same way as a one-room school; the physical arrangement inside the building changes little about the relationships among the children and between them and the teachers and other adults. It is still a close, somewhat intimate setting, where nobody is a stranger and where siblings and cousins are very likely to be in the same room. They do a number of activities together as one group, and from time to time, older and younger students are likely to be paired for reading or other lessons where the older one can act as a mentor. Children might take some pride at finally graduating to the "older group," but in general, the division is practical and not extremely rigid. What grade a child is in within his or her room group might even be ignored; when I was introduced to Mrs. Johnson's grade 3–5 room, each child identified him- or herself by name and age, not by grade. They are for the most part "the olders and the youngers."

Paula says, "I have been teaching or assistant-teaching on Long Island since 1974. I took some time off when my sons were toddlers, but have been full-time since 1985, with a few other years thrown in there. The school is much better off financially since leaving Portland, as expenditures can go where they do the most good. We were at the end of the Portland supply line for sure.

"What I miss is the larger group of staff to bounce things off of; however, we do much more staff development now in order to stay on top of new practices, etc. Portland did not pay for as much staff development, and we now have private funding which was not available when we were part of Portland."

Regarding the topic of island teacher turnover and term limits, she adds, "I think long-term staff brings some great institutional memory to the position as well as working relationships with parents and community. The key is to make sure the staff stays current with educational practices, technology, and so on. We do have a lot of responsibility beyond the classroom, such as for the building, heating, the fundraising issues, and so forth, but I assume that is true on most islands.

"It's very difficult having your own children in school. I had to work hard to make sure no one could accuse me of favoritism. I was harder on my own than on others, and they have always told me that. On the other hand, they did fine and all are college graduates, so I guess I didn't damage them too much.

"We try not to put too much emphasis on grades. We think each develops at his or her own rate and there are times when a child may need the 'gift of time' before he or she moves on. Also, everyone works at his or her own rate, so one may be doing fifth-grade work in fourth or even third, so grades are sort of irrelevant."

Mark Greene thoughtfully handed me an unexpected tuna sandwich to eat on the ferry ride as I got ready to leave Long Island; he'd been my island host, offering introductions, logistics advice, a brief tour, and a ride to the ferry. I asked Greene if he'd comment on Long Island's secession from Portland, an effort he was heavily involved with in the early 1990s:

> Our secession in 1992-1993 was a result of many years of many issues, but it boiled down to lack of local control over our island services and needs. To be sure, the 'spark that landed in the can of gasoline' was a massive tax increase on island properties; that began the work of the Town of Long Island Research Committee in 1991. Through the whole process, a long laundry list of past issues with the City of Portland was reviewed, and big on that list was a formal proposed closing of our elementary school a couple of decades before. There was subsequent informal talk of this by other city administrators in later years, but none as threatening as that one. It gained national attention [along with Cliff Island] and was dubbed by the media a 'boating plan' at a time when busing plans were under fire in major cities. It was dropped with the local and national attention and protest, but it was a big issue for many folks.

We would never be forced by anyone to close our elementary school if we were a town. We learned of island schools on Great Cranberry and, I think, Matinicus that were kept open by the local town with only one or two students. Our numbers have dropped to six or so in the past, but had the school been closed, we would not have the young families we have now. When it came time to vote Yes or No on secession, our proposed tax rate was not going to be much lower than Portland's if we left, due to startup costs and debt to the city, but folks voted overwhelmingly Yes anyway, mostly I think for the local control over such things as the school.

My short opinion is that Portland did a fair job with our school over the years (except threatening to close it!), but since incorporation the resources and community support of the school have been fantastic. It is the pride of this community. With the addition of the Learning Center, the facility is first-class. It certainly has made more work for Paula, with the paperwork mountain that comes from having your own stand-alone school district, but having Paula and Marci as two great local teachers has made a good school system absolutely great. They are teachers that *we* hired, totally with local resources.

Greene says of his island community, "It isn't all honey and cream out here, but we really do get along pretty well." What more could a small town ask?

Secession Keeps the School Open for Early Grades
Chebeague Island offers good home cooking—at school!

Chebeague Island in Casco Bay is Maine's "youngest" municipality, the island having seceded from the town of Cumberland in 2007. Schoolchildren from the sixth grade up commute daily to the mainland by way of a ferry to Cousin's Island and then by bus over the bridge to Cumberland. Chebeague is also served by Casco Bay Lines, and a trip from Portland to Cliff Island often makes a stop at Chebeague. Chebeague has a population large enough to support some recreational activities and more than just minimal community services, but is too small for much retail activity. It sustains a substantial number of native families, with commercial fishing still a part of the economy, while it is also close enough to the mainland and served by enough daily boats to make a commute possible. Chebeague is neither a truly remote island nor a suburb; it seems to be in between, perhaps "just right." According to the Island Institute's website: "After seceding from the town of Cumberland, Chebeague Island became Maine's newest independent town on July 1, 2007. The reason for the secession was to protect the future of its island elementary school, without which it would be extremely difficult to sustain a year-round population. Historically, Chebeague was a famous shipbuilding center; its 'stone sloops' transported granite up and down the coast. Chebeague's year-round population is approximately 360 people, with a summer population of approximately 1,600."

On Chebeague, the twenty-two children from pre-kindergarten through fifth grade could smell the homemade cookies baking down the hall as they took their vocabulary quizzes, prepared to read their writing aloud, and returned from the library. They may not realize how lucky they are, but their teachers do.

Food services director and cook Laura Summa is the farthest thing from the classic stereotype of the frumpy, intimidating school "lunch lady." As we were introduced, through the serving window into her modern kitchen in the three-classroom Chebeague Island

The Chebeague Island School. Much of the impetus for Chebeague's secession from the city of Portland in 2007 had to do with making sure this elementary school would remain open for island children. Eva Murray

School, she immediately asked me what I'd like on my pizza. That was all the invitation I needed! Homemade dough was being stretched onto a half-dozen pizza pans, and Laura had a penciled list on the wall indicating who wanted what for toppings. She smiled when I confessed that my favorite pizza was just plain cheese.

Earlier that day, as I traveled to the island from Portland on the Casco Bay Lines ferry, I ran into somebody I knew who now works for the Town of Chebeague (usually pronounced "sheh-BIG," by the way). "If you're going up to the school, make sure you stick around for lunchtime," he assured me. "It'll be worth it!"

Chebeague is getting a reputation for having the best school food anywhere. "I had three goals in mind for the lunch program when I started in the spring of 2010," explains Laura. "One, to eliminate processed foods from the menu; two, to serve a variety of fresh fruits and vegetables daily; and three, to minimize waste while pleasing children's fussy palettes and keeping costs in check."

When lunchtime came around, we (students, teachers, and visitors) all got a plate with a slice of pizza—topped as requested—with a serving of salad and a few slices of grapefruit. The best was yet to come, though: one of the students had a birthday that day. As the students, teachers, and ed techs sang "Happy Birthday" in English and then in Spanish (they are studying Spanish), Ms. Summa appeared at the door with a plate of chocolate cupcakes. The birthday girl got a large one, and everybody else was presented with a small one; plenty for the middle of the school day and, again, assuring only a few crumbs left over for the compost.

"We don't have sweets every day," one of the adults mentioned, "so it's special when we do."

Superintendent Alton "Bump" Hadley was at the Chebeague school that day. He and Laura joke with each other about the cost of the "fine cuisine" in school, but clearly, nobody really thinks the cost is in any way extravagant.

The Chebeague students tend a school garden in season, and grow some of the produce for their lunches. Says Laura, "I use fresh, whole foods whenever possible. The kids are happy to eat roasted garden potatoes that they grew, with olive oil and garlic, and fresh baked chicken strips with bread crumbs and parmesan cheese, instead of frozen French fries and chicken nuggets.

"I'm not against sugar, I'm not against bacon," she continued, explaining that the purpose was not to insist upon a strict dietary agenda. "I'm against fake food. We're making natural food, good food that people will actually eat. We feed any food scraps to a local flock of chickens in exchange for eggs, and compost whatever a chicken would not eat. The kids all eat the school lunch, very rarely bringing anything from home. Students are also pleased to report zero milk waste on a regular basis."

The Chebeague school website lists planned menus for each day: lasagna, homemade chicken soup, chicken pie, omelettes, pasta carbonara. Sandwiches and meatless entrees are available, and fresh fruit is typically the dessert. Sugary desserts are reserved for special occasions, and the day I visited I was lucky—there were two such occasions that day!

That afternoon, as part of their reading, language arts, and social studies work, the students had invited their parents and a few others in for a "publishing party." Each of the older students had done some research on a topic of interest and had written, illustrated, and bound a book to be presented at the party. The small group of parents and grandparents enjoying their visit to the school clearly all knew each other. The best part, however, was the smell of the fresh-baked chocolate chip cookies coming from Ms. Summa's kitchen down the hall! Sure enough, she appeared at the classroom door with a plate piled high with made-from-scratch cookies. Superintendent Hadley stopped in for a cookie, too.

Pre-K and kindergarten teacher Nancy Earnest describes how the good cooking has become a big part of the curriculum and the life of the school: "After a simple mention to Laura that we should do something special to enhance the children's cultural knowledge of Chinese cuisine, Laura went all out with a Chinese New Year's celebration, which was incredibly delicious!"

Deborah Bowman, the director of the Chebeague Library, who also worked on the Chinese lunch, told me that they "prepared and served crab rangoons, vegetable- and pork-fried rice, Hunan green beans, Chinese chips, teriyaki chicken on a stick, and pot stickers. Everyone had chopsticks and it was really fun!"

"When our class author was Dr. Seuss, and his birth date was coming up, she obliged us with green eggs and ham," said Nancy Earnest.

"The children love working in the garden. Beyond producing great local food, it provides opportunities for math, such as weight comparisons with pumpkins, and counting with cherry tomatoes—although somehow we had fewer at the end than when we started counting!"

Laura Summa adds, "In our school garden, we anticipate tomatoes, garlic, beets, carrots, potatoes, eggplant, asparagus, strawberries, and lettuce this year. Our lunches are hearty and homemade daily. When baking, I start from scratch. Muffins and fruit smoothies are a favorite snack choice. Each child is offered a choice of at least two fresh fruits and vegetables at snack time and lunchtime. I have found that choice is the key to children eating well and keeping waste to a minimum. A gentle reminder about finishing your milk has become part of our daily routine."

Protecting the Brick School at Peaks Island
A neighborhood of Portland?

Island residents are often asked by well-meaning mainlanders, "What do the islanders think about" this or that, or "How do the islanders feel" about some issue or another. An island, whether a freestanding municipality or not, is no more likely to be inhabited by like-minded people than is any other town. To be sure, certain issues of local interest—whether that be lobstering, shellfish harvesting, the reliability of the Internet, the frequency of the ferry service, or the quality of the school—are on everybody's minds, and the percentage of residents who are involved in community agencies is greater than it is in cities, but by no means do all islanders think the same thing or feel the same way about the concern of the day. Island dwellers are not schools of fish or flocks of starlings; they do not move as one, and they do not all take the same path.

Peaks Island, in Casco Bay, is just a few minutes' ferry ride from Portland. Far from being an isolated outer island like some of the others, Peaks is truly a suburb of Portland, with a branch of the Portland Public Library and a small Portland Police station a couple of blocks (yes—paved, typical city blocks) from the ferry terminal. A Peaks resident can take a short boat ride to Portland, dine at a very nice restaurant in the Old Port district or attend an event at the Civic Center, and get home again on a late boat without much trouble. However, Peaks' island identity should not be scoffed at; if you are feeling ill in the middle of the night on Peaks, you will be looking for the Portland fireboat—or some local mariner—to bring you to the mainland. Many aspects of one's daily routine still must be made to work around the ferry schedule, and in the winter after the tourists are gone, unfamiliar faces tend to be noticed.

Kindergarten-through-fifth-grade schoolchildren on Peaks Island attend a school which looks a lot like a miniature version of a typical flat-roofed urban elementary school. "The brick school," so called, is a regular City of Portland school facility, albeit a tiny one. With a year-round island population estimated between 800 and 1,000, and roughly 60 students in grades K–5, Peaks children grow up knowing their classmates. When I visited Peaks, the school had a kindergarten, a first-second-grade room, a third grade, and a fourth-fifth combined room. The configuration of multi-age classrooms varies with the children enrolled during any year. This year, there were more third-graders than any other age group, so they have a room to themselves. As lead teacher Cindy Nilsen gave me a little tour of the school, we saw that the chairs in the third- and the fourth-fifth-grade classrooms had been replaced by large exercise balls. "The kids really like those."

As on every island, the school is an essential component of Peaks Island's sense of itself as a community. How to describe or define that sense of community, however, is anything but simple, and that has a lot to do with the island's multifaceted and complex relationship with the City of Portland. Peaks is legally a part of the city, and unlike Cliff Island (which is also part of Portland but is truly physically distant, located in the outer reaches of Casco Bay), Peaks residents largely make their living in Portland. A fifteen-minute ferry ride over sheltered water with up to fifteen scheduled trips a day means Peaks Islanders don't kid themselves about being "way out in the ocean, all by ourselves." Nevertheless, people who move to islands, not to mention people who grew up on islands, are notoriously independent. Sometimes Peaks feels like "a neighborhood of Portland," as I have heard it described by a local, and sometimes it feels like an island. Upon hearing I lived on Matinicus, one Peaks friend immediately piped up, "I know, I know, you're going to tell me that Peaks isn't really an island. We hear that all the time," yet another Peaks resident, about to spend her second winter on the island, complained bitterly about the sense of isolation she felt there. Isolation—and insularity, if

Peaks Island Elementary, with three or four classrooms depending
upon the number of K–5 students each year, is called
"the brick school" by islanders. Craig Davis

I may—appear to be very subjective issues.

Peaks has considered and attempted secession from Portland several times, including in 2006-2007, following a 2004 revaluation of properties that resulted in an enormous tax hike, and most recently in 2010 as I was working on this book. So far, each effort has failed to get through the state legislature. Two other nearby islands, Long and Chebeague, "went independent" in recent years and for many it would seem logical that Peaks do the same. For others, however, the realities of running a town, one used to a fairly sophisticated level of public services, make secession from Portland a far more complicated issue than it may first appear. "Independence sounds good in theory," to paraphrase a couple of islanders who did not support the most recent secession attempt, "but who's going to plow the roads?"

Many say, "Just let the islanders vote!" and allow the secession by simple majority rule, regardless of the opinion of the legislature or the City of Portland, which people say takes in more in Peaks Island property taxes than it spends on Peaks Island public services. That sounds perfectly sensible, until other islanders counter with their well-considered fears. "This secession effort isn't the same as the previous one. This time there are different people involved, different people living here. This island isn't ready to go it alone. We don't have all of our plans made to get things done." That makes sense, too. As a mere visitor, I have no idea whether secession is a good plan or a bad one. Several islanders told me that the most recent secession campaign was not a rerun of the previous attempt, though; they told me that the island population had changed, and that "the facts" a few years ago are not "the facts" now. It does sound complicated.

All are in agreement about one thing, and that is that "the brick school" must remain open. The island's youngest children must not be expected to commute on the ferry. Whether ensuring the longevity of the school requires becoming an independent municipality or remaining a part of Portland is debated. Evidently, both sides worry that the school may be at risk if they do not prevail. Even those people who told me that they weren't convinced that secession was the best idea for now added that "Should Portland in the future ever seriously threaten to close our school, we would certainly vote to secede and keep the school here."

One full-time working resident of Peaks Island describes the complexity of the situation as follows:

> I do think that there are real fears about the school, but I think that those fears differ depending on which side of the secession issue people are on. I also feel that both sides like to use scare tactics, such as saying that the school will be closed down if we do not leave Portland. Honestly, I do not know what will happen in the future. I do not think we should leave Portland until the threat of closing the school becomes a reality. Right now the issue is split too evenly. If they ever closed the school, a line will have been crossed, and a lot more people will be on board with leaving the city. I have always thought it was better to stay with Portland if we can. When I moved here, it was because of the connection to Portland.

She also worries about how divisive the issue was this time around, and how neighbors disagreed sometimes less than amicably:

> My peer group seems to be able to disagree on the issue and stay friends, but I do hear a lot of gossip about other people not speaking to each other anymore because they were on opposing sides of the issue. I see how ugly the fight has been on both sides with slander, lies, and downright rudeness. Some of my friends, who do not

share my opinion, have been verbally attacked and had nasty things posted about them on social media sites. The other thing that sets my teeth on edge is having people constantly saying, "If we secede [or if we don't secede] I'm moving!" I say, GO. Go now. If they are going to bail out because they don't get their own way, then they are not in it for the long haul anyway.

Perhaps with a sense of irony she comments that, "I myself just think it is better for us all to hate Portland together (sort of like hating a big box store) than to have us hating each other."

She describes the concerns she and other islanders have with school decisions being made in Portland rather than locally:

I have, at times, come close to wanting to support the secession bill. At the end of one year, one of our teachers, who was on her probationary two-year contract, was not offered a contract for the next year. She is a woman who has strong ties to our community because her mother lives here and she and her kids come out for a lot of the summer. She is an excellent new teacher with a lot of room to grow and a great track record with the parents and the kids in her classroom. She was assessed by someone in the administration of the evil power called "the Central Office" in Portland and was deemed not worthy to continue working for the Portland Public Schools. Many parents wrote to the superintendent on her behalf, and a letter was given to him with seventy-eight signatures on it asking him to come to Peaks and explain why a school with only four teachers is losing someone we feel is so vital, especially after not having much continuity for the last few years. His blanket response has been that he could not comment on the teacher because it was a personnel issue.

He did agree to come and talk about the stability of our staffing, but would not address the fact that we wanted to keep our current teacher. Her job had already been listed. This is when I waver on leaving Portland. If we were our own town, this might not be happening—or at least we would have some control over it.

Luckily, the rest of the staff is fantastic, and if we left Portland we would definitely lose them.

A few months later, the same Peaks Island parent told me, "I don't think anybody has moved away because of secession, and I haven't heard any serious talk lately about trying again right now."

TWELVE-YEAR-OLD COMMUTERS
AND HIGH SCHOOL "AWAY"

Going to School by Boat
Cliff Island kids know the ferrymen by name.

The Casco Bay Lines ferry terminal is a hubbub of happy activity on a sunny, if cold and blustery, April afternoon. A woman waits with a big dog on a leash, and among the others are a man with a wheeled shopping basket and several bags of groceries, a couple of young men who might be college students or computer repairmen, a couple of older fellows in their veteran's ball caps, and one man in a suit, perhaps a Portland lawyer who lives on nearby Peaks Island. Other than just those few adults, the terminal is filled with teenagers.

It grows a bit quieter as a gang of younger kids, evidently middle-schoolers, disappear out the heavy doors and walk aboard the Peaks Island ferry. Older boys sit around reading each other questions from Trivial Pursuit cards and laughing and talking about taking their driver's license exams in borrowed pickup trucks. They talk about dogs. I hear the word "Somalia" a few times in their conversation.

It is clear that almost everyone here is a regular commuter. Before long, as summer brings tourists, the terminal will be full of strange faces, but not yet.

There are usually two Casco Bay Lines ferry routes. One goes back and forth to Peaks Island nearly every hour, and the other makes a circuit between Portland and Long Island, Little and Great Diamond, Chebeague, and Cliff Islands. Today there are also younger children aboard, students from Cliff Island's one-room school, returning from a Portland field trip. The kids all know the deckhands. One of them, who the kids hand around with, pester, and call by name ("Seth"), shows himself to be an expert line-handler, tossing a heavy hawser over the large bollard at each island's dock. The steel vessel makes a deafening screech as it slides against the wharf pilings, and for a couple of seconds, all conversation stops; just part of the routine.

The ride to Cliff is long, over an hour, but the *Maquoit II* has a few tables among the seats, and kids play Magic and other card games. The boat has recently been equipped with wireless Internet, to their delight. The volume tends steadily upward until a parent reminds them, "If Seth has to tell you to keep it down you'll feel pretty bad."

Amy, a mom from Cliff Island, has a preschooler, a sixth-grader who is in his first year of commuting to King Middle School, and two older teenagers in high school. She tells me, "The kids who ride the ferry every day go from being the older kids in an island school to being the younger ones in the commuter group. A lot of times they do their homework on the ferry, and they can ask their siblings and all their older friends for help. The older students are great about the little kids." Cade, her sixth-grader, and Julian, a fifth-grader in the Cliff school, play a complex game as they ride. The littler kids cluster around the two boys and ask questions.

Josh Holloway, Cliff Island's teacher, tells me, "The school kids get exempted from adult stress. Things get difficult, like they do in any remote place, but nobody dumps it on the kids. They seem to be an entirely happy, well-cared-for lot, and they seem to be enjoying the advantages of a tiny community without a sense that they'll be stuck here in a negative way."

Unlike Frenchboro and Matinicus, there are only a half-dozen or so lobster fishermen and -women on Cliff. The father of two of the schoolchildren writes software and another is a Portland firefighter; both ride the ferry to Portland regularly.

Josh says the Portland principal likes "the expeditionary learning style" of the Cliff school and supports it. A recent scare over the possible closing of the school by the City of Portland was, according to Josh, not a serious threat. I hope Josh is right; those rumors do circulate from time to time.

The Holloways talk about the Cliff Island preschool program, which is becoming more formalized as the teachers become certified in early childhood education. "It's good for the student population. The little ones come in the morning and do start-the-day stuff with the older kids. Then, we set the three of them up in the little library area doing their own activities for a while (somebody is with them). Then, we pair them up with an older student who reads to them. They all switch off from day to day, and they all love this. Then, we do some kind of work where the preschoolers can participate, like a science project or garden work or something; then they get a story and go home."

I asked Josh if he could ever really "go home from work." "Definitely," he said. He and Heidi, unlike teachers on some islands at some points, have not been treated like all-around public servants. "Cliff residents are very good that way. When we're out of school, we enjoy spending time with the kids, sledding, swimming; those things are fun for us. I'm still 'the schoolteacher,' I'm 'Mr. Holloway' in school and out of school, but it's been really good, it's fine.

"If you want to create enemies on the island, it's easy to do. You've got to live with people. I find if you want to get along with people, that's easy to do. We don't have a local school board; the boss is the City of Portland. In a lot of ways, I think that's a good thing. We share a principal with Peaks, so she makes it out once in a while, and we had the new superintendent come out to see the island; he enjoyed that—people who are in administrative tasks love coming out to something like this, they can meet everybody at once, the issues are less complicated. I don't know exactly what goes through their minds, but I do know that our principal loves this school; she's so supportive, she wishes she could spend more time out here."

On the Casco Bay islands—Cliff, Long, Chebeague, Great Diamond, and Peaks—a daily commute is part of the routine for students after the fifth grade. Rather than staying in their small, sometimes intimate, island community until suddenly moving away full-time at age fourteen, the Casco Bay commuter students adapt to early mornings and inflexible ferry schedules.

Josh Holloway talks about a student who moved to the island recently. "He goes to King Middle School in Portland, but whenever the city has a snow day, he comes in to school here and spends the day with the class. He's a sixth-grader and he commutes every day. He has to catch the 6:00 A.M. ferry each day—that's pretty tough. The kids can get the 2:45 ferry back, which drops them back on Cliff at 4 o'clock if they don't do sports, but he does, so the 5:45 P.M. is his only option. That gets him here at 7:00 P.M.; there are four boats a day, so it works out. It means that they have to use their time wisely. A sixth-grader has to be very mature.

"One of our students who graduated last year really shows that maturity. She does her homework on the boat, she's a driven student. With everything that they have to do, I think they learn time management. She has excelled at King Middle School; she's just received 'student of the month,' and it's a really big school. She gets a lot of As."

Josh describes another Cliff family where the fifth-grader has just graduated from the Cliff School and, since his older sister was already at King Middle School and both parents worked on the mainland, the family moved off so they wouldn't have the commute. They bought a house on the mainland and rented out their island home. The new sixth-grader "was very active in sports and very eager to have that opportunity, but also, I've talked to his mom and he has realized that a lot of the freedom is gone. As far as playing outside with his friends, they now have to do the scheduling-playdates kind of thing, because it's not the same kind of community. It's complicated. If he's going to go somewhere with friends, there are all kinds of activities but they all cost money. It's not just 'I want to go out for a hike to the bluffs.' He's realizing the loss there. He's got the sports, but—it's a give and take."

Josh explains that if King has a snow day, the middle-schoolers usually come over to the island school, "and help out or do things. Sometimes, if King has super-early-release, like if they're having conferences and the kids are out at 10:30 A.M. or something, it doesn't make sense for the kids to even bother going over. They'd be at the ferry terminal for hours anyway."

A Portland librarian, art teacher, music teacher, physical education teacher, and principal all visited the Cliff Island School regularly (these arrangements vary year to year). The librarian was there reading to the students when I arrived to visit Cliff; she then left to go to Peaks Island, but not before leaving the Cliff kids some cupcakes, so they work on their next assignments while eating cupcakes. The Holloways' toddler Kai is underfoot. We talk about how with all these other teachers coming in, "it's almost like a private-school education."

Samantha Crowley has lived on Cliff all her life. Her father is a Portland firefighter. Sam is in the eighth grade at King Middle School in Portland and has made the commute each day on the ferry from Cliff for three years. "I get up around five," she tells me, "to get the boat. We play cards, talk, or play games. I usually eat my breakfast aboard the boat." The trip from Cliff Island to Portland takes up to an hour and a half, depending upon conditions and the stops at the other islands.

"We stop at Chebeague usually, but the school kids don't get on. [Chebeague's older students take another boat in another direction and commute to school in Cumberland.] Then we stop at Long Island, which has a lot of kids. There is one younger kid who gets on at Great Diamond, a fifth-grader; he goes to Portland, to a private school.

"We get off the boat at around 7:30 A.M., wait for the ferry from Peaks to arrive, and take the school bus from the Casco Bay Lines terminal to King Middle School. After we get off at King, the bus goes on to Deering High school."

I ask Sam about participating in sports with such a schedule, since I'd heard she had been on the swim team this winter.

"With swimming, there is a bus you can make and still get the last boat. With soccer, you usually need to get a ride to the ferry."

Island parents had explained to me that they and the students arrange carpools a lot, and, as a rule, the students get cell phones before they begin this commuter life, to help organize transportation. I ask whether the bus drivers have much awareness of the island students' transportation issues.

"It depends," Sam says, "but the boat *is* supposed to wait for the bus. I think the bus driver can call the boat. The deckhands are pretty aware of who the students are, whether the students are there yet. The ferry isn't supposed to leave the students."

I asked what happened if she missed the last boat for some reason. Sam explains that her grandmother is on the mainland, not far away, and that most students have friends or relatives near enough so that a ride or a last-minute overnight visit can be managed. It sounds as though everybody within this network of extended family would be willing to help out a stranded island student, whether their actual relative or not.

Sam talks about the Casco Bay Lines deckhands with some affection. "They will get angry with you if you're doing the wrong thing— they have to keep it safe—but they're nice. The high-schoolers aren't always as friendly with the deckhands as us middle-schoolers are. We're really friends with them. Sometimes we even hang out with the captain."

Cheryl Crowley, Sam's mother, tells us that the deckhands keep an eye on the kids, that while "these guys joke around with them and play cards or whatever, they're monitoring." To that, Sam says, "Well, with the high-schoolers they are. The middle-schoolers—we don't really have problems."

I ask about stormy weather and rough boat rides. Much of Casco Bay is fairly sheltered, but Cliff Island, the farthest from Portland, can see some rough water.

"They cut it off at something like sustained winds at thirty miles an hour—the ferry might only go out as far as Long—but that's rare," explains Cheryl. "Especially with the school kids' schedule. That's rare. They might have a rough ride!"

Sam insists that "It's fun, with the waves."

Aboard the boat, besides talking with each other, eating breakfast, goofing around with the deckhands, and playing cards, the island kids might study. Headed for Cliff in the afternoon, it's social time until the majority of the students get off at Long Island; then the remaining students hit the books. "That's usually how it works," says Sam.

I ask whether having to deal with the boat makes her life different from other middle-schoolers. "You can't just decide at school that you're going to visit a friend at their house or go hang out. Everything has to be planned. You have to work out a ride to the boat, and make sure you get that last boat. People complain about waking up at 7:00 A.M. I say, 'I'm on the boat by seven!'"

In an unusual situation, one small child does make a regular, daily commute to school. A little boy named Kineo lives on Great Diamond Island, which has no school. As part of the City of Portland, Great Diamond students are welcome at Portland schools, but that commute (and subsequent school-bus ride) would be an awfully long haul for a kindergartner! Instead, he takes the ferry one "stop" to Long Island and joins the much smaller school group there. Long Island teacher Paula Johnson says:

The morning commute works fairly well for him. He arrives at about 8:40 A.M. and we ring the kids in at 8:30, so he doesn't miss much other than outside time with the other kids. He leaves on the 12:30 P.M. boat, which is during the lunch break. On Tuesdays he stays with us all day, since we have art and music in the afternoon.

Josh Holloway and the Cliff Island students join us [in 2011, the art and music teachers did not make the regular visits to Cliff]. Kineo then leaves with Josh and rides down the bay at the end of the day and then back to Great Diamond. His mom rides that boat with him. It makes for a long day for him. Fridays we get out at noon and he goes back to great Diamond on the noon boat. The City of Portland agreed he could come to school here, but would not pay tuition or switch out one of our tuitions that we pay to them. Kineo's parents are paying his tuition. We love having Kineo and he seems totally adjusted to the commute. It's only about ten to fifteen minutes in the morning.

The High School Options
Every man for himself.

One of the most common questions asked of island teachers, island parents, and islanders in general is, "Where do the island kids go to high school?" The assumption, in many cases, is that all students are *told* where they will go to high school and attend whichever local public school exists in their district.

But for many of the island students, there is no high school in their district. In some cases, the island, with its one-room elementary school, is the entire district. Even when an island is legally part of a larger school district, union, or municipality, commuting to high school may be undesirable, inconvenient, or truly impossible.

Three unbridged islands in Maine have high schools to serve the local students: Vinalhaven, North Haven, and Islesboro. Tiny by typical high-school standards, these schools still serve communities much larger than those we have been visiting. Students who grew up attending one- and two-room schools must manage a significant change in lifestyle when they reach high-school age. Most have to leave their island home, some with and some without their families.

On Isle au Haut, a small passenger and mail boat serves the island daily. Most of the Isle au Haut kids recently have gone to boarding school or their families have moved, but one island boy elected to take the boat each morning, then take a school bus to the Deer Isle–Stonington High School and come home each afternoon. This was a matter of choice, not expectation or obligation. His mother explains:

The commute worked well for the most part. The boat was

accommodating and the school worked Nicholas's schedule around the boat. His first class was always a study hall because he would not get to school till just before 9:00 A.M. The boat company even pushed back the last boat departure time so Nicholas would not have to miss part of his last class.

One time he got stuck on the mainland, and Josh, the mail-boat captain, took him in. All the other times that the boat just made one trip a day due to weather, Nicholas would stay home and the school made it an excused absence.

The downside to commuting was he could not do any extra activities after school because he would have to hop on the bus to catch the boat. In hindsight, I would not do this again, as Nicholas's only social life was at school or on the bus.

Kipp Quinby, of Isle au Haut, was homeschooled for high school on the island before going on to college. She explains how it worked:

For high school I homeschooled, with some less-than-usual quirks. For the first three years, I was on the island and worked a little with my parents and a lot with some very generous friends (a former bishop for Latin and literature; an island contractor for lofting and building a boat; other folks for field research, etc.). I did a lot of ITV courses from the University of Maine System—fifty-five credit hours in those three years, which were paid for by the town as a much, much cheaper alternative to regular tuition. For what would have been my fourth/senior year, I went to Finland through AFS, where I lived with a family and went to school there in Finnish. There was also plenty of the usual puttering about with projects. June Kantz Pemberton [also a Matinicus teacher] was actually my official teacher for the purposes of signing off for the state's paperwork.

For many Matinicus students in the middle of the twentieth century, Maine or other New England boarding schools were a common choice. The stereotypical notion that private school is either some Dickensian horror or a luxury reserved for the snobbish sons of Park Avenue and Beacon Hill is easily proven nonsense by the sons and daughters of lobstermen. Island students go to boarding school not because it is a luxury, but because it is expedient. For those who do not have a friend or a relative who lives near a high school and has a spare bed, and when financial aid is available, private school can actually be the easiest, least stressful option (after all, nearly everybody is "from out of town"!).

Of course, there is bound to be a period of adjustment. This was as much the case a generation or two ago as it is now. Lobsterman and former math teacher Edwin Mitchell of Matinicus, who attended Gould Academy in Bethel, Maine (now a magnet for skiers due to its close proximity to the Sunday River Ski area), tells the story of his transition to high school and his particular brush with sartorial splendor back in the 1950s:

> My family rarely left the island; in those days there wasn't as much reason to. Normally, we kids only got off the island about once a year, for a week in August when we went to visit the relatives in Bar Harbor. When I was getting ready to go to Gould, my mother ordered me three sets of new clothes from a catalog: a pair of Dickies twill pants and the matching shirt in green, and the same set in blue and the same set in khaki. Of course, over at Gould the guys were wearing sport jackets and whatever. At the first parents' weekend in October my folks came up to Bethel and I said, "Look, we have *got* to go shopping!"

Edwin chuckled over the whole thing as he told his story, but probably at the time—being fourteen years old and away from home for the first time—it was a tad stressful.

Ellen and Janan Bunker of Matinicus had a father who owned a small airplane. Their lobsterman father had learned to fly when their mother had been in treatment for cancer and had needed frequent trips to the mainland. Also Gould students, they and a few friends occasionally took the "flying school bus" between Matinicus and Bethel, all the way across the state, at the beginning or end of a school break. Almost forty years later, my husband, visiting our son at Gould Academy, got word from home that he had to hurry back to the island to be ready as lineman for the island power company when a severe storm with destructive winds was forecast for the next day. Penobscot Island Air, the air taxi service that carries the mail and freight to Matinicus and some of the other islands, was dispatched at no small expense across the middle of the state to the Bethel airport to pick him up. Dan Kunkle, Gould's headmaster, joked that day that "I have to deal with all kinds of pretty heavy-hitting parents, but we've never had anybody so important that they sent an airplane special for him!" This for the father of a scholarship student.

For all isolated island children and their parents, approaching high-school age means there will be decisions to make. For students from Matinicus, Monhegan, and Isle au Haut, which are not part of larger school districts (nor have they been historically), the mechanism for finding a high school is quite seriously "every man for himself." The steps a student goes through while deciding where to go to high school differ from island to island and from family to family. For many, it resembles an older teenager's search for a college. Catalogs and websites, school visits, and "shadow days" help with the decision; family finances and financial aid must be examined, questions of how far away is too far must be discussed, and a great deal of paperwork sometimes has to be done.

A few island students who have recently been through or are just beginning the process offer their thoughts. Eighth-grader Dalton of Monhegan was examining his options.

The decision of choosing a high school is a very special one for the seventh- and eighth-graders on Monhegan. For me, it was a little scary thinking of going off to a boarding school, but after I finished visiting five or six schools and talked with some friends, I did feel like I could live there for four years. The process of picking out schools to look at and eventually visit was exciting and nervewracking for me.

First, my mom and I looked at a website called boarding schoolreview.com, and we picked schools that looked interesting, or had my favorite sports. Then we had to visit them at a convenient time for both us and the school. Once we'd visited, we made a little list of pros and cons and we talked about the school. This process seems pretty easy to do, but the schools in New England are spread far and wide, so take a car with good gas mileage! I am feeling really excited about experiencing high school. My mom is glad that I will be going to a good school, because she went to Kent's Hill for three years and she understands how special boarding school is.

Emily T. of Islesford writes from Mount Allison University, Sackville, New Brunswick, Canada:

I have lived on Islesford for my entire life with the exception of attending high school and university. I'm the younger of two girls, with my father a lobsterman and my mother the librarian at the community library [her father first came to Islesford years ago as the schoolteacher and chose to remain on Little Cranberry]. Growing up on an island can have its difficulties, but I would not trade that experience for the world, particularly when it came time for me to leave the island. I was always very excited about school for two reasons: I had wonderful teachers and parents who were serious about education. They believed in it, and as a result, I do as well. I liked being able to have a small class size in elementary school. I believe my largest class was the year I graduated from eighth grade—we had one teacher for twelve students. It was a bit of a shock to go from twelve students in the school to sixteen students in a classroom!

My transition from island school to high school was interesting. I had decided to go to boarding school and eventually chose Northfield Mount Hermon, in Northfield, Massachusetts. I was very homesick my first semester there, but eventually settled in well and came to love and cherish my time there. In large part, my island roots allowed me to make that transition and to come to love the area. Even now, three years after graduating and about to graduate from university, I still consider NMH to be one of my "homes." Growing up on an island, going to an island school, allowed me the chance to learn differently, at my own pace and with my own style. The decision to attend boarding school was mine. It probably was not the initial plan my family had in mind, but it was what I wanted to do, and I did it. Once I got to NMH, I became heavily involved with the music program and the "ultimate Frisbee" team. I sang with the choir for three years and was in a smaller, all-auditioned choir for two years.

Twenty-first-century boarding school students use cell phones and Skype and Facebook all sorts of other communications to stay in touch with friends and family at home, so the sense of "leaving home" is not as overwhelming it used to be (and sometimes it is the parents, rather than the student, who expect daily communication, for better or worse). Many aspects of the move to boarding school have not changed over time, however. Moving is still difficult.

Things have not changed entirely in forty years. Jeanette Young Beaudoin grew up on Matinicus and was a boarding student at Kent's Hill School in Readfield, near Augusta, Maine, in the late 1960s. Air travel to Matinicus was relatively new in those days, with one pilot who owned a Piper Cub that could carry one passenger. There may only have been one pilot and one plane, but there were two airstrips in those days—one on the north end, where it is now, and one in a large field on the southern part of the island. Jeanette tells the story of flying home for Christmas vacation when the pilot (Arthur Harjula) discovered that he was unable to land at the north-end airstrip as expected, as snowdrifts had blocked it. He landed nearly two miles to the south where the airstrip was open but the road to it was not. Jeanette, dressed in a skirt and suede boots, slogged through the deep snow with her luggage halfway up the island to her grandparents' house before she could call anybody for a ride. She remembers that her grandfather gave her a big lecture about not being properly dressed to be out walking in the deep snow.

Jeanette told me more about going off to high school from the island more than a generation ago:

If you live on Matinicus, you know from the time you're in first grade that you're going to have to leave here for at least part of the year. I dreaded going. I was so homesick my first year at Kent's Hill, but that was because I was so entrenched in my extended family. [She was also only thirteen, having completed second and third grades in one year.] After that first year, I was fine, because I knew what to expect and I'd made friends.

We didn't have school trips when I was in school. We had the bird club! That's just how it was; the moms and dads didn't "want" their kids to leave, they'd miss them, but when you're done with eighth grade you go away to school. If my parents were stressing about it, they didn't say much. It was more about getting stuff ready, get your clothes organized and pack the trunk and everything, getting ready to move into a dormitory. There were more kids in school here, too, fifteen or twenty students, so here were more friends to be leaving behind.

My parents would come for family weekend; that hasn't

changed. I'd matured the first year; after that I realized it was okay to be away from my family. It wasn't as though I'd never been anywhere, but we didn't leave the island often.

I was meeting teenagers who were vastly more experienced with some social behavior. I had my own room, and I was lonesome in that little room by myself at night. Girls would be talking about kissing their boyfriends or having huge fights with their parents, or the older ones getting stopped by the cops for speeding. When I was thirteen, you might have a crush on a boy on the island, but you wouldn't have been dating!

The rules at Kent's Hill were very strict. They needed to be for some of the kids, and then along came me. I didn't understand why the girls had to be in the dormitory at 4:30 in the afternoon once the clocks had changed in the winter. I had come from a place where everybody trusted me. I didn't understand, initially, why people who didn't know me would think that they couldn't trust me. It took a while to get used to the rules. I respected authority, I wasn't mischievous, and I didn't see why they treated me like I was a potential troublemaker. They didn't have to worry about me breaking the rules.

Looking back now, I feel that I got a really good education. At Kent's Hill, we had to take a sport, and you had to do it every afternoon, Monday to Friday. I learned to ski, I learned archery, tennis—I loved learning the new sports. I was in the glee club—I loved glee club. Those were the bonuses. I got accepted to a lot of colleges. [Jeanette is a graduate of Boston University.] In my house there was always talk about "When you go off to college you'll have new adventures." It was expected that I would get good grades and my parents really hoped that I would go to college.

Jeanette's father, a Matinicus native from a large, longtime island family, was a lobsterman, as well as being the storekeeper, postmaster, and town historian. He was a Colby College graduate with a degree in mathematics.

Samantha Philbrook, Matinicus lobster-catcher and school-board member, describes her experience with private school after having rarely left her island home:

I originally found out about the Westover School through my

friend Crystal [another Matinicus student; Westover is a prestigious girls' prep school that encouraged island students to apply and offered a generous scholarship]. I went on an overnight trip with my dad to check the school out. It was close to Margret and Charlie, family friends who summer on Matinicus, and also near a great-aunt and -uncle of mine, so that was a factor—on some weekends I would be able to go and visit people I knew.

The overnight was interesting, to say the least, me coming off Matinicus where Crystal and I were the only girls the same age, to a place with fifty girls my own age, from all over the country—and the world, for that matter.

I also had looked into Maine Central Institute in Pittsfield because my brother Nick went there, and I thought about Vinalhaven, because I could have lived with my gram, aunts, or brother, but in the end Westover looked to be the best of the best.

I asked Samantha if she felt any kind of "culture shock." She was not a child who had spent a lot of time traveling or involved in activities off the island.

Oh my God, yes. I don't think that in the nine months I was there I ever got used to it, and I never stopped seeing or experiencing new cultural things. For you to get an idea: on my freshman floor there was a Muslim girl from Bangladesh, identical African American twins from the Bronx, another set of "southern belle to the extreme" twins, my roommate's parents were right off the boat from Portugal, and just around the corner on the sophomore floor were girls from the Philippines and Japan. They had an exchange program with South Africa, so there was a student from there, and two girls called "gappies," who were like teacher's aides, from Australia, and that doesn't even get to the junior and senior floors. But I myself— to the other girls—might as well have been from a foreign country as well. They couldn't believe that there was a place like Matinicus in the USA. From the one-room school to catching lobsters and dealing with bait, to already driving a car on my own, not to the mention the four-wheelers and dirt bikes and outboards, I was like an alien to all of them.

Through all of the differences in color, language, religion, and everything else, everyone got along for the most part, and if there were people who didn't like each other, it was only because they were teenage girls, and not because of ethnic differences.

Island High-Schoolers Correspond with Their Slightly Younger Neighbors
You guys should hold a big dance, and practice!

In addition to organizing the annual Island Middle-Schoolers' Retreat, the Reverend Rob Benson—minister aboard the *Sunbeam* and former teacher and coach—asks island high-schoolers for open letters "from the field" directed toward the students beginning to think about that big move. Published annually as "I 2 I" or "Eye 2 Eye," the assembled letters are "wisdom and hope for the journey off-island." Here are some excerpts from those letters, from the 2009 edition of the booklet.

I didn't start to feel nervous about high school until about three days before I left. I was hardly ever nervous about anything. I was mostly excited about living on my own, meeting new people, and not being confined to the small island I was living on. When I first got to school I couldn't wait to get rid of my parents and start living my new life. I didn't start to get homesick until about a week before Thanksgiving break, when I was ready to go home and sleep in my own bed.

I was scared to go to high school. I would think of all the things that could go wrong. I kept reassuring myself of what could go right. That is very nervewracking. The absolute hardest thing for me to do was leave the island for high school at the end of the summer. I remember looking out of the mail-boat window, seeing family and friends on the dock waving from the distance. When I first got to school all I could think about was everyone on the island and what they were doing at that moment. This was a very strong feeling of loneliness. The feeling does go away.

I remember being frustrated as the only eighth-grader and the oldest student in the school. I wanted to play sports and do things with other kids that everyone on the mainland had the chance to do. I wanted to be around more people my age. [On this student's island, programs have been put in place to encourage at least occasional off-island athletic experiences since she graduated.] I'm so glad that my little sister has been able to play soccer, cross-country, basketball, and outdoor track with other elementary schools on Mount Desert. I remember being twelve years old and wishing I had the chance to play sports.

One thing I remember was really strange to me when I first moved ashore was how people don't conserve resources—they aren't even aware of them. Lights are left on and water running. [This student was from Monhegan, where the electricity rates are quite possibly the highest in the country.]

Learn how to do things for yourself: do your own laundry, use a phone card, use an ATM, and manage your own spending money. Learn to cook the comfort foods you like [in the microwave].

The real thing I wish I'd learned is how to dance. Yes, this simple but useful tool is something that has proved itself to be absolutely vital in high school. The first dance I went to, I left traumatized and laughing at my own lack of talent. Needless to say, living on the island I didn't get much experience! You guys should hold a big dance and practice!

From Matinicus to Phillips Exeter
Quite a little hooligan.

Emily Murray, studying at Bowdoin College, remembers adapting to life at boarding school after a childhood on Matinicus:

I wasn't terribly shy or anything like that, but I didn't really have a lot of experience with how to throw myself into a group. I definitely hadn't been through all that horrible junior-high-school social climbing, all the posturing, learning how to be mean and manipulative [she laughs]. That was okay. It took me a while to realize what they were doing when people would start with that stuff—like if somebody was trying to sort of trick me into saying something so they could run around and tell everybody else what I'd said. Thankfully, we didn't have to deal with lots of teenage-politics, rights-of-passage stuff, but there is always some.

On the other hand, I was better than most of them at coping with some things, like when you realize you've forgotten or run out of something you need. I was fine with borrowing and lending and making do without things. On the island, if you don't have a part you need, you have to improvise. If you run out of eggs in the middle of a recipe, you borrow some, and it's perfectly normal to do that. If somebody else needs something, you don't say no. Dorm life is somewhat like island life. We are to a certain extent "all in this together." Communal living like that was not new to me. The only thing that was strange to me was the adolescent game-playing, but that's not very important. My roommate that first year is someone who I'm sure I'll stay in touch with for life—we're really good friends now—but she was pretty impatient with my [and here she smiles again] "savagery." I ran around barefoot most of freshman year until the teachers were worried that I would get frostbite. Quite a little hooligan.

Emily went to Phillips Exeter Academy in southern New Hampshire as a ninth-grader with a pocket full of Allen wrenches, a hard drive full of Celtic folk-rock music, and a cheap bicycle. Her Matinicus summers really had been spent sleeping outdoors and running barefoot, but purely by choice. She expressed some concern about school dress codes ("What do you mean, 'slacks?' All my pants have hammer loops!"). She had never been on a basketball team or won a T-ball trophy, but she'd won the pin chase on the *Harvey Gamage* and hiked in the Grand Canyon. She'd grown up playing with boys, slightly older and slightly bigger, and was as tough as they were.

Somewhere around Thanksgiving, Emily e-mailed a photograph home of herself in a slinky formal dress and high heels for a dance. Her neighbors hardly recognized her.

"I know that some islands kids go off to high school and never come back," she tells me. "That wasn't how I felt. I'm not trying to buy a boat and go lobstering, but I also wasn't trying like hell to get out of there," meaning the island. She plays me a song that she says she would often enjoy listening to that first year away from Matinicus, "Home," by Enter the Haggis. It's really about Ireland but, as she says, "There's a lot in there that sounds like Maine":

> I long for my home
> For my family and friends on the island

But I cannot return
'Till I find who I am
Perhaps I'll go home when I'm sleeping.

And the lightning does crash
And the thunder it rolls
As the storm comes across
From the harbour

Where the cruise ships are tied
With the big corporate yachts
But no fishing boats roll
On the whitecaps

So I'm watching the storm
Is it calling me back
I can feel it well up from inside me
And it's guiding my hand
With my pen or the strings
And it's leading me back to my island. . . .

© Enter the Haggis, with permission.

Emily was invited to attend a pre-orientation event called "Sampler," where students from overseas or for whom the move to boarding school was likely to represent an especially significant upheaval had a few extra days to socialize, get to know the area, and get organized before the craziness began. Many of the friends she made at Sampler, she is certain, will be friends forever. "The first day I was at Exeter, during Sampler, I was in my room by myself messing around with my computer, not really sure what to do with myself, and Noon [a student from Thailand] came in and sat down on my bed. She said, 'Hi, I'm Noon,' and just started talking." Noon and Emily had absolutely nothing else in common except Exeter Sampler, but they made friends right away. Noon, from a very wealthy family in Bangkok, helped Emily learn how to gracefully handle a room full of strangers, and Emily helped Noon learn how to operate a washing machine.

In recent years, boarding schools have often been within the reach of island families because of available scholarship aid. The schools have discovered that islanders add to the diversity of their student body much the way a student from another country or from an under-represented state does. Emily grinned as she told her island friends over Christmas break, "I guess I'm a student from overseas!"

Not every student would wish to do this, but Emily had some fun with her "foreign-ness," playing up the cultural differences between herself and her suburban classmates. Never having participated in coached activities, or ever before worn protective gear like shin guards, she enjoyed the startled expressions of her new friends when she showed them the scars of her childhood roughhousing. An avowed "gearhead," she arrived at boarding school with a full toolbox, and before orientation was over, she had become the class mechanic, repairing several bicycles, a music player, and a couple of pairs of eye-glasses. Never having been involved with team sports, she was never-theless an eager athlete, and the coaches at Exeter noticed. The cycling coach recruited her for his extremely competitive team, and before freshman year was over, she was a varsity bicycle racer, riding with the fastest in New England. The following year she took up ice hockey.

Kids who haven't been in sports since they were little shouldn't worry. If you're fairly athletic and you enjoy it and you do what-ever the coach tells you to do, you can get in shape in one season. You can learn the sport at sixteen. All that stuff you do when you're four years old, I think, is mostly learning teamwork and stuff. Certainly, the kids that have played for a few years before high school are better at it, but you do not have to do it from the time you're four years old. Junior varsity is for learning the fine points of the game. With a few exceptions, like men's hockey, most of the teams can find a place for anybody who is willing to work on their skills and really participate. You don't have to already know everything before high school.

Exeter has a first-year phys-ed program in which students can try out a number of sports without making a commitment to any. For most students, this will be the first time they've ever had the chance to try sports like crew or squash or diving or water polo. Emily was in the swimming and diving session when the coach asked if anybody would volunteer to go to the end of the diving board, turn around, and jump in. Most of the kids said something like "You've got to be out of your mind!" Our island roustabout, thinking of her summers spent diving with the other kids somewhat recklessly off the ferry wharf into the harbor, said, "Okay, why not?"

She also became the "Animal Control Officer of Bancroft Hall," as it was discovered that among several dozen girls she was one of the few not apt to scream at the sight of a spider in the shower or a mouse in the basement. She was often called to other girls' rooms to remove some insect that had flown in, and once spent half an hour chasing a chipmunk up and down the Bancroft stairwell as other girls screeched, fearing it was a less cute rodent like a rat.

One day in April of Emily's junior year, as she was practicing with the varsity cycling team and anticipating her best season ever in that highly demanding sport, she experienced a sudden level of pain severe enough to practically knock her off the bike. Coach Don Mills, known for his hard-core training regimen and his very high expectations for his athletes, knew that dedicated racer Emily wouldn't exaggerate something minor, and allowed her to return to the school's health center. Barely able to make it up the steps alone, and after a call to her island parents, she was taken to the Exeter Hospital Emergency Department with kidney stones.

When a boarding student needs help or the kind of support usually offered by family, the modern boarding school can really shine. Coaches, deans, students. and teachers rallied, trying to make sure she was never left to feel like she had to deal with this alone. Coach Steve and teammate Eva from the cycling team, best friends Liam and Neil, German teacher Herr Reiter, dorm parent Mrs. Braile, and many others visited her and offered everything they could to help. They did everything from making sure teachers knew what was going on so she wouldn't get into academic trouble to bringing her homemade muffins, and most important, remaining by her side to the extent they could. They were her extended family and, in the best sense of the word, her neighbors. Still, as soon as the exhausted student was back in class, she was expected to keep up and to put in very full days.

Emily makes sure to point out that boarding school is not babysitting. "You have to be ready, in your own head, to deal with life independently. People shouldn't think that the school is going to surround them with all sorts of coddling every time they get a hangnail. Being at boarding school still can be hard—very hard—and you have to realize that there is a difference between an emergency and just a kid being a little nervous about some problem. You have to be willing to start growing up."

A Big Change at Home, Too
It was sad when her room was empty.

The move off-island to high school can be hard for Mom and Dad. For many families, sending a child off the island, away from home, whether it be to a friend's or relative's home to attend a public school or to a boarding school, is initially a painful upheaval. When a child has grown up anticipating this transition, following in the footsteps of older siblings, cousins, and neighbors, the normal jitters are usually tempered with a fair bit of excitement about the "coming of age" aspect of going away to school.

High school sophomore Lydia Twombly-Hussey, a student at the Putney School, Putney, Vermont, and her father, Nat Hussey of Matinicus, share some thoughts on getting through such a big change. I asked Nat whether there was some sort of moment of realization— a wake-up call, as it were—about Lydia leaving for high school.

I didn't get the wake-up call until the day before she was leaving, actually. It didn't really register. We did all the applications and went through the process and I was never bothered by it, and then I just cried like a baby all day when she was getting ready to leave. For a few days after that I was flattened by it, and then I was happy again, because [and here he turns to Lydia] I thought you were in a really cool place. I actually think that the private school is a good thing—it gives the kids one step up—but the wake-up call for me wasn't until it was way too late.

I asked what the family had considered, together and separately, as realistic options for high school.

Aside from other boarding schools, not really. We didn't talk about moving off, we didn't talk about setting her up in Rockland or on Vinalhaven with another family.

We discussed how some families have certain options and other families have different ones.

For somebody who has twenty-seven cousins on Vinalhaven, it might just seem logical to go there. If we lived on an island that had a one-hour ferry, or really anything daily, we might have done that, but we didn't really have any options except boarding.

Lydia explained, "Mom looked at the boarding schools on the Internet that she thought would be good for me. Mostly we looked at small schools that had strong arts programs."

The application process is very similar to applying for college. The student has to take a standardized exam (the SSAT), which means registering for the exam and getting to the mainland when it is offered at a larger school somewhere. Application forms ask for details on all your sports, academic awards, hobbies, community service involvement, arts activities, memberships, and employment; there are several essays to write, letters of recommendation to get, and official transcripts to be requested from the middle school. Little of the island eighth-grader's world is represented in these questions, and some of these requested documents take some creativity to construct. Island students often write their application essays about some reality of island living, from going sternman on a lobster boat to fighting a forest fire to the one-room school experience itself. "We don't call community service 'community service,'" Lydia pointed out. "It's just doing stuff," loading the recycling truck or whatever. "The applications asked for things and I'd say, "Well, we don't have that, but we have this instead. . . .""

I asked about letters of recommendation, remembering that my son had his written by the air-service pilots, the *Sunbeam* minister, and a local artist who did some workshops with the kids.

"All written by the school teacher," Lydia said. "They wanted my English teacher and math teacher and science teacher and one arts person. I only had one teacher, so she wrote all of them."

Nat volunteered some thoughts about a parent's natural worry over his child's safety away at school:

Lydia's temperament wasn't such that I was worried about her going wild, flying off the handle, being out of control. There were rough patches with learning to communicate, learning to work with others who were in loco parentis for us—learning to delegate supervision, checking in—instead of two people, it's now lots of people who have some oversight concern for her welfare. Also, to let go of some things—your daily management of children is not the same when they are three states away.

It's really special now when I see out of the corner of my eye that extra bedroom door open or her light on. I like it when she comes home.

I asked Lydia if Putney was what she imagined high school would be like.

> The whole business of being independent of the family structure wasn't difficult for me. Navigating the social structure of boarding school was a lot more difficult. I was in school on Matinicus with a bunch of small children. Living in a building with a whole bunch of teenage girls—I hadn't been around many teenage girls before. They were always having this drama and stuff. My first roommate was all about personal drama. I said, "I don't know how to handle your big emotional thing that's going on." Some of them thought I was weird. That takes care of itself.
>
> Putney has a program where we all work at jobs. That kind of thing was easier for me—the outdoor jobs, the kitchen jobs— were a lot easier for me than for a lot of the other kids. They didn't know how to help out.
>
> I had a lot of expectations about what things would be like, and a couple of weeks in, I realized I had no idea what I should have expected, what it would be like.
>
> I was really into visual arts before I went to Putney, and now I'm really into performing arts. I'm doing a lot of music, I'm in the theater program, in the musical, I'm taking some dance classes— I'd never thought I was going to like dance! I'm still awkward and gawky, but I like it. Fencing, too!

We talked about keeping the tie to home. Lydia admitted, "Communication is not always the easiest. A lot of the time when I'm online, my parents are not online. We have very different schedules. I have classes all day, extracurriculars, rehearsals. Usually the time I have to talk to people is 9:00, 9:30 P.M., and they've all gone to bed." (Lydia has two young siblings and Nat fishes, necessitating rising early.) Nat adds, "Skype is great."

I asked about the distance from home, and whether that was an issue when choosing a school. Lydia said, "It was a concern for my parents. I honestly didn't really think about the distance that much, and I still don't, but I know that for my parents it was far away. It is far away, I guess. Usually, one of my grandparents comes down and gets me [for vacations] or I sometimes get rides with a kid who lives in the same town as my grandparents."

Nat adds, "You become more 'professional' about all these logistics things as you go. You get a routine down. We have a kind of menu of options. When we first moved to Matinicus, I used to get incredibly stressed out just getting to town for groceries, getting them to the plane, all that. Then add to that going to Vermont. I hate that drive. You get used to it. [He indicates curving, winding back roads with his finger.] You drive about three road miles for every mile closer to your destination."

Nat speaks reassuringly, I suspect, as much to himself as to us: "Just do it, stay in touch, make contact when you can, and have some trust. You can imagine all kinds of horrible things happening, and they can, but usually they don't. You have to have some faith in the world and faith in the child and faith in the people at the school. It was sad when her room was empty, when her bedroom door was closed."

Lydia smiles and adds, "I was too busy being nervous to be home-sick! This year I felt very much at home. Last year—I didn't really have trouble with being away from home, but everything was a new experience. I was pretty timid."

Nat says, "It's very hard to let your first-born go. It's hard to feel like you are doing your parental duties when problems come up—and they do come up. It's hard to feel like you're being a responsible parent by having other people, who have very fragmented attention, deal with those problems. You feel some guilt for not being right there when there are problems, and frustration about trying to deal with everything through various offices and on cell phones. . . ."

I asked Lydia if she felt adequately supported at school.

"I didn't feel like I needed that much support. I was very independent. I didn't really feel like I needed somebody there all the time, making sure I was doing all right. I felt like I was doing all right on my own."

Two Gould Academy Graduates Reminisce
Ski Patrol changed my life!

Matinicus native Eric Murray remembers:

> We toured a bunch of schools. The theater program at Gould stuck out, because I thought I wanted to be involved in either tech or acting. The proximity of Sunday River was a draw for me; I

wasn't into skiing or snowboarding yet, but I wanted to be. Ultimately, I went with Gould just because it felt good. We toured around the McLaughlin Science Center at Gould and it was brand-new, a beautiful facility. It just felt comfortable.

There were plenty of other kids there from out in the sticks. Maybe I was a little more emotionally and philosophically developed than some of them. I liked arguing and I liked thinking and I liked talking about politics and religion and stuff like that; I thrived on [verbal] conflict. Was I from a different lifestyle? Not really. There were other kids from really small communities. Kids from Isle au Haut came to Gould, kids from little tiny towns out in the woods—one of my friends was from Mason Township, which has about fourteen people in it. There were people from big communities, too; my friend Rachel came from Seoul, Korea. There were kids from New York. There were kids from tiny villages in the Middle East. The salutatorian, or the kid we invited to speak my year at graduation, a kid named Sikander, was from the middle of Afghanistan.

While I was there, I felt like I was benefiting from knowing these kids from various places. I think I understood the thinking of Muslims more than a lot of kids do, I got to interact with kids from Korea and Japan and China and other Asian countries; we had exchange students from Germany and from a couple of places in Eastern Europe There was a lot more of a global viewpoint than there probably would be at a regular public school in Maine just because there were so many kids from different places. Talking to them is better than reading books about those places. My roommates were from all over this country, and we had a group of friends from all over the map.

Transitioning to a school with 260 kids in it (even if that seems small) was a big change, so a little bit of regimentation probably helped. As far as the sports go, I didn't really like the fact that I was required to do a competitive sport, but by the end of my freshman year I had gotten into mountain biking, which I enjoyed. Sophomore year was my peak—I did really well with it, I was going to race varsity the next year, but I lost interest in the competing. The group of people changed and it wasn't as much fun. I went over to doing theater tech full time, which I loved. The requirement that you do an extracurricular—that is beneficial. You might not realize it at the time, but if I hadn't been told to do something, I might not have gotten into some of these things that I found I enjoyed. A little bit of regimented, scheduled time is a good thing. I needed a little bit of structure.

Part of what I liked about Gould is that it's beautiful here all year 'round. Bethel doesn't have a mud season. Looking out here, it's like, wow, you could be in Scotland some of the time. It's a beautiful place, one of the most beautiful places I've ever been.

I missed the ocean sometimes. For the first few days, I noticed not hearing waves. We're in the middle of the mountains. It wouldn't have been the same thing if I'd moved to the Midwest in a cornfield, or to a big city, though; this was a comfortable transition, kind of from one wilderness to another. It was good because I knew I loved both places. I also missed swimming, but we had the polar bear club for that—idiots who liked to get up early and jump in freezing-cold water, I guess. As soon as the ice melted off Songo Pond, we'd head on down there at six o'clock in the morning and jump in, and then get back on the bus and go have breakfast. It was a good time. It was a bonding experience—people who under normal circumstances wouldn't spend much time together. The geek squad would go socialize with the girly-girl types, there were faculty brats there, all kinds of people. Freezing-cold water makes everybody friends, I guess. You'd look at some kid you thought was an annoying jerk and say, "Well at least I know he's hard-core enough to go and jump in the freezing water with me." It was a great time.

When I was a freshman, the majority of my closest friends were seniors, actually. It's how I got into snowboarding. One of these guys was a jacketed [certified] ski patroller. He taught me to ride the way one of his older friends had taught him to snowboard. He told me I was supposed to do the same thing, teach somebody how to snowboard. I did. Having expert skiers around wasn't a bad thing because they were experts who were willing to take the time to help. There were guys—patrollers—who would check up on me. Our OEC [Outdoor Emergency Care] instructor was a wonderful human being; she taught me to snowboard, and her husband, who is about seven feet tall and rides a snowboard more gracefully than I've ever seen anybody do, would take me down the harder trails. I learned to snowboard by following people who were really skilled. There were a lot of people there who were great. I had already had some experience with the medical side [first responders], so it was "Go out and learn to snowboard." By the end of my sophomore year, I could tear all over the mountain like everybody else could.

One thing about Gould was there was a distinct lack of "Let's hassle the freshmen." I remember one guy had had that attitude, but most of the seniors were really nice guys. There was no unwritten rule that you only hang out with people in your own grade. I happened to get along with the computer science geeks, the tech crew guys. Some of the seniors sort of protected the freshmen; there were a few sophomores who liked to mess with the freshmen. It was a little sad when some of the seniors from my first year graduated. We all got along great.

Vicki MacDonald from Isle au Haut was a couple of years younger than Eric, also attended Gould, and also joined the Ski Patrol. She was born on Isle au Haut and went through nine years of elementary school there.

My dad is a fisherman in the summertime, and in the winter, snowplow man, oil delivery man, meter reader—all kinds of jobs. For a long time my mother was on multiple things like school board, town boards, and she worked at the store. When my sister and I were around nine or ten, my dad couldn't afford to hire a sternman, so he had to go out to haul traps on his own a lot. My mom didn't like that. He wouldn't let me go out on the boat with him until I was ten years old, although I painted the buoys and stuff like that. Once I turned ten, my sister and I went sternman every summer. We didn't have a choice! [She laughs.] My sister would go out one day and I'd go the next.

I was the only one in my eighth-grade class. I got lucky when I came to Gould because Eric was already here and so was another girl from Isle au Haut. My sister went to an all-girls school in Massachusetts [Miss Hall's]. I didn't want to go to an all-girls school.

When I first got here, even though it is a boarding school, a lot of people had somehow met each other before. The ski racers knew each other, and there were a lot of local kids that year—faculty kids, day students—that doesn't happen every year, it just happened to be that way. So I didn't make a lot of freshman friends, but lots of upperclassmen friends instead. I was fine with that.

On Isle au Haut the eighth-graders hung around all the time with the first- and second-graders. I definitely felt that growing up on an island was a big reason why I was comfortable hanging out with juniors and seniors. The freshmen my year sort of "fit in" together, and I didn't feel I was like them. A lot of them also seemed to be pretty well off, money-wise. Some of the older kids I hung around with were easier to make friends with.

Growing up, we knew just about everybody, and even someone you didn't know—like a summer person—you'd smile and say hi and keep doing whatever you were doing. I was feeling very small that first day at high school with so many new people. But a friend grabbed my plate and lugged it over to her table where she was sitting with Eric and this big gang of guys. That's kind of a Gould thing: you see a lonely freshman and you snag them and give them someone to hang out with. I wasn't really homesick; I was too busy to be homesick.

I am really happy that I went to boarding school. I wanted to go away. Going to boarding school makes you appreciate your parents so much more because they're not there all the time. The things you took for granted, you start to realize. I never realized how good a cook my mother is until I went to boarding school—and Gould has really good food! The food here is amazing but it isn't my mom's. Things like that.

I wasn't used to having homework every day. When I was in school on the island, if we didn't finish something, that was homework for the day. In high school they assigned additional stuff and scheduled two hours for homework time every night. Of course, the teachers gave you about six hours of homework!

Soccer! Every kid in America knows how to play soccer—except island kids! The soccer on Isle au Haut was a crazy mix of rugby, football, and traditional soccer. The only rule was you had to kick it with your foot. Playing soccer in high school, I had a few problems at first; I'd never had a set position on the island. At Gould they put me on defense and I had no idea where I was supposed to be. You can't just run around and take people out! [She smiles.] The coach had some sudden insight and asked me, "Have you ever thought about playing goalie?" She said, "You're a freshman, you're coachable, and you're not afraid of anything." I must have missed the gene for self-preservation. If I'm supposed to think "That's going to hurt me," I don't. I'm not afraid to get in front of some player's foot. I scream like a banshee. I love being a goalie. A couple of people told me I was playing better than these other girls who were bigger and who'd had all this previous training playing sports as kids. I remember one game at Kent's Hill, I stood out there in a snowstorm in my goalie uniform for an hour and a half. Another game, same school, I stopped forty shots in the first half.

I'm glad I grew up they way I did, running around, without organized sports and the competitive attitude that the parents can get. Some kids— they're good, they know it, and they have an attitude about it. We'd play kickball, tag, a lot of running around, sardines, hide and seek, sledding, "quote-unquote snowboarding" on the five-foot hill behind the school. You'd see the island kids outside on bikes all the time.

I have had experiences I would never have had if I hadn't come to Gould. Snowboarding was *not* an option growing up. Even here I didn't think it was going to be an option until I was told that in Ski Patrol training the pass is free! I'd always wanted to snowboard, for years, before I came here. [Gould Academy is a few minutes' shuttle-bus ride from the Sunday River ski area.]

Ski Patrol changed my life! I've gotten such a confidence in myself that I didn't used to have. Earlier this year a couple of people got hurt, and they were in the ski center. One of them was a young guy, sort of cute, and I might have been shy around him in the past, but when I walked in there, I put my hand on his chin and said, "Don't move your head!" After I helped put him in the ambulance, I realized, "Wow, I have changed a lot!"

The Gould Academy Ski Patrol training program is a big deal, and the only one like it in the country. Being an emergency responder is probably the most unchildish thing a teenager can do.

It is as if you consciously elect to outgrow being squeamish, waiting for somebody else to tell you what to do, being peer-pressured, being stopped by your nerves, being irresponsible and reckless— it's kind of like saying out loud to yourself and all your friends and neighbors, "I choose to outgrow those things." I've matured a lot. That's what I've heard from my mother.

Doug Alford, who teaches Spanish, directs the spring musical, and helps lead Gould Academy's unique ski-patrol training program, teaching committed teenagers to become certified emergency responders on the ski slope, observes "The one thing I have noticed across the board is that island students speak their mind. They're not afraid to speak up. I think that comes from not growing up separated from the adults in their community."

PILOTS, RANCHERS, MINERS,
AND LOGGERS

In 2011 I initiated some correspondence with a few teachers in western states—Alaska, Colorado, Montana, and North Dakota—who worked in schools which are similar in many ways to our Maine island schools: a small group of students, relative isolation, weather-related travel concerns, and the ever-present threat of shrinking down to a population of zero. The students from Matinicus began corresponding with some of their western counterparts as well. Here, a few of the teachers describe their schools, their workday, and their students.

Cold Bay, Alaska
We also have to contend with brown bears.
Teacher Stephanie DeVault writes from Cold Bay, Alaska, where a two-room, K–12 school serves a community built around an air station:

> Well, it sounds like there are many similarities and a few differences [from the Maine islands]. We are far further from civilization (we call it the "real world" around here because we actually are on the mainland), about 800 miles from Anchorage. However, we get far more air traffic because of our runway. We serve as the hub for other communities in the area. Our one air carrier flies from Anchorage with a Saab 340, which seats roughly thirty people. From here, people hop to nearby villages in six-to-eight-seaters. Because of our location between Anchorage and Asia, we also get many jets stopping here for fuel. We've had the Antonov, the second largest jet in the world, on the ground a number of times, along with any number of other cargo carriers. And we also serve as a Coast Guard station during the king and opilio crab fishery in the Bering Sea, which you might have seen on *The Deadliest Catch*. Oh, and in the summer we move between 1 and 2 million pounds of red salmon across our dock from a fishing tender to the runway to be flown to markets in the lower forty-eight

and Asia. So because of those things, we have a clinic here that is staffed with a mid-level practitioner. Most of the communities in the area that are as small as Cold Bay only have a certified health aide—a position that, to my knowledge, only exists in rural Alaska. But because we serve as the medivac site for much of the fishing fleet and the surrounding communities (including one with a population of about 700), we nearly always have a nurse practitioner or physician's assistant on hand.

As for other transportation, we get a ferry that comes twice a month from April through October. It can bring vehicles as well as passengers, and is truly exciting because it has a restaurant aboard. As fate would have it, it arrives here on Friday right around lunchtime, so the whole community usually turns out for Ferry Friday to eat the one restaurant meal we get. We also have a freight boat that docks here roughly every other week bringing everything from groceries to large appliances. The downside of the freight boat is that, while it departs Seattle on schedule, every-thing after that is up to the weather and the time it takes them to offload at each community. So getting up at 3:00 A.M. to get gro-ceries is a pretty common occurrence.

Our year-round population is a bit more stable, since most of the folks here work for the government. The state DOT main-tains the runway and the roads in town. The FAA has two full-time employees and many itinerants who do air traffic control and maintain the lights and communication equipment for the airport. We also have a National Weather Service station and a National Wildlife Refuge, the latter of which employs an increasing num-ber of people. We do have a crowd that comes in the summertime as hunting and fishing guides. We have some of the best water-fowl-hunting in the world in the fall, and the largest bears in Alaska—so both bring quite a few rich folks here to live the Alaskan dream.

As for the school, we're actually pretty spoiled. It was built in the 1980s when the population was quite a bit larger in Cold Bay. We have three HUGE classrooms, a three-quarters-size gym, a kitchen, and a library. We've been here for six years and our largest group in school was thirteen, and now we're down to our smallest ever at eight. In order for the state to fully fund a school, it has to have ten students, so that is always our goal in the fall. It appears as though next year might be the first that we don't make it.

We have all of the technological advantages available today—very fast Internet, laptop and desktop computers, and brand-new iPads. We also have videoconferencing services throughout the district, so our in-service training, board meetings, and even some classes are done through the TV.

Right now in my class, I have students in grades 1–5. My husband (who teaches the high-schoolers—which recently dropped to just one kid!) takes some of the students for math, and I have an aide who happens to be a certified teacher from South Carolina (her husband moved here with the Weather Service). So our teacher/student ratio is pretty amazing. Most of our kids are working above grade level, because it's so easy to do here. For instance, my second-grade math students (actually one second-grader and one first-grader) are about to finish up the second-grade math program (we use Saxon), so we'll just pull out the third-grade materials and keep right on cruising. I love the small-school model, and while it can be a tremendous amount of work, I don't think I'd ever want my kids in a single-graded classroom again.

We don't do a lot with other schools, and if the weather permits we try to get outside as much as possible. (Sounds like our weather is a lot like yours!) During the spring and fall we also have to contend with the brown bears, so any field trips outside the community get a little dicey and require a firearm. Luckily everyone carries a firearm here, so it's not a big deal, though we still obviously don't allow them on school property.

Maybell, Colorado
A three-day weekend to recuperate.

Rhonda Counts Willingham recently taught at the school in Maybell, Colorado, where long commutes and winter weather dictate the school schedule:

My students travel up to sixty miles each way for their trip to school. This is about a one-hour trip in good weather conditions, obviously longer in bad weather. There are days when the weather is bad and the trip just doesn't happen. We can e-mail parts or all of lessons to parents or make it up when they are back at school. We just remember to be flexible, and the parents are so key in that effort. [There's that word *flexible* again, so common in discussion of teaching on the islands!]

We have a bus that is actually a minivan to pick up the students each morning. Our driver meets the parents of our Brown's Park students and brings them to school. The students' ride to and from school takes somewhere between two and three hours each day, depending on the weather, the wildlife, etc. These four students are really resilient kids. Three of them live on the Brown's Park Wildlife Refuge which is a very beautiful place in a very western way. Brown's Park was the hideout of the Hole in the Wall gang, notorious outlaws and criminals—now there's something to be proud of!

Three of the students' fathers work at the Refuge, while the fourth student lives on Sombrero Horse Ranch, which is a huge ranch that supplies horses across Colorado. Her mom meets the bus on horseback occasionally if she is out working in that direction. These are great kids, but honestly, the length of their commute takes its toll on them. We have school four days a week most weeks, which gives them a three-day weekend to recuperate.

Each year we have at least a week or two when the temperatures are -30° to -50° F. This year [2010-2011] seemed especially brutal, and we had a few days when the students just stayed home if they had very far to travel. We have several feet of snow pretty much all winter; this doesn't usually upset our routine. If the wind blows or if the temps drop to extremes, then we have issues. We never have official snow days; only once in my fifty years do I remember that happening. I just encourage parents to please use their judgment, and mostly this works pretty well. Our other students ride the bus various distances. Most live in the next town, Sunbeam, Colorado, which is not really a town at all. I suppose at one point in time it was, many years ago.

I am a local; my family has been in this area for over a hundred years. I think this has been key to my acceptance and success in the school. I knew many of the community members before I started this job, and I felt a connection with them. I worked for the school district teaching high school and was offered this position because they thought I would be a good fit for the school. I felt like I was welcomed into the community before I started the job, and I was excited about that. I had taught ninth-grade science, with over a hundred students daily through my door, and repeated the same lesson all day long. What a switch to teach fourteen students in five different grades! I do remember wondering if I had lost my mind. What I was thinking?

We actually have good technology; we have six desktops and four laptops with Internet access. The struggle is that we use satellite Internet, which is slower than I would like. If the weather is bad, we have no reception. But it is still functional and gives us a connection to the cyber world. We use several Internet-based programs, including a math and a literacy program.

The best thing about my job is that I do have autonomy to a point. Of course we work within the constraints of state and district standards, but I have a little more flexibility in how that is accomplished. I love the fact that I am able to teach a student at the level that is most appropriate. I have two students who basically work a year ahead of their grade. I also have a high number of special-ed kids, which makes a challenge. My principal is very supportive of me, and that is helpful. We work with the special-ed teacher to meet the needs of those students. Everything we do is small-group and intervention.

I actually commute sixty miles daily, so my day starts early. I have one regular ed paraprofessional [same as ed tech or aide] and one special-ed para, so I do have help at school. We also have a woman who is our "lunch lady" and our janitor. The first two years I taught at the school, we had minimal janitorial and no hot lunch services. The third year we had increased services that made my life easier. I didn't mind the extra duties; I actually had great kids that were a great help.

We have had members of the Rotary Club reading to us and with us this year. They drive thirty miles each way to do this for us. One of the men who comes to read is actually older and went to a one-room school in Brown's Park. Many of the area locals attended one-room schools because the county is so huge (my parents and their siblings included).

We are always up in the air as to whether or not we will have children next year, or any year after. The Maybell community has changed from being a very ranch-oriented community to a community that has a very mobile population. While we have some longtime families, we have had an increasing number of children that have moved in and out of the community, which gives us a somewhat unstable group. We are looking at two kindergartners for next year and will be losing one fifth-grader, a first-grader, and a second-grader. This will bring our class size down to twelve, and the district has to have eleven students to make expenses. There is a big bus that could potentially take the students to the elementary school in Craig, but the trip would be close to two hours each way for our Brown's Park students. The school board doesn't want to close the school, partly because of the backlash it would create, but I also know that Colorado has severely cut the education budget, and the district is in a financial bind.

The most overwhelming part of my day is the concern I have for my students if they are not working at the level they should be. I lose sleep trying to sort out how I can help them be more successful.

Decker, Montana
The school is on a dirt road, nestled in the foothills.

"My name is Creighton Teter and I am the teacher at Spring Creek School, Decker, Montana," begins another letter. Spring Creek and Matinicus have become pen pals, and seem to have as much in common as not:

Spring Creek School is located thirty-five miles northeast of Sheridan, Wyoming. All that Decker, Montana, is comprised of is a post office. The school sits next to Tongue River Reservoir. I have nine students this year [2010-2011] in seven grade levels: two in kindergarten, two in first, and one each in second, third, fourth, sixth, and seventh grades. I have two full-time instructional aides who work with me, and one is also the bus driver. My dog, Libby, a Chocolate Lab/Chesapeake Bay Retriever cross, is at school with us every day.

The main industries around the area are coal mining and ranching. The Decker Coal and Spring Creek Coal mines are close by. The school is on a dirt road, nestled in the foothills.

We have been really busy lately. We just had a reporter come from the *L.A. Times* to see the school and interview me and the kids. We have been getting a lot of publicity in April in the newspapers. It is pretty crazy!" [Spring Creek was also mentioned in a *Wall Street Journal* article in 2011.]

I am able to go home from school every day. I live in a cabin in the hills about five miles from the school. I take papers and student work home to grade and correct. I am "on call," though, all the time for the school. I do get the occasional phone call at night or in the mornings from a parent concerning a student or field trip or something going on with the school.

My superintendent is seventy-five miles away in Hardin, Montana, and if I have anything major come up, I can e-mail him or call him. However, we are pretty much on our own out here. I love it! I have a good rapport with the community. They are friendly and treat me well. Sheridan, Wyoming, is our nearest city, thirty-five miles away. Many people drive 125 miles to Billings, Montana, to stock up at Costco or Sam's Club once a month or every couple of months. Billings has about 120,000 people.

Malea is in first grade: She lives about forty miles from the school. (We have a little school bus that picks up all the kids and drop them off.) She lives on the Cheyenne reservation. She likes to color and to ride horses.

Caden is in kindergarten: He lives down the road about fourteen miles on a cattle ranch where his family has lived for many years. His dad went to our school while he was growing up. Caden is on a wrestling team during the winter and goes to many rodeos during the summer.

Katelyn is in sixth grade and writes: "I like to play outside and play catch with a football. I also like to read, draw pictures, and ride my horse."

Chase is in fourth grade: He likes to fish in the mountains, and he helps his grandpa stack hay in the summer. He likes to take care of his 4-H pig.

Chase's brother Calder is in third grade: He says, "I like to feed my 4-H pig, shoot my gun at cans and targets, play football, and help my family work on the ranch."

Ashton is in second grade. (Katelyn and Ashton are brother

and sister.) He likes to play with his dogs outside, and go fishing.

J.D. is in seventh grade: He likes fishing, hunting, camping, and riding his dirt bike.

The school is on a gravel road about two miles long. It is maintained by the county. It can get pretty muddy in the springtime. We have telephone, power, and Internet. The highway to town is in good condition; you can drive 65–70 mph, no problem. We had four snow days this year. It can snow and blow around here!

After eighth grade at Spring Creek School, the kids tend to go to Sheridan High School or Big Horn or Tongue River High School. Big Horn and Tongue River are smaller areas, and those schools have about 150 students. The Sheridan High School student population is 800–900.

I will tell you a bit about the parents and the community. We all feel really positive about the future of our school. We have a new coal mine that is supposed to open soon. We had two new students this year and two new ones coming next year. Most of the people who live in this area are long-term people either in ranching or mining. Parents always stay very active in our school and are on top of everything going on, which helps us a lot.

Third-grader Calder describes Thanksgiving at Spring Creek: "At school we celebrate Thanksgiving together. My teacher fried a turkey for us to eat. I brought pickles, rolls, stuffing, mashed potatoes, and sweet potatoes. Other students brought corn, stuffing, green-bean casserole, pecan pie, and pumpkin pie. After we ate we took a hike down to the lake and back to the school, about 2.5 miles. We read about the first Thanksgiving, and how it lasted three days! We had leftovers the next day so I didn't have to pack a lunch."

We have a little yellow bus that heads up the road every morning about 6:40 A.M. Our last pickup is about thirty-eight miles up the road, and then it turns around and comes back to the school, another thirty-eight miles. We usually let the students walk up the dirt road a little ways in the morning on their way to school to get a little exercise. We get the school day started about 8:30 by saying the Pledge. The younger students do the calendar to help them work on the months, days of the week, and the year, and also important holidays. After we make a few daily announcements we move on to "mad minute." The kids all love this. We give them thirty or forty math problems in addition, subtraction, multiplication, or division, and they see how many they can get done correctly in less than four minutes. After that, they all have a few daily worksheets for math and language arts to work on independently at their desks while we start working with each grade level on the regular classes, which are math, spelling, geography, and reading. We try to find a project for each student to do along with the story they are reading. We try to alternate science and social studies in the afternoon every other week. We have a little snack about 10:00 A.M. and then recess about noon, with lunch afterward. We hold them responsible for completing their daily independent work before recess. About 3:15 each of the students has a job to do to help keep the school clean. They all pitch in and get their jobs completed, then get on the little bus and head back up the road, some riding the thirty-eight miles to the last drop-off. The bus comes back to school till the next morning.

We are really lucky here because we have two aides who also teach. That helps us get everything covered in a day. If we weren't lucky enough to have that much help, it would get a little crazy.

Bismarck, North Dakota
We have students who ride their mules or horses to school.
Rachel Steffen, a teacher in the one-room Manning School, located about twelve miles southeast of Bismarck North Dakota, notes:
Our school is a public K–8 school system. This year I have nine students. I am considered the principal/teacher, music teacher, and PE teacher. I also assist with lunches, and am the janitor at the end of the day.

We have students who ride their mules or horses to school when the weather is nice.

Mandan, North Dakota
There are fewer and fewer of us.
Sherilyn Johnson, principal/teacher at Sweet Briar School, Mandan, North Dakota, tells us:
The very nature of a one-room country school with one teacher, one aide, and twelve bright-eyed, full-of-energy K–8 students is

BUSY. I am working with children the entire day. Prep time? Spell that for me! That is what evenings and weekends are for!

I have developed a "Student Assignment Tracker." It's in a small spreadsheet format about 4 x 6 inches with all times and subjects listed. Each student's name and grade are at the top. Every assignment for the day is on the tracker. Every morning, I tape each individual tracker on each desk. After the morning opener (Pledge, calendar, announcements, and "Ask Me" questions), the students settle into their math assignments. My aide and I make the rounds from grade to grade explaining the main topic and giving examples until each student feels comfortable with his or her assignment. They work independently, asking questions when needed. If I'm working with another grade level, they'll ask an older student to help. Each grade level works at its own level for math, reading, language arts, etc. Some projects are "all-school" projects.

They are wonderful, bright, cheerful, responsible (most of the time!), and very helpful. They are paired up with "buddies" for "all-school" projects like music, art, PE, some science, math, health, and language arts projects. The "older kids" (third through eighth grade, six of them) are partnered with the "younger kids" (kindergarten and first grade, six of them). At the end of each day, they all get with their partners and do their JOBS: flag, mail, clean the microwaves (we have no hot lunch program).

In kindergarten and first grade, they take home a leveled book every night for "Backpack Reading," which they read to their parents and bring back the next day. In the morning, while I'm helping the older kids with math, they pair up with their Book Buddies and take turns reading their books to each other and ask "Great Questions" about the setting and the characters. All of my kindergartners and first-graders love to read and are very good readers. (*Goosebumps!*)

There are fewer and fewer of us in North Dakota, as we are slowly losing enrollment and consolidating with larger districts. It's very sad, and I get emotional to think that this "rich culture" and very wholesome way of life and teaching may one day be absorbed by the big schools. I am very thankful that "my children" have the opportunity to build a solid educational foundation, to develop positive leadership skills, and that when they leave Sweet Briar School they will know who they are and where they have come from with confidence and pride!

The Last Two Inland One-Room Schools in Maine Close
Watch for moose!

In the spring of 2009, I visited the last two one-room schools still open on the mainland in Maine. The town of Shirley, about eight miles south of Greenville, was listed in the *Maine Atlas and Gazetteer* a few years ago as having a population of 183. Rockwood (or "Rockwood Strip"), halfway up the west side of Moosehead Lake, doesn't even have a population, according to the same reference. If you look at a map, you'll notice that no cities are nearby. (Greenville, the largest town in the area at the south end of forty-mile-long Moosehead Lake, has a population of roughly 1,600.) Bangor, with the nearest shopping mall, is well over an hour to the southeast. In this part of Maine, it is quite common to see the moose for which so much in the area is named; particularly in the spring, they are often in the roads and drivers must be cautious. There are a few incorporated towns in the area, but if you look at a map, you will find most of the area divided into plantations, townships, and big sections of the state of Maine designated as "unorganized territories." Large sections of northern Maine geography are designated not with city or town names but with numerical grids and archaic boundary references. For example, one piece of woods appears on the map as "Township 7 Range 9 North of Waldo Patent."

Historically, most of this part of Maine was paper-company land, millions of acres of forest harvested by full-time loggers for the spruce and fir pulp that makes America's newsprint, office paper, and toilet tissue. Scott Paper Company, Great Northern, and a few others ran huge paper mills and employed thousands of men with chainsaws and skidders. Most of this "north woods" is technically private property, but Mainers for generations have been permitted access to it for their annual deer-hunting trip, a vacation on a snow machine speeding from one small-town restaurant to the next, or a few spring weekends spent fishing in hard-to-access sections of rivers or the many small streams, lakes, and ponds. Now, the paper mills are closed, there are far fewer jobs in the woods, and the small amount of back-country tourism that has sprung up, with a few related construction jobs, cannot hope to take the place of those lucrative paper-company jobs. Families have been leaving the Moosehead Lake region for years.

I felt like I was driving the only minivan in Piscataquis County as I headed for Shirley and Rockwood. For those visits I based, myself in Greenville, on the south end of Moosehead Lake. It had been a couple of decades since I'd visited anybody in Greenville (in those days I owned a perfectly respectable pickup truck, too), and things had changed a little. There was less evidence of a town built around the men who cut wood, and more efforts toward tourism. Still, in April, between seasons, there was darned little there for an out-of-towner. I was noticeably, conspicuously, "not from around there," me and my minivan.

Such is the oral historian's work.

On that trip I saw five moose and a complete rainbow over the lake; I also saw a young man crossing the street in Dover-Foxcroft carrying a very large snake. I saw that the police department in Greenville has a pickup truck. Driving north on Maine Route 15, when you come over that hill and suddenly see Moosehead Lake, it takes your breath away.

As someone from away with no idea where to eat, sleep, or get information, I was delighted to find K.J.'s Variety in Greenville for coffee and sandwiches. It appeared to be one of those little neighborhood places with a table where the regulars hang around, where they all stop talking and look up at any new face coming through the door, ready to roll their eyes at the usual dumb questions or the strange accent or the request for a soy caramel macchiato or something equally unlikely.

The woman behind the counter was friendly, and I was admittedly relieved. We chatted a little the first time I ventured in for a cup of coffee, and I told her about my interest in the one-room schools. She told me, "There's nothing here for the youth."

Rockwood

Bill Folsom was the teaching principal of the Rockwood School in 2009, the last year the school was open. A native of the northern Maine woods, he worked from 1972-1986 as a teacher and teaching principal in School Administrative District 25 (the Sherman Station area, another sparsely populated expanse of Maine woods). Then, he says, "They added another school for me to supervise." Folsom had recently been in a snowmobile accident and decided it was "too much." He married and took a job in Rockwood in 1986 as an ed tech at the River School, where his wife and his father-in-law had been students. According to the *Bangor Daily News,* he left to further his education and to work as a superintendent for the Greenville and Ashland districts, and then returned to Rockwood to teach in his current position in 1991 when this new Rockwood School opened with ten students. He has evidently held just about every job one can have within a school district in this area, from aide to superintendent. "I used to drive the bus, but with the new regulation, you have to be a superperson to have a bus-driver's license" (he grins at the bus driver who walks through his office at that moment). The Rockwood School building is lovely, modern, and expansive with every amenity—much like the school on Swan's Island.

Rockwood, like many small towns, used to have at least two oneroom schools, the River School and the Village School, and so in a sense has already experienced consolidation. With just three students, it would seem logical to many that the cost is awfully high to operate the school, but consider that with the closing of the Rockwood School at least one of the students will have to travel roughly forty miles each way from her home to Greenville, partly on primitive dirt roads, in a part of the country where winters are long and severe.

Folsom's little cluster of students—all young girls—are building birdhouses. This project requires that they do the math to figure out the measurements and the angles, and that they divide fractions. Mr. Folsom reminds them to "invert and multiply." They use and discuss the old tools he has brought in, such as a large bit-brace hand drill, and they wear their safety goggles. He teaches the girls how to be careful and prevent the pieces of pine from splitting.

Mrs. Sargent, the ed tech and cook, remains behind her desk for the most part. She finds a pair of pliers to tighten the bit brace. Folsom describes how several of his students are from families new to the area: one recently moved from New Jersey, another from Europe. The three children and couple of adults do seem almost lost in the large building, but it certainly looks as though the students lack for nothing. They work on computers, editing writing and looking up informa-

The Rockwood School, closed in 2009. Eva Murray

tion. There seems to be a surplus of equipment: supplies are piled up in the storage area, boxes full of school materials that came from the town of Benedicta when that small school closed not long ago.

In a *Bangor Daily News* article dated November 11, 2008 ("Rockwood school not viable economically"), teacher Bill Folsom observed, "I expected it, but that doesn't make it easy." One parent is quoted by the *BDN* saying, "Our child has blossomed. For us it has made it so much easier to belong to this community. Marta needed help with English and Folsom provided that help."

"For Jenny M— of Pittston Farm," the article continues, "the closing of the school will mean her granddaughter will have about a one-and-a-half-hour drive to the Greenville school. 'We hate to see the school come to a close, but we can understand, economically, with only two students it's pretty hard' (since that interview, a third student had joined the group)."

The newspaper article continues: "It used to be that the state would reimburse parents who have a lengthy commute to the bus stop, but the Legislature passed a law last session that forbid the state from continuing that, according to the Commissioner of Education. The Legislature felt that was the parents' responsibility."

Bill Folsom in the classroom, Rockwood, Maine. Folsom was Rockwood's last teacher. A native of the area, he had been a student, an educational technician, a teacher, a principal, and a superintendent in northern Maine woods towns. Eva Murray

Folsom tells me that parents are concerned about socialization issues. "The worry of parents is that the children are missing something. I have a piano in there [he points to another room within the school]. Marta uses it many mornings. She goes to Greenville for private piano lessons. Danielle and Nicole are going to Greenville after school tonight for soccer. I think they have the best of both worlds. That's a big commitment on the part of parents. Parents have good trust in me, and I have faith in them."

He has a sense of humor about the fact that he's been here seemingly forever. "These girls walk all over me. I don't want to be intimidating. I can give a stern look. They know by my tone of voice when enough is enough. I want them to leave here with a smile, and I want them to come back the next day with a smile—and with their homework done."

We talk about local pride, and whether these kids have a sense of belonging to this place. "Everybody likes to take pride in their area. My wife—she's from Rockwood! I'm not; I'm from across the lake! In the year 1990, when there was the census, I was across the lake ice fishing and I didn't come back before the first of April when they did the census, so I am listed as the only resident of Day's Academy Grant!"

There seem to be town line signs about every hundred feet all the way up the side of the lake from Greenville. Folsom tells me, "Marta lives in Sandbar Tract, Nicole lives in Rockwood Strip, and Danielle lives in Pittston Academy Grant. This school sits on the township line between Rockwood Township and Taunton & Raynham. 'Misery Gore' is exactly thirty miles long and probably 3,000 feet wide at the widest, but down here on Route 15, it's less than a hundred yards." He tells how "Pittston Farm" had telephone service before the towns of Rockwood and Greenville did, because of forest-fire watch service. Folsom's mother was the telephone operator.

As he describes his school days with the three girls, Folsom talks about a play they are doing, a humorous historical piece. "We can do it with three students. It's about the westward movement. They talked me into being the 'Delivery Girl.' I'm supposed to be delivering the Golden Spike and I end up delivering a bowling ball, and then some cookies. The play goes on about how President Thomas Jefferson was very impressed with the French, how he loved French toast [he laughs]."

Shirley

Until the early 1980s, Shirley was part of the Greenville school district. Kathryn Armstrong, whose husband, John Stolecki, was on the school board in Shirley at the time, tells the story of that town's secession from the district in order to save the one-room school:

My boys were born in 1975 and '77. It was a two-room school then, K–3 and 4–6. Greenville decided in the early 1980s sometime that they should close the Shirley school and the kids should be bused to Greenville. The citizenry of Shirley—about 100 to 150 people— did not want their kids to get stuck on the school bus all the way to Greenville every day, so they seceded from the school, lost lots of federal monies, and maintained the school themselves. The school board, people like my husband, did stuff like roof the school, they rewired the school, they took all that responsibility themselves. They involved anybody in town who was willing to participate. Because the school is sort of the heart of the community, people wanted to support the school and keep it open—they didn't want to see the school closed. The men in town did the work themselves. Charlie, who was the K–3 teacher, was also a Scout leader, so they had Cub Scouts there; they did the Pinewood Derby at school. Part of the school budget went to buying sleds for every kid in school. I think there were about twenty kids in school in the early 1980s. Every day at recess in the winter, they could all go sledding because everyone had his or her own sled at school.

I spent a day with Joyce Lessard, teacher of the K–5 Shirley Elementary School. That school year had begun with five students. At the time of my visit there were two: second- and third-graders Dean (age eight) and Ian (age nine). Ian and Dean were articulate, well-spoken boys, but that day they were noticeably dejected. Each was acutely aware of what had happened at the meeting the night before, and they weren't happy about it. Dean told a *Bangor Daily News* reporter who visited shortly after I did, "It's sad to see this school go because I really enjoyed it. Greenville was good, but here I did way better." Ian added, "I really like this place." The boys wore T-shirts on the last day of school sporting a picture of the Shirley school and reading: "The last student in grade 2" and "The last student in grade 3."

In a sad coincidence, my visit to the Shirley school fell the day after the town meeting was held where the vote had been to close the school. The referendum vote had been 60–30, in a town with 175 registered voters, following a 3–2 vote of the school board to close the school. The boys were quiet, reserved, and clearly not in agreement with the opinions of the adults around them. Still, few of us can fault a small community's following what seems "common sense."

Shirley Elementary was a traditional one-room schoolhouse; the inside was warm and welcoming and full of color. The hardwood floor and old-fashioned trim, the school bell, and the schoolhouse architecture reminded us how generations of local kids had learned their basics here, and now, in a few weeks, the last couple of Shirley Elementary students would leave for summer vacation and not come back. "They just love it here. They want to go to school here," says teacher Joyce Lessard. "Yes, they knew I was retiring, but that didn't faze them; they assumed somebody else would come in."

I asked her why the population of children had shrunk to the point where it wasn't possible to keep the school open. What had changed?

Shirley Elementary, closed in 2009 by a referendum of the town.
Eva Murray

Greenville had the logging industry, and for a while the construction industry was going very well. That's not happening now. Carpenters and electricians aren't getting the work. Everything seems to be at a standstill. After the initial homes and camps were built, everything stopped. We've had some stores close in town. There have been generations go through this school. Ian's mother went here. We've had families where the grandparents went to this school. This school has been here since 1835; there are a few old names in towns that go back several generations.

A month later, Joyce Lessard explained to a newspaper reporter that "There aren't any large families around anymore. A lot of people were renters, and they left. There are quite a few homeschoolers, but they tend to homeschool for religious purposes."

Changes in the economy, changes in the worldwide need for newsprint and other paper products, and rapid mechanization of the woodcutter's job are just a few of the factors that have turned many prosperous northern communities into mere shadows of their former selves. Now, fishing guides, innkeepers, owners of sporting camps, and the skeleton crew of usual small-town businesses get by on what

The Shirley school library. Some of Maine's smallest schools are (or were) more generously equipped than are many urban elementary schools.
Eva Murray

income a slowly growing tourism trade provides, but the days when the restaurants and bars were filled with woodsmen who had money in their pockets are gone. With the end of a reliable source of year-round employment went the reliable flow of school-aged children through Shirley Elementary. Joyce Lessard is not a native of the area. I asked what had brought her to Shirley.

I started in a one-room schoolhouse; I went to three of them in East Pittston before I went to West Gardiner High School [in south-central Maine]. My husband was working on our camp up here at First Roach Pond, which was going to become our retirement home, but turned into our home. I was in Gardiner still teaching, and came up every weekend. This job opened up and I thought, "I can do this for three years." I started my education this way and now I'm ending my education this way! I always thought that would be fun to do. It isn't the highest paying three years of my teaching career, but I enjoy it.

Lessard had planned to retire after that year all along, with or without the closure of the school.

I asked her about being "on call 24-7" or being treated like a "public servant," as some of the island teachers have described. "Fortunately or unfortunately, I live twenty-eight miles away!

We talked about how some of the special monies such as REAP (Rural Education Achievement Program, described earlier), which cannot be used for the huge normal expenses such as utilities, when spread among so few students for "special" things can really make a difference. Lessard was hesitant to admit that a school closing for being "too expensive" had surplus money for some things, but it wasn't the same pot of money. That wasn't the local taxpayer's portion.

Here, when they came to do the evaluation visit, every child had his or her own computer. You don't get that in a class of twenty-four unless you have, maybe, a lab in the building. I replaced old computers, and I went through and picked out science kits for the next year, new kits that would really work for the students I had.

We have a recumbent bicycle for each of them, different sizes; Dean's so tall he needs the adult size. They have a great library of books, they all have snowshoes, and we rented cross-county skis. In past years we took them once a month to the Dover-Foxcroft Y, about thirty miles away, but it takes a long time to get there and come back. One year when we had a large number of kids it

Shirley Elementary's last teacher, Joyce Lessard. Eva Murray

worked out well. We borrowed kayaks one year, got them out on Shirley Pond kayaking.

We did a lot of snowshoeing; we put one of the little boys in snowshoes and we could hardly keep up with him; we have the skidder trails around here, so we put him on that, he broke trail, he loved that. Once we got him going, I had a hard time keeping up with him. We'd hear, "I'm way ahead of you, Mrs. Lessard!"

One of the boys actually lives in Greenville. "The superintendent lets him come down here to be in the smaller environment," says Lessard. He has chosen to attend a one-room school, and that school simply shrunk out from under him. He'll go back to Greenville next year, as will his friend, who knows people in Greenville and isn't too worried about it. They'll just miss their little school.

Dean does his spelling out loud, including "Piscataquis," the county name. He gets 100 percent. Ian is doing "subject and predicate." I note that a lot of students have never heard of a "predicate" these days. It seems to me that Dean and Ian are getting a wonderful education.

"One of the boys loves science." Ian overhears this and pipes up, "We did the boreal forest, the deciduous forest, the tundra. . . ." Mrs. Lessard says, "He usually asks, 'What are we going to study next?' He watches everything he can like *Nature* and *Nova,* and if he doesn't see it, his grandfather tapes it for him." Science vocabulary words were up on the walls: ecosystem, chlorophyll, transpiration, understory, periwinkle, reserve, parasitic, emergent, liana, canopy. Remember, these boys are second- and third-graders!

"We've done scads of things in the last three years, lots of science: electricity, magnets, senses, matter—I planned my three years of science before I came. I've taught a lot of fourth-grade science." We talked about curriculum. Lessard specifically talks about science, which is clearly her specialty. "I am the teacher, principal, curriculum planner, the whole bit. I have third- and fourth-grade science materials for next year; I hope the Greenville teachers will be interested in them, because they're wonderful things, from a really good company."

Mrs. Lessard teaches a literature-based reading program which connects science, art, and other subjects with the reading. I observed a wonderful reading lesson that involved sophisticated vocabulary and challenging content, which truly suited the boys' capability and interest, not just their ages. We agreed that you're not doing a child any favors by boring them. "They feel very successful about it, they enjoy it, they go home and tell their parents 'This is what we're doing,' like the worm lab associated with reading *How to Eat Fried Worms*."

Chapter 25 of *How to Eat Fried Worms* is called "Pearl Harbor." Mrs. Lessard asks the boys if they know what that refers to. "They got bombed," says Dean, "by the Japanese." Lessard explains:

The kids just read *Charlotte's Web*. So we did some research on spiders—including sorting out the facts from the misconceptions about spiders. One of the boys has all this knowledge that he throws at us and sometimes he, well, he might not have it exactly straight [she smiles]! We did a whole bulletin board full of writing activities. *Charlotte's Web* has a lot of good vocabulary. We did a lot of art with that book. Some books have a lot of social studies activities you can do, you know, pull out the maps. . . .

We're reading a series, the *Treehouse Books,* where the kids go back in time to different periods in history; there's one where the boy goes back to Revolutionary War times. Then the kids will say, "Let's do this one, I want to know something about this period in time."

We may read *Lost on a Mountain in Maine* this year. They'll probably do it in Greenville in the fourth grade again, but I think these two would like it. I know Ian has been to Baxter [State Park]. He hasn't climbed Mount Katahdin [where the story takes place], but his parents have talked about it; he's climbed other mountains around it. And it's a book you can read more than once."

She also mentions a planned field trip to the coast, where they hope to climb Mt. Battie in Camden.

The ice is out early this year, in First Roach and in Moosehead. Two years ago on our field trip at the end of the year, we were able to use a friend's boat and we took the kids up to Mount Kineo by boat; that was a great experience because they hadn't all been way up the lake.

We talked about how sometimes you don't go enjoy your local sights because you take them for granted. "That's why we started the program of getting them all on snowshoes and skis, and we borrowed kayaks and canoes. If you're going to live in the Moosehead Lake area, you ought to know how to do these things. They're lifelong activities."

LOOKING AHEAD

Who Does Best in a One-Room School?
Not being all things to all people.

If I dared to be so presumptuous as to answer my own question, I would offer that it is the younger student with a stable family and/or community life and not many hard-to-meet needs. But of course, I have no proof of any of that.

A one-room school with a small handful of students will ideally suit some children, and be a bit of a bore to others. It will embrace and reassure some, boosting confidence, encouraging their initiative, and comforting them with the closeness of home. Others will long for things—and for opportunities—they haven't got. Most students find things to like and to dislike about their school no matter the size or location, and most students, as long as they are not neglected, mistreated, threatened, or humiliated, will get enough good out of school to make it worthwhile. Some surely have it better than others, and that is certainly not fair, but relatively few outside of the nation's most dangerous neighborhoods give serious thought to moving because the local school isn't perfectly to their liking. Most island children find moving away bittersweet at best.

By way of my own observation and through conversation with many others, a few patterns do emerge. Who thrives and who is shortchanged cannot be calculated by any formula, and the group of students represented is far too small for statistical analysis to be much help, but allow me to suggest how, in only the most general terms, things appear. Three considerations seem relevant when looking at the student's "satisfaction level" with a very tiny school.

Age: In many cases, younger children are happier with the situation than are middle-schoolers. Teenagers are not universally enamored of being schooled and treated in much the same way as they were when they were six (although this isn't necessarily an accurate portrayal of their education—it's more a matter of their perception). Most of the students I got to know, or with whom I worked, had a deep affection for their island home and were in no particular hurry to leave, but they usually did express some interest in expanding their world. Their warm feeling for their tiny home conflicted with their eagerness to grow up, to do new things, to play sports or play in a band or get away from being "the only big kid and everybody's babysitter." The reality for many island seventh- and eighth-graders is that they spend a lot of their time keeping an eye on the littler kids. For those not engaged in meaningful, gainful employment or immersed in some time-consuming activity of their passion, the grass may well look greener off-island. Younger students may be more aware of what they DO have (from tangible privileges like maybe their own laptops, to intangibles like much more freedom and a sense of safety, and perhaps fewer rules or more attention), while the eighth-graders may be thinking about what they don't have in a K–8 school. After years of nature walks, math on the beach, and swings in the tree branches, the "perks" may seem a bit routine, as they look forward to football games and teen parties.

This having been said, the attitude of boredom and ennui common among adolescents is only partially real. Many teens cultivate a veneer of dissatisfaction as part of the natural process of growing away from being a family dependent, and yet deep down, most harbor a genuine affection for the details of home (including their small neighborhood school). Another very real variable is whether the student group happens to consist of primarily older or mostly younger students at any given time, and this ratio can change greatly from year to year. Tal Birdsey's intentional (and relatively new) one-room middle school in Ripton, Vermont, was exclusively for twelve-to-fourteen-year-olds—no recess-time babysitting required. Older students, as a general rule, prefer not to be treated like "little kids." Recall the story told by student Jacqui Mitchell of Matinicus: One year a new teacher, who didn't know about the traditional and customary invisible line between the "big kids' side" and "little kids' side" of the classroom, seated middle-schoolers innocently on the wrong side of this imaginary boundary. This resulted in deep indignation! If the one-room-school teacher caters to the older students as such, and grants them a few privileges or agreeable responsibilities to differentiate them from the youngers, and the teacher isn't outside of his or her comfort level teaching teenagers, observation leads me to believe that the satisfaction level will be higher.

Family or community stability: It appears, just based on casual observation, that students who come from stable families or who at least have a real sense of belonging within the community might appreciate and thrive in these schools better than those students who, for whatever reason, feel somewhat adrift. Some who have been neglected at home or have had to manage without much for parental support, and those who are very transient and move frequently, and a few students who are new to the island and cannot for the life of them understand what their parents were thinking to move there may be less ready for the independent study, long stretches of solitude, and self-motivation necessary to succeed in this setting. Some of these children need adult friends and role models, mentors perhaps, more structure, and sometimes professional counseling; they might be happier in a larger school.

For a period of time while my own children were in elementary school, the majority of enrolled students were members of very transient families. Each lobster fisherman employs a helper, a sternman, and many of the sternmen are not from the island. Such an employee may move to the island, with girlfriend or wife and their (or her) children, thinking he has made a long-term career move, but in reality these jobs come and go, satisfaction with the position often wanes fast, and the sternman may be "looking for another berth" within months. The children in such a family are in the same educational predicament as those of many migrant agricultural laborers: they move so often, with so little preparation or advance notice, that their education cannot help but suffer.

In some cases, here as anywhere, certain adults who have severe problems of their own are barely able to parent their children. Often, they attempt to "run from" their troubles and may think a remote island a good place to escape to—after all, there are no "authorities" here! These people need help they can't get, and their children often need mentoring, academic support, or counseling they aren't getting, or perhaps just friends they aren't making. For such children, a one-room school in a remote location may not be the best of all possible worlds. On the other hand, if what they really need is more attention from the teacher than they've ever had before, they might just love it.

Serious special-education needs: Students with mild learning disabilities who benefit from increased one-on-one instruction, more time in school spent with an adult who understands their learning requirements, and a teacher who can tailor the activities and the curriculum to the student's needs may find that a tiny school suits them very well. They may in fact receive a superior education for these reasons. However, if a student has a significant disability, including a major behavioral struggle, there is no way to deny that a larger school is likely to do a better job for him or her. The island districts understand the law and do their absolute best to provide the best education possible for all students. Still, a larger and more specialized staff may be necessary to truly provide what a given student should have for services. An Individual Education Program stating, with the force of law, that "this child needs occupational therapy, physical therapy, and speech therapy" does not mean that such therapists will exist on the island, and remember: on some of the islands commuting is not a possibility. The fact that small towns can be warm, nurturing places and island students in recent years have been fortunate to suffer far less bullying, peer pressure, or social stratification than exists in some larger schools does not mean that every student gets exactly what he or she needs all the time. Parents of children with special needs should not kid themselves; moving from a large community to an isolated island will not ensure a better education for their child.

Critical Mass
How few students are too few?

As I write, several of the island schools I have visited over the past couple of years are looking at the possibility of decreasing enrollment—decreasing, that is, to fewer students than you can count on one hand. A quarter-mile down the road from my home, the Matinicus Island School began the 2011-2012 year with nine—briefly, ten—students, a well-rounded group with roughly one student in each grade. Before long, though, two families had to move off-island for the winter, one for health reasons, another out of economic necessity. When the children returned after the Thanksgiving break, the student body was down to four. Two of those were the new teacher's children, without roots here, both nearing high-school age and probably not intending to be long-term islanders. In communities this small, the inevitable and personal business of just one or two families can create an enormous change, percentage-wise, in a school population. The reality exists that our entire student group at some point might consist of a pair of siblings. Should this be the case, we sincerely hope that more children will join them before long, but for that to happen, the parents of those prospective island students will have to be able to make their living on an isolated island. That is often easier said than done.

When possible, island communities do take a proactive approach to this problem, as we've explored earlier. Not every Maine island community has an organization that can offer housing to new residents, but some do, or are currently exploring the possibility.

There is small, and then there is really small. Most of the teachers with whom I spoke would agree that a classroom with seven or eight children is an entirely different experience (for those children) than is a school with only a couple of kids. However, does that mean that it isn't "real school" or isn't an adequate learning environment, or that a school isn't worthy of taxpayer support if it dips below some certain magic number of children? "By 1965," a 1974 newspaper article said of Frenchboro, "there were too few children to open the schoolhouse," meaning that there were three students. These days, islanders know better than to think three "too few." For islands that operate their own school districts and do not have to justify this decision to a larger bureaucracy, even zero might not be too few students to at least maintain the building and keep the paperwork going—not if there is any chance that more children may enroll in the future. True, legal closure of a school, we know, means closure for good, and that does not bode well for the future of a year-round community.

So, should there be such a thing as "too few students to have a school"? Based on observation, teaching experience, parenting experience, school finance experience, and research I would say, "No." The two boys who attend the Monhegan school as I write, and the two boys who attended the Shirley school until it was closed, and the teachers who worked with pairs or even single students over the years would also say no.

That doesn't mean they, or we, are oblivious to the differences in the school experience. Ideally, a larger group of students is enrolled. But sometimes that larger group simply does not exist (or perhaps that is the case only for a year or two). We make a mistake if we conclude that a child will actually be harmed by a slightly-shy-of-optimal experience. Many children nationwide attend schools that are insufficient, stiflingly overcrowded, even dangerous. I would sooner make a case for getting those students out of those truly bad situations than for worrying that a slightly-less-than-ideal number, a scarcity of students in a well-outfitted, safe, friendly rural school is a significant educational shortcoming. Having too few children in attendance is simply not that caliber of problem.

Clearly, if given an option, island teachers would recommend not making the group of students any smaller than can be helped. One example where this issue is being confronted is on the Cranberry Isles, where school buildings exist on both Great Cranberry (the Longfellow School) and Islesford, or Little Cranberry (the Ashley Bryan School). Not that long ago, each island had enough resident children to warrant a schoolhouse of its own. As in all the island communities, the year-round population has shrunk a lot in recent decades. That two-island (actually, five-island) community is struggling with how to keep the maximum number of students together while balancing that concern against the need, now, for a few young children to make a daily mail-boat commute. It never seems fair to the families on the "other island." "Why should my kid have to commute rather than those other kids doing it?" That isn't an easy question to answer.

On Cliff Island, in Casco Bay, the teachers are taking the graduate courses in early childhood education required to establish a formal, official preschool program (rather than just inviting the youngsters to stop by once a week or for storytime or whatever). Having a real preschool program—a solution that does not fit every school or every teacher or every island community—is one way to minimize the chance that the school will become a one-student show.

As I write, an online conversation is taking place about Monhegan Island. Summer visitors and friends are bemoaning what they see as "Monhegan dying." Islanders cite the reduction in the fishing fleet, quite a few of their neighbors moving off-island for all sorts of reasons, and, of course, worry about keeping the school open. The collaborative academic work, inter-island social experiences, and telecommunications options available now through the Outer Islands Teaching and Learning Collaborative have made all the difference to that one Monhegan family; they might have considered leaving the

The Van Dyne family: Emma, Jeremy, Beth, and Maxwell. Emma and Max may be the only students enrolled at the Matinicus school in September of 2012; their father Jeremy graduated from eighth grade on the island in 1985, and his mother's family has lived on Matinicus for many generations. EVA MURRAY

island if the two brothers had nothing but each other and the four walls all year long. As Dalton gets ready to graduate from eighth grade and move on to high school, his mom and his brother Quinn have a decision to make. Does Quinn want to go to school alone, or nearly alone, being the lone middle-schooler with a first-grade classmate? The alternatives may not be much easier, though, and all would include moving.

Having lived through the bottom of the curve, as it were, when Matinicus as a community was faced with a year with no enrolled students a decade ago, I feel emboldened to recommend to any small town confronted with this issue that they not give up too soon. Once a school is legally closed, is it extremely unlikely to open again; the tiny town simply wouldn't be able to afford it. A school with no students enrolled is not necessarily "closed." The Longfellow School on Great Cranberry has not been in use for several years, but it is not officially out of business. If a community is faced with a lack of students, better to vote a maintenance budget and "hold turn," as they say; it may be that children will come. No small town should think they can just "open" the school again at will if it has been legally closed. Opening a brand-new school would obligate the community to meet a set of school building-code and facilities requirements never dreamed of when these one-room schoolhouses were constructed. The cost would very likely just be too high. However, if no school exists on the island, no new families with children will ever decide to move there (I suppose barring the occasional homeschooler, but don't hold your breath). Mothball the schoolhouse, perhaps, but do not give up the legal agency.

A major issue seems to be: "What do we, the adults, expect of an elementary school?" If the purpose of school is recognized to be academics, is seems ridiculous to argue that there is such a thing as "too few students." One or two adults working with a small group of students guarantees lots of one-on-one time, academics precisely tailored to the students' readiness, no wasted time, and the potential to accomplish a lot more work in a year than usual. Private tutoring used to be the privilege of the wealthiest children. Of course, most adults who have attended public school will tell you that academics alone are not what we expect from school (or they assume this understanding is just a given, whether they think about it or not). Social activities, sports, and learning how to interact well with others—to wait your turn, to be serious and attentive at the proper time, to care for the shared equipment—are expected to be part of the experience. Those things presumably fall by the wayside when there aren't many kids.

Is that true, and does that or does that not matter? Well, both.

I believe that those social skills are important, but they don't have to be solely the responsibility of school. Whether or not the student will get as much out of the "private-tutor" experience as he or she might get out of a larger school community seems to have a lot to do with the personality of the child involved. That is problematic, because adults feel they need to make school policy based on just about anything but what the children might prefer. One thing we ought not forget is that the assumption that children just naturally belong in age-segregated social groupings is an artifact of our large schools, a byproduct, not a reason to have large schools. Much of what we think of as "traditional school routine" is about safety and crowd control and has nothing whatsoever to do with academic education. Although children will most generally seek out, appreciate, and enjoy having the company of other kids at least some of the time, and that is healthy and makes sense, it is by no means important that they learn all their social lessons—how to work in a group, how to play on a team, how to be patient, how to deal with other people's needs—from other children alone. If anything, it is easier and more effective to learn these lessons from the community at large, including children of all ages, adults, and preschoolers. Children who have grown up socializing with and working with adults, and occasionally being responsible for toddlers, are often far ahead of their strictly age-segregated peers in "real world" social skills, responsibility, and maturity.

So, academics can be learned in a group of any size, or alone, or using communications technology; social skills can certainly be learned without homogeneous age groups, and as for sports, my experience has been that for most children, the high-intensity competitive stuff can wait until middle or high school. There is no real need to be signed up for everything as a youngster, as long as options for physical fitness and outdoor recreation exist somehow (and they always do).

However, asserting that "whether or not a school this small is adequate depends upon the students involved" does not help the decision-makers much. We like to have something quantifiable upon which to make decisions that involve, frankly, so much money. We need science or that wobbly target called social science, or we need accounting facts or we need test scores or we need to pass the decision on to somebody else (small town voters, perhaps, who may or may not be in a position to examine every side of the question). I have met middle-schoolers who are bored in their tiny school; I have met children who were deeply saddened by the closing of their school; and I have met children who were finding plenty of socialization, physical activities, and real-world experience in their community even though there weren't enough children for group activities, team sports, or standing in line for anything. The total sum of people involved in this lifestyle, and tackling these questions, is simply too small for a pattern to emerge. Statistics don't help. These are truly case-by-case decisions. We should not make the mistake of saying, however, that "such a tiny school is not common, and thus it is not 'normal,' and thus it is not good." In many cases, a tiny school will be excellent. Surely, if we go back to looking at academics as the primary purpose of school, there should be no argument.

Maine's one-room island school staff are definitely excited about advanced telecommunications technology, as we have seen. The technology available now also makes an enormous difference to the isolated student and teacher. It cannot replace real face-to-face interaction, but when students from four or five isolated schools have book group together on Skype, they access a learning opportunity they wouldn't have otherwise. When they get together to explore real field science with graduate students or full-time researchers and naturalists, activities rarely if ever available to students in huge schools, they are in a very privileged position. In recent years the handful of island schoolchildren has been invited to participate in very special off-island enrichment activities that no large school group could possibly undertake. For everything they don't get by virtue of being small, something else—some other unique learning opportunity—seems to be available exclusively to them.

An important consideration, also, is that we not penalize any student or family for being the "last one left." With a school like Shirley that had twenty students not too long ago (roughly the same size as the Long and Chebeague Island schools, both of which are thriving and expanding their resources), it is hardly the "fault" of a local family or two who happen to still be in town after others have moved away. Do we (and who are "we" to say this?) say to the remaining local families, "Well, we expect you to move away for the sake of your kids' education because other people have chosen to move away for other reasons." That is what we do say when we talk about closing a school because "the number of children doesn't justify keeping it open." We ask those last few families to strike the death blow to the school and, in some cases, to the year-round community.

A word about the cost, when the per-pupil cost begins to reach for the moon; tiny schools have extremely high per-pupil costs, obviously, because the large, fixed expenses such as teacher salary and insurance and utility bills are divided over so few students. Consider it the other way, however: if the taxpayers are willing to spend $150,000, for example, to educate six or eight students, who is to tell them that it's wrong to spend that same money to educate one or two? In the real world of the very small town, it isn't about the "per-pupil cost." There is no "per-pupil cost." The cost of operating the one-room school is very close to exactly the same whether there are two or six or fifteen enrolled. It isn't a matter of comparing this set of educational expenses to theoretical others. There isn't usually a range of options; it is "do we have a school or don't we?" Typically, it's about the total lump sum of money: Is the money going to something we consider worthwhile, is it something we can afford at all, and is it a wise investment?

Who's going to be the last one left? Will doing without the benefits of a larger school (despite the possible benefits of a tiny one) look like a mistake in retrospect later? What does a community member do when what's good for your family is bad for your friends? Should we stay or should we go?

Supposing you were the second-to-last family left on an island, or in a small town with just a few children in school, and you decided to leave, for whatever perfectly good reason, leaving just one or two children in school? What if you were the parent of those last children? Would you feel obligated to move? What if your home, your work situation, or your finances made that very difficult? What if you had no other reason in life to move and nowhere in particular to move— you had a good home, a good job, friends and family—but for reasons outside of your control the local elementary school was down to just a couple of kids, maybe just yours? What is the right thing to do?

I urge readers not to oversimplify this.

The misconception, common, I fear, among people in positions of authority off-island, is that families casually elect to move to the islands and could just as well live anywhere. This inaccurate picture leaves out the natives, the long-term residents, and the people with essential jobs who are not easily replaced. My husband is the electrician/mechanic responsible for the day-to-day operation of the island's power station, and we had the only two school-aged children on Matinicus at one point. (The island has no cable to the mainland and supports one of the country's smallest regulated municipal utilities.) Should anybody have told him that he should leave the island just so his kids could go to a larger school? There was nobody waiting in the wings to take over running the generator plant, and the children did not seem either unhappy or undereducated. Both children successfully attended high school on the mainland and are now in college. No harm was done.

One year, about a decade ago, Matinicus Elementary had no enrolled students. The following year, one student and then a second and a third moved to the island for family reasons; before long a more typical number of year-round students were in attendance. Those first two returning students were the grandson and son of island natives, children dealing with family struggles and moving back to where their families had come from, hoping for the nurturing experience of a small town and an extended family. Those boys were hardly idealists and were certainly not homesteaders invited in to save the school. They might be better described as "angry young men," preferring a community of fishermen to too much civilization. That year, they received an education that approximated private tutoring, while they began the process of sorting out their family lives. Both are now lobster fishermen. The taxpayers of Matinicus did a very good thing when they decided the year before to keep the school legally open, even if no children were enrolled and no teacher was hired. We paid the insurance bill, passed a budget, and kept the fuel tank full, and we waited for the children to come back. They did.

Oral History
Everybody is doing a story on the one-room schools!
I worked on this project for four years. Some of the students we met are now in high school or even college. As I wrap up in the early days of 2012, the people of Peaks Island and Matinicus Island mourn the passing of their neighbor, teacher, and lobster-fisher June Kantz Pemberton. One of the children from Matinicus spent last winter on the mainland with his family for medical reasons and received a liver transplant at Boston Children's Hospital in February of 2012. Graduating eighth-grader Dalton from Monhegan is headed for the Putney School in Vermont, and graduating eighth-grader Meg from Islesford is headed for Mount Desert Island High School. Maine kids are still corresponding with students from Decker, Montana.

I happened to be in Rockwood, meeting teacher Bill Folsom and the three girls at the Rockwood School on the day the Oprah Winfrey television show aired its story about Frenchboro Island. I did not see the broadcast myself. Oprah's camera crew had been on Frenchboro just a short time before my first visit there. My assertion that "I'm doing a story about the one-room schools" was met with "Everybody is doing a story about the one-room schools!" Something like that. The islanders have had their fill of media types.

Doing oral history around here is hard work, and here's why: Oprah's crew may have been a delightful group of people, but some writers are intrusive, rude, insensitive, high-maintenance pests. Reporters, photographers, documentarians, and freelancers from everywhere descend on the Maine islands every year and some of them, frankly, irritate the heck out of the working people. They all seem to think themselves the first writer ever to have thought of doing a story on some aspect of Maine island life. The islanders yawn, look at their watches, and sometimes quite literally hide. As a full-time Matinicus Island resident, I have been the subject of these writers' inquiries and it isn't always fun. So when I show up somewhere I do not belong and begin asking questions, people are likely to be a bit tired of answering questions.

To all of my respondents, all my old and new friends who helped me with this project, who not only told their stories and welcomed me into their schools and board meetings and aboard their boats, but who answered questions and gave me directions, fixed me tuna sandwiches for the ferry ride, showed me the good hiking trails, fed me garlic soup or beer or cookies, and stayed up late just talking, islander to islander—thank you. I cannot say thank you enough.

ACKNOWLEDGMENTS

I am grateful for the assistance of so many people, for hundreds of hours of interviews, for storytelling and reminiscing; for photographs, letters, and advice; for room and board, lunches on ferries, rides, and for all sorts of other hospitality. I am certain that there are many others I have neglected to name here; please accept my sincere thanks.

Emma Van Dyne

Anne Bardaglio and Lana Cannon

Robin Tarkleson

Captain Mike Johnson, Captain Storey King, Pat Dutille, Sharon Daley, RN, and the Reverend Rob Benson, crew of the *Sunbeam*

Phil Conkling, Rob Snyder, Ruth Kermish-Allen, Gillian Thompson, and many others at the Island Institute

Past Matinicus teachers Betty Carleton Thompson Heald, Sari Ryder Bunker, Suzanne Winkelman, Tom and Kristy Rogers McKibben, Christina Quigley Young, Kate Finn Nolette, June Kantz Pemberton, Mary Tetreault, Patricia Walchli, Dorothy Carter, Heather Wells, David and Rachel Duncan, and Lisa Rogers

Josh and Heidi Holloway, Cheryl and Dave Crowley, Roger Berle, and Amy Sandoval of Cliff Island

Paula Johnson, Marci Train, and Mark Greene of Long Island

Donna Damon, Laura Summa, Kristin Westra, Tammy Hoidal, Nancy Earnest, and Beverly Johnson of Chebeague Island

Alden Finney and Tracy Sommers of Great Diamond Island

Ellen Mahoney, Celeste and Peter Bridgford, Scott Kelley, Cindy Nilsen, Heather Wasklewicz, Lisa Lynch, Eric Eaton, Ronda Berg, Ann Cannon, Fran Houston, Craig Davis, and all my new friends on Peaks Island

Jessie Campbell, Jackie Boegel and Bill Boynton, Kathie Iannicelli, Donna Cundy, Angela Iannicelli and Travis Dow, Barbara Hitchcock, Tara Hire, Richard Farrell, Livka Farrell, Jes Stevens, Lisa Brackett, Gabe Church, Marion Chioffi, and Zoe Zanidakis

of Monhegan Island

Paula Greatorex, Lisa Turner, Dianne Bowen, Victoria MacDonald, Sue, Dan, Geneva and Belva MacDonald, Ted Hoskins, Brenda Clark, Joy Seaver, Kipp Quinby, Payson Barter, Bill Barter, Anne-Claude Cotty, and Rudy Graf of Isle au Haut.

Doug and Michelle Finn, Rebecca Smart Lenfestey, Rachel Bishop, Lance Bishop, Erica Davis, and Beverly Roxby of Frenchboro

Lindsay Eysnogle, Donna and Henry Isaacs, Sally Rowen, Emily Thomas, Melissa Amuso, Kate Chaplin, Barbara Meyers, and Marya Spurling of the Cranberry Isles

Mimi and Gary Rainford, Donna Wiegle, and Sonja Philbrook of Swan's Island

Natalie Ames, Suzanne Rankin, Samantha Philbrook, Nat and Lisa Twombly-Hussey, Lydia Twombly-Hussey, Charlotte Strong Ames, Patricia Harmon, Jeanette Young Beaudoin, Laurie Webber, Maureen Mitchell, Jacqui Mitchell, Kathryn Armstrong, Bruce Ives, Jerry White, Emily Murray, and Eric Murray of Matinicus Island

Creighton Teter, Stephanie DeVault, Rhonda Counts Willingham, Rachel Steffen, Sherilyn Johnson, Bill Folsom, and Joyce Lessard

Doug Alford, Gould Academy

Lucy Judecki, Almeda Urquhart, Hal Owen, Nick Snow, Norma Staples, and Dick Waldron for stories of school in the early twentieth century

Reverend Bobby Ives

The Maine Islands Coalition

Jennifer Bunting, at Tilbury House, Publishers

Finally, my thanks to everybody at Rock City Café, Rockland, Maine

In memory of June Kantz Pemberton, 1952–2012

SELECTED RESOURCES

Historic Material and Island Background:

Boyce, Alice, and Eunice Curran, Ellin Gallant, Reta Morrill, and Joyce O'Brien. *A Glimpse of Old Peaks Island—Through Rose-Colored Glasses.* Xlibris: 2009. Island history and recollections of five women who grew up on Peaks Island.

Conkling, Philip. *Islands in Time: A Natural and Cultural History of the Islands of the Gulf of Maine.* Rockland, ME: The Island Institute, 1991 (second edition, 2011).

Cronin, Stephen. *The Island: A Young Boy's Journey to Manhood on Matinicus Island.* Lincoln, NE: iUniverse, Inc., 2007. Autobiographical reminiscence of island life in the mid-1800s, when population was at its highest, as told to Cronin's niece; book assembled by Cronin's great-grandson.

Emmons, Celia Philbrook. *Highlights of Life on Matinicus Island.* Westbrook, ME: H. S. Cobb Printing Co., 1960. Considered by many islanders to be the informal continuation of Charles Long's book (see below). Matinicus genealogy is continued through male lines, however, and is therefore not entirely complete.

Long, Charles A. E. *Matinicus Isle: Its Story and Its People.* Lewiston, ME: Lewiston Journal Printshop, 1926. Reprinted by Higginson Book Company, Salem, MA, 1999. Referred to by islanders simply as "the Matinicus book," this volume or the reprint has a place of honor in nearly every island home. The genealogy is continued by Emmons. Brief sections on geography, aspects of early social life and institutions, industry, transportation, etc., paint a picture of Matinicus Island history, mostly through the 1800s.

Lunt, Dean L. *Hauling By Hand: The Life and Times of a Maine Island.* Yarmouth, ME: Islandport Press, 2007. Lunt, a Frenchboro native and graduate of the island school, offers a comprehensive history of the island from his intimate perspective.

McLane, Charles B. *Islands of the Mid-Maine Coast Series* in four volumes: *Penobscot Bay, Mount Desert to Machias, Muscongus Bay and Monhegan Island,* and *Pemaquid Point to the Kennebec River.* Gardiner, ME: Tilbury House, various years. Short island histories, census records, many photographs, and island stories.

Simpson, Dorothy. *The Island's True Child: A Memoir of Growing Up on Criehaven.* Camden, ME: Down East Books, 2003. Memories of Criehaven when there was a year-round community on the island (which is no longer the case).

———. *The Maine Islands in Story and Legend.* Philadelphia: J. B. Lippincott Company, 1960. Material compiled by the Maine Writers Research Club. Includes an interesting historical section on early settlement of Matinicus, including Ebenezer Hall and the Penobscots, and the story of Matinicus Rock lighthouse heroine Abbie Burgess.

Starkey, Glenn W. *Maine: Its History, Resources and Government.* Boston: Silver Burdett Company, 1938. Includes a section on early history of public schools in the state.

Thorndike, Virginia L. *Islanders: Real Life on the Maine Islands.* Camden, ME: Down East Books, 2005. A peek into many aspects of daily life on Maine inhabited islands; I am interviewed and quoted quite a bit (sometimes by name, sometimes anonymously).

One-Room Schools and Small Rural Schools:

Apps, Jerry. *One-Room Country Schools: History and Recollections.* Woodruff, WI: The Guest Cottage Inc., 1996. A thorough and straightforward description of small rural Wisconsin schools in the early twentieth century. Neither academic and judgmental nor sentimental and romantic, this detailed but accessible account makes interesting reading. I recommend this book to anybody interested in this topic. One of the best general books I have found on rural one-room schools.

Bial, Raymond. *One-Room School.* Boston: Houghton Mifflin Company, 1999. A well-done, short historical book for younger readers, with plenty of photographs.

Birdsey, Tal. *A Room for Learning: The Making of a School in Vermont.* New York: St. Martin's Press, 2009. Account of the formation of the North Branch School, an intentional, modern-day, one-room, multi-age alternative school in rural Vermont. Opened in 2001, this school is still in operation. www.northbranchschool.org.

Dart, Gladys, and Alfred Wright. *In Deed, Indeed: Teaching and Learning in a One-Room School.* Denver: Outskirts Press, 2010. Autobiographical memoir of teaching in rural Alaska for several decades with additional observations by a local teenager; this book is a warm collaboration between the retired Gladys and then-tenth-grader Alfred, which brings us up to the present. The Manley Hot Springs community had no school in the 1950s, and enough local interest was spurred to "reopen" the K–12 school, which is still in operation. Color photographs invite the reader into the life of the school. Quick read.

Gambell, V. C. *The Schoohouse Farthest West: St. Lawrence Island, Alaska.* New York: Women's Board of Home Missions of the Presbyterian Church, 1898. Reprint by Nabu Press, 2010. Memoir of teaching on this very remote Alaskan island, the same island on which the present teachers at Frenchboro taught just a few years ago. Keep in mind that this was written in 1898; modern sensitivities with regard to describing Native peoples differ from those of the authors.

Gjelten, Tom. *Schooling in Isolated Communities.* North Haven, ME: North Haven Project for Career Development, 1978. Journalist Tom Gjelten and his wife taught on North Haven Island in the early 1970s. This short book describes many of the realities shared by all the island schools.

Hausherr, Rosemary. *The One-Room School at Squabble Hollow.* New York: Four Winds Press, 1988. Nonfiction for younger readers, with lots of black-and- white photos, about one of Vermont's last one-room schools (now closed).

Montell, William L. *Tales from Kentucky One-Room School Teachers.* Lexington, KY: University Press of Kentucky, 2011. Short memoirs and comments from many teachers, arranged by topic.

Rocheleau, Paul. *The One-Room Schoolhouse: A Tribute to a Beloved National Icon.* New York: Universe Publishing, 2003. High-quality photo essay; includes a segment on the Isle au Haut school.

Simonson, Dorothy. *The Diary of an Isle Royale School Teacher: A Memoir of a Winter on an Isolated Island in Lake Superior During the Great Depression.* Hancock, MI: Book Concern Printers, 2004. Diary entries tell of good food and bad weather, both familiar to "isolated islanders" anywhere.

Wickenden, Dorothy. *Nothing Daunted: The Unexpected Education of Two Society Girls in the West*. New York: Scribner, 2011. A well-done reconstructed historical account of two easterners who traveled to northwestern Colorado to teach in a one-room school in 1916-1917. Enjoyable reading, and we do notice some similarities with the present day.

Zimmerman, Jonathan. *Small Wonder: The Little Red Schoolhouse in History and Memory*. New Haven: Yale University Press, 2009. A quick—and at times starkly unsentimental—survey of the one-room school as a malleable American symbol. Zimmerman tends to emphasize the more impoverished schools and the negatives of a rural education; his point has more to do with these schools as an American icon.

Historical Fiction:

Lord, Cynthia. *Touch Blue*. New York: Scholastic Press, 2010. This story for young readers is based on Frenchboro history.

Unpublished Resources:

Benson, Rob, ed. *I 2 I: A Booklet of Wisdom and Hope for the Journey Off-Island and Beyond*. Printed by the Maine Sea Coast Mission, 2009. Advice to island middle schoolers from island high-school students.

Bunker, Sari R. *The History of Education on Matinicus Island*. Unpublished research paper, 2002.

American Education in General:

Colangelo, N., S. G. Assouline, and M. U. W. Gross. *A Nation Deceived: How Schools Hold Back America's Brightest Students*. Philadelphia: John Templeton Foundation, 2004. This report in support of various forms of acceleration for the most able students shines a positive light on the one-room, multi-grade schools of the past.

Delisle, James R. *Barefoot Irreverence: A Guide to Critical Issues in Gifted Child Education*. Waco, TX: Prufrock Press, 2002.

Foote, Donna. *Relentless Pursuit*. New York: Random House, 2008. What it's like to be involved with Teach for America.

Grant, Gerald. *Hope and Despair in the American City*. Cambridge, MA: Harvard University Press, 2009.

Hochschild, Jennifer L., and Nathan Scovronick. *The American Dream and the Public Schools*. New York: Oxford University Press, 2003. Discusses many of the well-known issues and controversies related to public schools nationwide. Not light reading. Exhaustive list of references may be helpful to those interested in further study.

Kidder, Tracy. *Among Schoolchildren*. Boston: Houghton Mifflin, 1989.

Kohl, Herbert. *On Teaching*. New York: Schocken Books, 1976, 1986.

Levine, Eliot. *One Kid at a Time: Big Lessons from a Small School*. New York: Teachers College Press (Columbia University), 2002.

Lortie, Dan C. *Schoolteacher: A Sociological Study*. Chicago: University of Chicago Press, 1975.

Mondale, Sarah, and Sarah Curran Bernard, eds. *School: The Story of American Public Education*. Boston: Beacon Press, 2001. Companion to a PBS series. Brief history of American education including numerous black-and-white photos taken in early American schools.

Montessori, Maria (translated by Claremont). *The Absorbent Mind*. New York: Dell Publishing, 1967.

———— (translated by Costelloe). *The Discovery of the Child*. New York: Ballantine, 1967.

Nieto, Sonia, ed. *Why We Teach*. New York: Teachers College Press, 2005. A collection of essays by inspiring teachers reflecting on their motivation to enter or stick with classroom teaching as a profession.

Pope, Denise Clark. *"Doing School": How We Are Creating a Generation of Stressed Out, Materialistic, and Miseducated Students*. New Haven: Yale University Press, 2001.

Postman, Neil. *Teaching as a Conserving Activity*. New York: Dell Publishing, 1979.

Postman, Neil, and Charles Weingartner, *Teaching as a Subversive Activity*. New York: Dell Publishing, 1969.

Ravitch, Diane. *The Death and Life of the Great American School System*. New York: Basic Books, 2010.

————. *EdSpeak*. Alexandria, VA: Association for Supervision and Curriculum Development, 2007. "A glossary of education terms, phrases, buzzwords and jargon." A helpful resource, but I have noticed that this listing does not include everything!

———. *Left Back: A Century of Failed School Reforms.* New York: Simon and Schuster, 2000.

Rochester, J. Martin. *Class Warfare.* San Francisco: Encounter Books, 2002. Rochester makes an impassioned argument *against* multi-age classrooms (page 101), which, although I disagree with him, is of interest in this discussion.

Schwahn, Charles, and Beatrice McGarvey. *Inevitable: Mass Customized Learning.* CreateSpace, 2011. In 2011 Superintendent of Instruction Don Siviski, an assistant to Maine State Department of Education Commissioner Stephen Bowen, told an audience of island teachers that 200 copies of this book had been ordered for the entire Department of Education staff and all of Maine's district superintendents.

Tomlinson, Carol Ann. *How to Differentiate Instruction in Mixed-Ability Classrooms.* Upper Saddle River, NJ: Pearson, 2001. One of several short books by Tomlinson on differentiation intended for classroom teachers.

For people thinking about moving to an island to teach or for any other reason, I recommend the following reading list:

Icebound, by Maryanne Vollers and Jerri Nielsen
Danny, the Champion of the World, by Roald Dahl
The Water is Wide, by Pat Conroy
The Guernsey Literary and Potato Peel Pie Society, by Mary Ann Shaffer and Annie Barrows
The Crofter and the Laird, by John McPhee

None of these claims to be about Maine. They don't have to be.

INDEX

Eva Murray taught at Matinicus Island's one-room school in 1987-1988. She expected to stay on the island for one year, having been accepted to law school. Instead, she made the island her home, marrying and raising a family on Matinicus. Since teaching there she has served as classroom volunteer and volunteer art teacher, substitute teacher, school district bookkeeper, and is now a member of the district's school board.

A Phi Beta Kappa graduate of Bates College (1985), Murray also studied at the University of Maine. She is a certified elementary teacher and continues to take graduate courses in education now that distance learning is available to Maine's islands. She is an emergency medical technician and wilderness responder, founded her community's recycling program, and spends her summers working as the island baker.

ADDISON DELISLE

Murray's essays have appeared in a number of Maine publications since 2003; she is a regular contributor to *Maine Boats, Homes & Harbors* magazine, *Working Waterfront,* and others. Her first book, *Well Out to Sea — Year-Round on Matinicus Island,* was published by Tilbury House in 2010.